FRANCIS BLAKE
An Inventor's Life
1850-1913

Francis Blake, Jr. By William A. Webster (Waltham, Mass.), 1901. #57.793

FRANCIS BLAKE

An Inventor's Life

1850-1913

Elton W. Hall

By

ELTON W. HALL

©2003 Massachusetts Historical Society

All Rights Reserved

Published at the Charge of the Publication Fund

Designed by Dede Cummings Designs

ISBN 0-934909-84-9 (cloth)

Boston, Mass.

Distributed by Northeastern University Press

Library of Congress Cataloging-in-Publication Data

Hall, Elton Wayland
Francis Blake: an inventor's life 1850–1913 / by Elton W. Hall
p. cm.
Includes bibliographical referrences and index.
ISBN 0-934909-84-9
1. Blake, Francis, 1850–1913. 2. Inventors—United States—Biography.
3. Telephone. 4. Photography, Instantaneious. I. Title.

TK5143.B37H35.2003
609.2ˉDC21
[B]
2003046462

For Ruth Blake Oliver

TABLE OF CONTENTS

INTRODUCTION

O<small>N MAY 30</small>, 1866, fifteen-year-old Francis Blake, Jr., reported for duty at the Washington office of the United States Coast Survey. The Coast Survey charted ocean currents and depths, measured wind speeds, made precise oceanographic maps that mariners and naval commanders relied upon, and established accurate longitude and latitude. That so young a boy could leave the family hearth so early and succeed so rapidly in the demanding world of adults testifies to his fortitude, industry, mathematical gift, and absorbent mind. These enviable talents made Blake an ideal candidate to head the Coast Survey, where he would have led a distinguished but largely unremarkable life. Instead, they propelled him out of government service and into a fascinating career as a leading American inventor.

His major inventions, the telephone transmitter, innovations in high-speed photography, and Keewaydin, his estate in Weston, Massachusetts, symbolize how Blake created and recreated himself. Although related to such distinguished New England families as the Trumbulls and Paines, Blake's own family lived a peripatetic existence, always running just a few steps ahead of the wolf, and at times dependent upon relatives for shelter and support. Indeed, it was his father's professional instability that forced Blake into an adult career at so tender an age. His intense search for the success and respectability that eluded his father made Blake exacting, precise, proud, and inflexible. He also possessed his father's mercurial temper, which erupted at opposition to his opinions or the vaguest possible slight to his honor or pride. Blake's volcanic relationship with his well-to-do father-in-law reflected the insecurities of a young man struggling with his humble origins and an unquenchable desire for respectability.

Possessing an irrepressibly inquisitive mind and the wisdom (or luck) to marry into wealth, Blake gradually diminished his role in the Coast Survey and instead applied his enormous energy to a series of important and lucrative telephonic inventions. The most famous of these, the "Blake Transmitter," became the world's standard telephone voice transmitter. Virtually anyone in the United States who spoke into Alexander Graham Bell's device in the last twenty years of the nineteenth century looked directly at Blake's name. The great wealth his inventions and business deals produced and the inheritance that came to him through his wife, Elizabeth Hubbard, allowed Blake to indulge his passions and follow his restless curiosity. Blake invested an enormous amount of this wealth, energy, and talent into Keewaydin, the estate he created in Weston, Massachusetts, just outside of Boston. The largely self-contained compound, which included homes for his in-laws and his children and adjoined the even larger estate of his father-in-law, Charles T. Hubbard, reflected Blake's passion for precision, beauty, and order. It became his obsessive preoccupation, the one place he could exercise unchallenged mastery and command the social respectability he desired.

Although the fabulous Keewaydin estate did not endure, Blake's photographic images of it and of countless other subjects remain. Indeed, Blake's experimental camera work placed him in the forefront of the photographic world in the 1880s. His high-speed photographs are unmatched in clarity, crispness, and composition, remaining as fresh today as when he first snapped them over a hundred years ago. Although little known today, Blake helped revolutionize photography, and his work represented a fundamental change in the social role of the photograph in American society. Disregarding his work in science and philanthropy, Blake's photography alone marks him as a significant figure at the dawn of the twentieth century.

But at the height of his success and wealth Blake became intensely private, shunning fame and ambition for personal research, private life, and the continual re-creation of his vast estate. Having attained wealth, power, and privilege with his telephonic inventions, Blake used his time and resources to employ his genius as he saw fit. He did not court publicity; indeed, Blake deliberately avoided it and never promoted any of his celebrated photographs. When he developed later inventions, he exerted little or no effort to benefit financially from them. After completion of the major portions of his estate, he opened it to the public for tours one day a week, but did so out of a sense of public duty rather than to accrue public notice. Ironically, Keewaydin, the one "invention" of Blake's that absorbed so much of his time and energy, served no broad public purpose or much outlived its creator. If the Blake name is unrecognizable today, this is no reflection of his accomplishments, which were significant, but of Blake's loathing for publicity and public attention. Ultimately, Blake reached the goals he sought and achieved the anonymity he preferred. Whatever lesson that offers us today, the significance of Blake's life and his inventions endures. His story is a compelling and fascinating chronicle of unbounded energy, independence, and genius.

ACKNOWLEDGEMENTS

I N 1964 THE DESCENDANTS of Francis Blake were cleaning out his great house in Weston. In a closet under the staircase they found many boxes containing their grandfather's personal and professional papers. Blake's granddaughter, Ruth Blake Oliver, and her husband, Andrew Oliver, realized the potential importance of the papers and arranged for the family to give them to the Massachusetts Historical Society. In 1988, Ruth Oliver provided funds to have this enormous collection processed. Linda C. Genovese completed the work and produced an inventory of the collection, which comprised eighty-three boxes and forty-six volumes. Mrs. Oliver then sought someone to write a monograph on her grandfather based on the papers, and that led her to me. The project took longer than either of us ever contemplated, but we were fascinated by the story as it emerged from the papers, and we had many enjoyable meetings talking about it, sometimes over a glass of Blake's own 1846 Blandy's Madeira. I am very grateful to her for giving me the chance to do it and only regret that she did not live to see the book.

The staff of the Massachusetts Historical Society was immensely helpful during the time I worked my way through the papers. Peter Drummey, Brenda Lawson, Kathy Griffin, and Chris Steele were always ready to provide whatever help I needed. Because Blake's activities encompassed a variety of disciplines, I sometimes ventured to other institutions in search of information and advice. For help with Blake's work for the United States Coast Survey, I thank William J. H. Andrewes, Curator of the Science Center at Harvard University and Prof. Owen Gingerich of the Harvard-Smithsonian Center for Astrophysics. Carlene E. Stephens, Curator of Mechanical and Civil Engineering, and Deborah Jean Warner, Curator of the History of Physical Sciences, both at the National Museum of American History, discussed the work that Blake did in the precise determination of differences of longitude and showed me some instruments that Blake used. Bernard Finn, Curator of Electricity at the National Museum of American History, and Sheldon Hochheiser of the A. T. & T. Archives provided information and material concerning Blake's work on the telephone. Marianne Curling, Curator of The Mark Twain House, brought the large volume of plans for Keewaydin, which had been given to The Mark Twain House before the bulk of the Blake papers was discovered, to the Massachusetts Historical Society on long term loan and eventually arranged for its gift to the Society. Some of these helpful and amiable people have moved on to other positions since my work on Blake began. Others helped, listened, and advised as well. My failure to mention them all by name should not be interpreted as ingratitude.

ELTON W. HALL
Dartmouth, Massachusetts
November, 2002.

LIST OF ILLUSTRATIONS

IMAGES ARE FROM THE BLAKE family photographs (photograph collection 39) and the Francis Blake photographs (photograph collection 57), Massachusetts Historical Society

CHAPTER 1

BEGINNINGS

STRONG CHARACTER AND A SPIRIT of adventure ran in Blake blood. Francis Blake's paternal and maternal ancestors, hardy New Englanders whom he eagerly read and wrote about as a young man, offered him models of character and ambition. William and Agnes Blake, founding English members of the Blake clan, left Pitminster, Somerset County, England, for Dorchester, Massachusetts, about 1635. They joined Dorchester's First Church, founded in 1636, and William quickly became a freeman and member of the exclusive Ancient and Honorable Artillery Company. He also served the town as selectman, constable, and clerk. Blake's father, Francis Blake, the ninth child of prominent Worcester lawyer Francis Blake and his wife Eliza Chandler Blake, was born on July 7, 1812. Originally, Francis was christened with a different name, after other family patriarchs. But the death of a sibling, distressingly common in New England families then, led his parents to change his name to Francis. Little else is known about Blake's father until his name appeared in Boston city directories in 1841 as a businessman.[1]

Blake also descended from the Trumbull family (spelled Trumble until the late eighteenth century), who first settled in Ipswich, Massachusetts, in 1645. During the 1680s, the Trumbulls made their way to Connecticut, primarily Suffolk and Lebanon, and Blake counted the state's Revolutionary War governor Jonathan Trumbull (1710–1785) and the patriot-artist John Trumbull (1756–1843) among his collateral ancestors. Dr. Joseph Trumbull (1756–1824), second cousin to the artist, was born in

Suffield and practiced medicine in Petersham, Massachusetts, before removing to Worcester in about 1803. In 1786, he married Elizabeth Paine, daughter of Timothy and Sarah Chandler Paine, and settled into a house that for half a century before had served as Worcester's courthouse and had been moved to an area still known today as Trumbull Square.[2]

George Augustus Trumbull, Joseph and Elizabeth's only son, was born in Petersham on January 23, 1792, attended Phillips Exeter Academy, and ventured into the book selling business. In 1819, he took over publication of the *Massachusetts Spy* following the death of the newspaper's legendary owner, Isaiah Thomas. By 1829, he had given up the newspaper and toiled as a bank cashier until his retirement in 1858. During this period he suffered financial reversals that crippled his fortunes but not his spirit. His wife, Louisa Clapp, was the daughter of Capt. Caleb Clapp, who had fought at Lexington during the Revolution and had become an original member of the Society of the Cincinnati. Their third child, Caroline Burling Trumbull, born on June 24, 1820, married Frank's father on June 14, 1842. Francis Blake, Sr., quickly benefited from his connection to the Trumbulls. As early as 1841, he had become the partner of his future brother-in-law, George Clapp Trumbull, a Boston dealer in wines and teas. The Blakes shared a home with Trumbull at 32 Oxford Street until April 1845, when Blake purchased the property for the considerable sum of $6,400. Under puzzling circumstances, Trumbull then dissolved his partnership with Blake and joined the commission merchant house of C. S. Brown & Co. Blake apparently abandoned the business two years later and moved to Newton Lower Falls on the Charles River.[3]

Dissatisfied—or unsuccessful—living the life of a merchant, Blake applied for a position as a purser in the United States Navy. To secure an appointment from the secretary of the Navy, he solicited letters of endorsement from the great jurist Rufus Choate, former governor Levi Lincoln, Jr., a Trumbull relative, and the merchant-prince Abbott Lawrence, but nothing came of the effort. In August 1850, Blake sold his house on Oxford Street and temporarily abandoned the city and his mercantile pursuits to raise his family and become a "yeoman" of Needham. The first two of his children died in infancy, but Louisa Trumbull Blake was born in 1846, followed by Charles Henry Mills Blake two years later. The fifth and final child, Francis Blake, Jr., was born on Christmas Day 1850, at the family's home in rural Newton Lower Falls.[4]

Francis Blake, Sr., renewed his efforts to locate work in Boston, having done poorly at farming, and joined the partnership of Whiting, Blake & Hindro, dealers in shoes and leather. About 1854, the Blakes moved to familiar family terrain in Worcester, where they remained for the next few years. The elder Francis Blake and his son, Charles, traveled to Richmond, Virginia, in an attempt to enter the tobacco business, but after eight months returned home largely empty-handed. Still casting about for a livelihood, Blake removed his family to New York City in May 1858, where he sought to continue his struggling tobacco business. Reflecting Blake's fortunes as a businessman, the family frequently moved around the city, even occupying a boarding house for a time.[5]

In 1861, about two weeks after the Confederate attack on Fort Sumter, the Blakes abandoned New York, traveled by steamer to Norwich, Connecticut, and then proceeded by train back to Worcester. "I staid at my Aunt Elizabeth Lincoln's until August," the young Francis Blake recalled, "going to School at the Sycamore St. School House."[6] William Lincoln, son and grandson of the two governors, had married one of the Trumbull daughters and lived on a farm on May Street about a mile from the school. Frankie, as the Blakes called their youngest child, appeared unaffected by his family's financial uncertainties and enjoyed visiting his grandparents and numerous Trumbull relatives in Worcester. He became a fast friend of his cousin Winslow Lincoln and remained close to him for many years. The elder Francis Blake's activities from May to August 1861 are not recorded, but likely he searched for a new position to support his family.

The Blakes achieved some financial stability in August 1861, when Francis's father won an appointment as a bond clerk at the Boston Custom House. But this meant again uprooting the family and returning to Boston. For the first winter they boarded in the house of an elderly widow named Mrs. Lemuel Pope who lived on Appleton Place—now Pilgrim Road—in the Longwood section of Roxbury. All traces of that neighborhood long since have been eradicated, replaced by Simmons and Wheelock colleges.[7]

In March 1862, the Blakes secured a more permanent residence when they moved into a brick house on Plymouth Street owned by the wealthy merchant and developer David Sears. Sears had acquired an extensive tract of land during the 1850s, principally in Brookline, with the intention of developing a peaceful neighborhood in which sober and intelligent people could live quietly. In an early example of a planned community, Sears built a church overlooking the Muddy River, laid out streets, and sold land to those most likely to realize the secure and respectable neighborhood he envisioned. Sears also built within the community blocks of brick rental houses, homes meant for families of good quality but limited means. The Blakes lived on the west side of Plymouth Street in a house with a back yard that extended down to Muddy River, giving the Blake boys plenty of room to play. In those pre-Olmstead days, the river was a dirty stream that snaked through a marsh in which the celebrated Longwood mosquito bred profusely. On the far bank ran the Brookline branch of the Boston & Worcester Railroad, its Chapel Station providing convenient transportation into Boston. The Longwood Post Office, situated in the railroad station, served as the Blakes' mailing address.[8]

Details concerning Frankie's school days are scarce. However, an astonishing note that appeared in an August 1862 issue of the *Worcester Spy* survives:

Nearly a Fatal Accident. As Frank Blake, son of Francis Blake, Esq. of Boston, now on a visit to the family of Col. William S. Lincoln, of this city, was playing with a gun a few days since, he accidentally shot the domestic. The gun had been discharged at a hawk and subsequently reloaded. Not aware of the latter fact, Blake pointed the gun at the girl exclaiming, "Now I'll shoot you." The full charge took effect in the neck and shoulders, inflicting a bad but not a fatal wound.[9]

It was an extraordinarily careless act, even for a youth of eleven. Whatever disciplinary action the family took, the Lincolns forgave Frankie and continued to welcome him into their home. Blake, unfortunately, left no record of his remorse or any other reaction to the accidental shooting. We know that he continued to own firearms, but he became meticulously careful and mindful of the consequences of his actions. Perhaps the unfortunate incident proved a valuable lesson that stayed with Blake for the rest of his life.

From 1861 through the spring of 1866, Frank attended school in Brookline. The Pierce Grammar School, located between School and Washington streets, was a sixteen-minute walk from the Blake house. On a fine day the commute was surely pleasant, although in winter the trip home into the teeth of a northeast storm must have been a struggle. Of the many subjects taught at Pierce, map drawing was one that would later prove very helpful to Blake.[10] Frankie entered high school in 1864, three months before his fourteenth birthday, and about five months younger than the average entering student. Brookline High School, built in 1857, stood at the corner of School and Prospect streets. Frank held the school principal, John Emory Horr (Harvard A.M., 1852), in high esteem and remained in touch with him even after he left the school. In those days the school year began on the first Monday in September and was divided into four terms. Teachers conducted classes between eight A.M. and one P.M. from April to September, and then between two P.M. and nine P.M. from October to March. The curriculum included algebra and geometry, French, Latin, natural philosophy and history, rhetoric and composition, music, and drawing. Unfortunately, the academic records of nineteenth-century Brookline students have not survived, but if Frank's performance in later life is any indication, he most likely pursued his studies conscientiously and with unusual skill.[11]

With money chronically short, the Blakes expected their male children to begin adult lives early. Frank's older brother Charles had already left home with an appointment to the Naval Academy. Charles had obtained his good fortune through the influence of an uncle, Commodore George

Smith Blake, who had been superintendent of the Naval Academy during the Civil War. In an effort to help balance the family budget, Uncle George and Aunt Mary Blake had moved into the Plymouth Street home of Frank's father in May 1866. "We are now members of Frank's household upon terms which seem favorable & satisfactory all round & here we remain for the *present*."[12] George and Mary Blake viewed their stay as strictly temporary while they hunted for a house of their own. For the present, however, the arrangement proved mutually beneficial.

The resourceful and respected commodore proved a godsend to Frank, Sr., and his family. Just when Blake family finances reached some stability, another threat loomed. As the Custom House appraiser, Blake's father discovered that maintaining his integrity and retaining his job could prove contradictory goals. On May 3, 1866, George Blake recorded in his diary that his brother Frank, Sr., had been resisting the attempts of several Boston merchants, led by one Philo Shelton, to defraud the government. These men also sought to remove Blake from his position, as he was an obvious impediment to their schemes. The commodore wrote an assistant secretary of the Navy to warn of the trouble, which fortunately proved sufficient to end the threat.[13]

As lighthouse inspector for the district of Massachusetts and a former high-ranking naval officer, Uncle George could find other ways to assist his struggling brother and his family. Beginning in 1835, as a Navy lieutenant, George Blake had commanded the schooner *Experiment* during long-term duty with the Coast Survey and served there for eleven years, until the outbreak of the Mexican War. He knew his way around, and had won the friendship and respect of his fellow officers. He generously used his influence to secure a position there for Frank, Jr. His contact at the Survey, Julius E. Hilgard, "very kindly" offered Frankie "50 dollars per month in the drawing division at the office in Washington."[14] Without the commodore's intervention, obtaining such a position would have remained far out of Blake's reach.

Hilgard explained in a letter to George Blake that the appointment of a young man in an entry-level position, even at very low pay, implied the prospect of an eventual promotion. But the ranks were full at this time, and unless congressional appropriations considerably increased, there would be no such opportunity for Blake. Nevertheless, Hilgard made the offer with the suggestion that it would be for a year and would provide young Frank the chance to gain some professional experience. "He would be at first employed in tracing maps, and would have a opportunity of developing a good style and acquiring a knowledge of topography. I do not of course mean that his engagement must necessarily terminate by that time, but that is as far as I can now make any promise."[15] Uncle George also made arrangements for Frankie to have a room with the family of Professor Joseph E. Nourse, formerly of the Naval Academy and, at the time, librarian of the Naval Observatory. The Nourses agreed to "take Frankie into their family upon very reasonable terms. This provides for the boy, very comfortably, in every respect."[16]

Although Frankie attended Brookline High School for only about two years, he had in this brief time gained the respect and admiration of John Horr, his principal and teacher. In a general letter of recommendation he gave to Frank, Horr wrote that as "a young man and as a scholar" Blake had "acquitted himself honorably to a very high degree. For one of his age he has attained even to excellence in some departments. He is animated by a generous ambition and a high sense of honor. . . . I foresee for him a successful future, and I have the fullest assurance in commending him to the confidence of any one with whom he may come into business or social relations." Frankie recorded in a diary that he had just begun to keep, that May 25, 1866, was his last day of high school. Clearly, though, his education had just begun.[17]

Endnotes

1. Francis Blake, Jr., *A Record of the Blakes of Somersetshire, Especially in the Line of William Blake, of Dorchester, Mass., the Emigrant to New England: With one Branch of his Descendants, from the Notes of the Late Horatio G. Somerby* (Boston, 1881); Francis E. Blake, *Increase Blake of Boston, His Ancestors and Descendants with a Full Account of William Blake of Dorchester and his Five Children* (Boston, 1898); *New England Historical and Genealogical Register,*

January 1891, reprint in vol. 31 of the Francis Blake papers (hereafter FBP); J. Henry Lea, *A Genealogy of the Ancestors and Descendants of George Augustus and Louisa (Clap) Trumbull of Trumbull Square, Worcester, Mass.* (Worcester, Mass., 1886).

2. Mary Louisa Trumbull Cogswell, "The Trumbull Mansion and Its Occupants," in *Proceedings of the Worcester Society of Antiquity*, September, 1900.

3. Suffolk County Deeds, Bk. 551, L. 45; Norfolk County Deeds, Bk. 172, L. 50 location; *Boston City Directory*, 1853.

4. Vol. 31, FBP, Massachusetts Historical Society (hereafter, MHS). Unless otherwise indicated, all Blake papers cited are those housed in the collections of the MHS.

5. Information contained in a memorandum in Blake's handwriting in the rear of Blake's 1869 diary. Beginning in 1866, Francis Blake kept a separate diary for each year and continued the practice for the rest of his life. All diaries are in the Francis Blake papers and hereafter will be cited as Blake, Diary, FBP.

6. Blake memorandum, Blake, Diary, 1869, FBP.

7. Blake memorandum, Blake, Diary, 1869, FBP; *Boston City Directory*, 1862–1869.

8. Blake memorandum, Blake, Diary, 1869, FBP; Herbert H. Fletcher, *A History of the Church of Our Savior* (Brookline, Mass., 1936).

9. *Worcester Spy*, August 1862. Clipping, 1869, in Blake scrapbook, vol. 42, FBP.

10. Blake memorandum, Blake, Diary, 1869, FBP.

11. *Report of the School Committee for the Town of Brookline for the Year, 1865–1866* (Boston, 1866).

12. George S. Blake, Diary, May 1, 1866, (1866–1867), MHS.

13. George S. Blake, Diary, May 3, 7, 1866, (1866–1867), MHS.

14. Francis Blake, Jr., *Memorial to George S. Blake* (Boston, 1871); George S. Blake, Diary, May 18, 1866 (1866–1867), MHS.

15. George S. Blake, Diary, May 18, 1866, (1866–1867), MHS; copy in Francis Blake's handwriting of letter from Julius E. Hilgard to George S. Blake, May 14, 1866, FBP.

16. George S. Blake, Diary, May 25, 1866 (1866–1867), MHS.

17. Open letter from J. E. Horr, May 25, 1866, FBP; Blake, Diary, May 25, 1866, FBP.

CHAPTER 2

BEGINNING WITH
THE COAST SURVEY

O N SUNDAY, MAY 27, 1866, Frank Blake began his long trek to the nation's capital. His commodore uncle recorded in his diary that it was a "dull day. Light rain & quite mild. Just the weather for vegetation. Frankie left us today for Worcester, & will continue on to Washington tomorrow. It is his first essay in the struggle of the world, & is made, I think, under favorable auspices." In the days before Alexander Cassatt's great rail gateway at Pennsylvania Station in New York City, the trip from Massachusetts to Washington, D.C., required at least two days. Frank met his cousin Willie Lincoln and his grandmother Trumbull in Worcester, and then proceeded on toward Washington the next morning. He traveled by train from Worcester to New London, Connecticut, where he boarded a steamer for New York. The following morning, a ferry took him across the Hudson River to Jersey City where he boarded a Washington-bound train. He arrived at the Nourse home in Georgetown feeling "awful dizzy & sick." On May 30, Frank reported for duty at the office of the United States Coast Survey, then located on New Jersey Avenue on Capital Hill. Julius E. Hilgard, the commodore's contact, was away in New York, so Frank presented his credentials to W. W. Cooper, the head clerk, and agreed to start work the following day.[1]

Congress established the Coast Survey in 1807 at the recommendation of President Thomas Jefferson. When Congress completed organization of the Survey in 1816, it appointed Ferdinand R. Hassler, a Swiss engineer of remarkable ability and exacting standards, as the first superintendent. Hassler divided the United States Coast Survey's (USCS) operations into three groups: geodetic, topographic, and hydrographic, and set standards of excellence that earned the USCS the scientific world's highest regard. But in the political world of Congress, the Survey's painstaking work and slow schedule invited frequent criticisms. In 1842, a congressional committee subjected the Survey to hostile scrutiny. Hassler's excellent work could not be undermined, though, and the resulting report proved a resounding endorsement. Following Hassler's death the next year, Alexander Dallas Bache, the great grandson of Benjamin Franklin, assumed leadership of the USCS, maintaining Hassler's high standards and weathering the same congressional assaults. Bache, however, earned Congress's confidence and in 1858 won the acclaim of the American Association for the Advancement of Science. Under Bache, the AAAS considered the USCS's work to be unsurpassed anywhere in the world.[2]

For a young man with Frank Blake's talents and temperament, the USCS represented the best possible schooling; the experience would shape the rest of his career. But within the space of five days, this very young man had left behind the secure life of a schoolboy to enter the alien, adult world of government bureaucracy. He felt homesick, particularly for his dog Dukie, and he worried about his future. Edwin Hergesheimer, head of the drawing division, would not permit his young employee the luxury of time to fret and immediately set him to work—in those times, six days a week. Hergesheimer liked Frank's first effort at map drawing and assigned a similar task, which also drew praise. Support from home began to buoy Frank's spirits and confidence, especially his father's assurances that his family—even Dukie—missed him. If Frank wondered about his family's concern for him, the voluminous correspondence that arrived from Massachusetts surely erased any doubt. During his first month in Washington, Frank received twenty-one letters from family and friends, which he characteristically recorded in his diary and carefully preserved.[3]

Blake's intellectual curiosity and enthusiasm began to attract the attention of his superiors. Frank showed his sextant to Hergesheimer, who responded by explaining the workings of the lock level. He took Frank to the instrument shop to show him a theodolite, a prismatic compass, and the alidade part of a plane table, important tools of Coast Survey work. Hergesheimer perceived in Blake the makings of a very good draftsman, and spent considerable time discussing drawing, surveying, and other USCS work with his young employee. But this attention did not assuage Frank's continued loneliness and sagging confidence. Sundays brought him some comfort as he imagined his family attending Episcopal services back in Boston, but homesickness still gnawed at him: "A week ago I was home! it seems like a year," he pined.[4]

During his second week in Washington, Frank was delighted by a surprise visit from his father, who had been summoned to Washington by the secretary of the Treasury. Frank and his father discussed Frank's work with Hergesheimer, met with several Survey colleagues and discussed his future. After his father's return to Massachusetts, Frank's mother wrote to him, concerned about the report she had received from her husband. She reminded him that he had been given an enviable position: "You are receiving a salary that not one in many thousands your age have, receiving the very best training to fit you for as good an occupation as any especially with your tastes."[5]

Although the first few weeks were difficult ones, Frank's talents and dedication were bound to attract the attention and help an uncertain fifteen-year-old boy would need to launch a career. His landlord, Joseph E. Nourse, took Frank on a tour of the Naval Observatory, then located at Twenty-third and D Streets, N. W., where he met the naval observatory superintendent, Adm. Charles H. Davis (1807–1877). Davis, a Civil War hero, Massachusetts native, and a founder of the National Academy of Sciences, was a friend of Commodore Blake and Frank Blake, Sr. He received the young man very cordially and took the youth to his home to meet his wife, a first cousin of Frank's father. The visit proved a milestone in Frank's career. Thereafter, he regularly visited both the observatory and the Davis home, where he found other celestial attractions in Admiral Davis's daughters, Nannie and Daisy (one eventually married Brooks Adams and the other Henry Cabot Lodge). Flag officers are not known to suffer fools gladly. Thus, Davis's interest in Frank provided him powerful support and a much-needed injection of professional confidence. The two met whenever both visited Boston and continued to strengthen their bond through years of correspondence. They remained friends for the rest of Davis's life.[6]

About two weeks after beginning his new job, Blake met the man who would be his principal mentor and senior colleague during his entire service with the Coast Survey. Julius Erasmus Hilgard (1825–1891), born in Bavaria, immigrated to the United States at age ten. Initially educated by his father, Hilgard began the study of civil engineering in 1843. He later met Alexander Dallas Bache, who offered him an appointment as an assistant in the Coast Survey. He soon rose to the position of assistant-in-charge, and during Bache's final years of ill health he assumed daily responsibility for the Survey. An influential professional, Hilgard was an original member of the National Academy of Sciences as well as its home secretary. He was also a delegate to the International Metric Commission and a member of the International Bureau of Weights and Measures. In 1874, he became president of the American Association for the Advancement of Science. His contacts would prove critical to Blake's career.[7]

Hilgard quickly perceived Blake's talents, but Blake's weak penmanship kept him from entering the Survey's "computer department." In those days a computer was a good mathematician with a pencil, responsible for the reduction of astronomical observations. The Coast Survey maintained an excellent team of them. Alert to every suggestion, Blake went to work to improve his handwriting. Of his first meeting with Hilgard, the young boy wrote, "He was very frank, & said that if he found that it wouldn't be best for me to keep on, he would tell me." The next day Hilgard examined Frank's work and pronounced it very well done, although noting that Blake did not yet understand the hachure—a system of lines used to indicate slopes on topographical maps. Hergesheimer reassured Frank that he would eventually learn about the hachure. Blake showed Hilgard a map of Longwood he had crafted, about which Hilgard commented, "Well, I must say, all this looks very finely."[8]

Hergesheimer and Blake became friends. They talked about family relations, and Hergesheimer must have told Blake about his childhood, including the fact that he was examined in cube root and quadratic equations when only nine years old. Training at the Survey continued with exercises in drawing and lettering, and Blake continued to win Hilgard's approval. As time passed, Frank explored the Coast Survey's other activities and from time to time sought advice from his Uncle George. On July 8, 1866, the commodore acknowledged receiving a drawing of Hull Head, Massachusetts, that Frank had sent him: "You have already laid a good foundation in topographical drawing under a master who is admitted to be the best in this country." The following day Hergesheimer noticed Frank carrying a copy of Vega's *Logarithmic Tables*,[9] which Hilgard had lent him. After some discussion, Hergesheimer suggested that Frank participate in a USCS triangulation party. Blake asked if it wouldn't be better for him to learn something about drawing first. "I don't want to discourage you," Hergesheimer said, "you are doing very well, only I think your tastes run in that line—still you will have spent the year very profitably if you stay here." Blake wasted no time in beginning work with his logarithmic tables. He calculated a triangle to show Hilgard and was put in G. A. Schott's office where he copied and read proofs. At Hilgard's suggestion, he asked Schott for some work in tertiary triangles to practice at home. Frank's mathematical wizardry soon outpaced the adults in the office, who, understandably, resented the brilliance of a mere boy. "I asked Mr. Schott if he didn't think the person who calculated. . . [a measurement] might have made a mistake. He said no! I asked Mr. Courtenay to go over it, which he did and agreed with me. I told Mr. Schott who looked the other computation over and tore it up."[10]

Idleness made Frank uncomfortable. Hergesheimer was away during the first week in August, leaving Frank without an immediate boss. He improved the time as well as he could, studying, practicing, and looking for ways to be useful, but yearned for more work. Frank had acquired an impressive amount of professional knowledge, earned the friendship and support of a number of senior colleagues, and made the transition from home to independent life. His supervisors believed he was ready to take to the field. In early December 1866, Frank joined Assistant Frederick T. Nes for hydrographic work at Havre de Grace, Maryland, at the mouth of the Susquehanna River. They took soundings and bearings to precisely chart water depths, all the time fighting bitter cold, gusty northwest winds, and dangerous ice flows. Frank kept up his personal correspondence and apprised his family and the commodore of his labors. At Christmas, Frank Blake turned sixteen years old.[11]

Shortly after New Year's Day 1867, Hilgard declared his intention to send Blake back to the field, this time to accompany Assistant W. S. Edwards for hydrographic work in Florida. After the blustery sojourn to Maryland, Florida must have sounded enticing. Frank traveled to Boston to visit family and friends and prepare for his new adventure. Despite the near-tragic incident with his cousin's servant, he purchased a new .31 caliber Remington powder and ball five-shot revolver. At the end of the month, he packed his Remington and other gear, bid his family goodbye, kissed his dog Dukie, and boarded the sleeper-train for New York by the inland route. He then sailed from New York with Edwards and the Survey team for Key West aboard the steamer *Euterpe*.

The Florida venture proved exciting. Headquartered aboard the U. S. Survey Schooner *George M. Bache*, Blake and his colleagues were hit by a "norther" on their first morning aboard. The gusts caused the vessel to drag anchor, and the next morning found the wind still blowing hard. When the storm subsided, Frank and two friends went ashore and took a three-mile walk along the beach collecting shells, coral, and natural curiosities. He saw coconut trees heavily laden with fruit and other exotic plant life. On February 14, Blake transferred to the *Corwin* for hydrographic work in Havana, Cuba, carrying his valise, mapping pens, and two very hard pencils.

"Everything looked strange and very pretty," Frank later wrote. He went ashore to savor the local refreshments: "Vino Catalina" and soda water at five cents per glass. On Sunday, Blake and several colleagues visited Regulus to see a bull fight; the killing of five bulls struck Frank as unsuitable Sunday activity. Three years later, Blake wrote about his experience and expressed considerable disgust for the torture and killing of innocent animals for the amusement of "ladies and gentlemen" of Havana's aristocracy. "Thus, throughout that bright pleasant Sunday afternoon, we were, for the first and last time, spectators of the wild sport which ceased only with the setting of that sun which God has made to shine upon the wicked as well as the good."[12]

The party remained in Havana until February 26, occupied principally in taking soundings. Then, in preparation for leaving, Blake gathered a supply of fresh oranges and on his last day in Havana purchased a lawn dress for his mother. Back in Key West, Blake kept a meteorological journal, recording three times a day the temperature, barometric pressure, direction and force of the wind, and cloud cover. In mid-March, Blake's vessel left for Charlotte Harbor on the west coast of Florida, a two-day passage up the shoreline, for additional hydrographic work. The relatively large amount of free time and Florida's bountiful flora and fauna permitted Blake to indulge his interest in nature. He caught fish, including sharks, and turtles, gathered the eggs of pelicans, cormorants, oyster catchers, blue herons, and mocking birds, and collected birds from hunting expeditions. Blake's eye for detail and acute sense of composition coupled with the appreciation of beauty he developed on this excursion later found expression in his marvelous photographic work.

By the end of April the expedition had nearly finished its tasks. A headwind delayed its departure, but soon the vessel reached Boca Grande, at the outer entrance to Charlotte Harbor, where the crew spent about three weeks surveying. Frank worked the twenty-three pound deep-sea lead; one morning he cast and hauled the line twenty-seven times, and then sixty-five times the next morning. The exercise strengthened Blake considerably. "Last night my breast measured 33 inches," he noted proudly. A day of inclement weather allowed the crew to catch up on record-keeping. During a trip ashore, Blake set fire to some palmetto trees, which burned splendidly at the edge of a lagoon, and gathered more birds' eggs. Between such high jinks and his official duties, Frank continued his studies, spending a good deal of time with Hackley's *Trigonometry*.[13]

With work complete, the group sailed for Key West on May 21. Beating out of the harbor in the afternoon with a headwind but fair tide, they headed south. The next day a squall overtook them. They ran it without sail, fortunately in the right direction, and arrived in Key West two days later. They spent the next four days cleaning up the vessel, making inventories, copying drawings, bringing journals up to date, collecting a few last souvenirs, and packing their gear for the steamer home. The record of their accomplishment, contained in the *Annual Report of the Coast Survey* for 1867, includes the survey of Charlotte Harbor, placement of twenty-five signals, determination of 1,838 angles, and 20,656 soundings.[14]

By good fortune, when Frank arrived home in Boston, he encountered W. W. Cooper, clerk in the Coast Survey Office, accompanied by Professor Benjamin Peirce, the Survey's new superintendent. Peirce's wife, Sarah, was a first cousin of Frank's father and a sister of Admiral Davis's wife. Cooper introduced them, and after some conversation, Pierce said he would try to have Blake assigned to Professor Joseph Winlock at Harvard, where Frank could continue his studies in astronomy and live at home. For the next seven weeks, as Frank awaited orders from the Survey, he was free to do as he pleased. His Florida egg collection aroused considerable interest, and on June 6, he showed some samples to Edward A. Samuels, assistant to the secretary of the Massachusetts State Board of Agriculture and a distinguished ornithologist and author of *Ornithology and Oology of New England*. The following day, he took his entire collection to Samuels and they traded specimens. Over the course of the next few weeks, Frank gathered more egg specimens and made a complete catalog of the collection classified according to Samuels's method. His collection eventually included eighty-six species labeled with their English and Latin names, source, and identifying Samuels number.

After a brief and laborious document-copying job for the Survey, Frank met George W. Dean, a USCS assistant, and Edward Goodfellow,

Assistant in Astronomical Observation, at the Harvard Observatory on August 8. As with the Naval Observatory, the Coast Survey had very close ties with the Harvard Observatory, cooperating with them on many projects and sharing information, publications, instruments, and staff. Several Harvard professors of astronomy simultaneously held appointments with the Coast Survey. The observatory was a well-run facility, held in high esteem by the international astronomical community. Talent paired with family connections again brought Blake an important opportunity.[15]

The Coast Survey employed a variety of astronomical procedures, all requiring accurate calculations on the positions of stars. Observers had obtained such information as they could from a variety of catalogs, but they needed a more efficient and accurate resource. To supply this need, Benjamin Apthorp Gould (1824–1896) produced *Standard Mean Right Ascensions of Circumpolar and Time Stars*, which became Blake's constant companion for as long as he engaged in astronomical work. A skilled, Harvard-trained mathematician, Gould recognized the advantages of the telegraphic method of determining longitude and adapted it to the work of the Survey. He was first to determine the difference in longitude between Greenwich, England, and Washington, D.C., over the Atlantic Cable.[16] Gould had collected fifteen years of longitudinal observations and Frank was asked to arrange the material.

Under the direction of Goodfellow, Frank spent the rest of the year at the Observatory. As he usually did, Frank made a good impression on his superiors, and he received a tempting offer from Professor Winlock, director of the Observatory, to work full-time for him. Although grateful for the vote of confidence, Frank preferred to remain with the Coast Survey. His colleagues came to rely on the accuracy of his work, and by November 1867 Frank was reading chronograph sheets. The chronograph was an instrument used in telegraphic longitude operations to provide an accurate record of clock beats and the precise time of transit of an observed star. Blake learned fast and worked hard. Although still only sixteen, his supervisors asked him to join another field party, this time in Texas.

New Year's Day 1868 was not a holiday for Blake. He was up early and off to Cambridge where he met his colleague S. E. Chandler and called on Dr. Gould to retrieve some Coast Survey instruments he needed for the Texas longitude work. On Chandler's recommendation, Blake bought himself a copy of Chauvenet's *Spherical and Practical Astronomy*, knowing that his next assignment would leave him much time to master it.[17] Three days later he sailed on the *Kensington* for New Orleans. This time Blake traveled in style, occupying a stateroom that his father came to inspect before they sailed. Chandler brought a friend, and they had a "bon voyage" party, feasting on ale, cake, figs, and candy. When Frank arose the next morning the vessel was already hauling off. It was a fine morning, clear and cold, as they departed from Boston. He enjoyed the passage, improving the time by reading *The Cricket on the Hearth*, practicing navigation, and making celestial observations.

Upon arriving in New Orleans on January 15, Blake secured a room at 38 Carondelet Street—at $1.50 per day. He toured the French Quarter, went to the Varieties Theatre to see Joe Jefferson in "Rip Van Winkle," and visited the Crescent Billiard Room, equipped with twenty-three tables, the most elegant he had ever seen. At the St. Charles Theatre he saw "Colleen Baron," followed by "The Dutchman in Difficulty or the original John Smith." The "house was nearly empty," Blake noted in his diary and considered the play to be "the most miserable I ever witnessed." Blake left the excitement of New Orleans for Galveston on January 20, and arrived four days later.[18]

The first order of business was the erection of a portable observatory, which required a solid and level foundation to mount the clock, transit, and chronograph. Frank took his turn at the shovel, and after a strenuous day's labor in the cold the crew completed most of the work. On January 29, they mounted the transit and the Kessels clock and ran a wire to the local telegraph office to provide direct communication with the observatory in New Orleans. That evening after supper, Blake and his colleagues made their first observations. Goodfellow read eight stars while Blake marked the time on the sidereal chronometer, computed clock and azimuth corrections, comparison of chronometers, and reduction of time to arc, as well as performing other tasks. That afternoon, he went out to the observatory where Goodfellow had been installing the chronograph. The telegraph operator communicated with the operator at Houston. When they connected the clock to the wire, the office received the signal clearly. With the instruments in place and operating, there followed a period of instrument corrections, rating the clock and chronometers, preparing forms for meteorological observations, and practicing at the telegraph key. The chronograph began to malfunction, catching at intervals, so they tinkered with it for an afternoon with only moderate success. Finally, on February 7, they received a telegram from George Dean at New Orleans asking if they would be ready to exchange signals that night. They were able to reply, "Ready at 9."[19]

On the night of February 17, they obtained good observations, with the clocks beating together for the first time. After their second exchange, Dean sent word from New Orleans, "If you have got good time tonight we will close this campaign." Frank noted that the chronograph sheets "were the prettiest I have ever seen," and Goodfellow concluded that, "We have good time." The longitude between New Orleans and Galveston was settled at last in what Goodfellow described as the most successful campaign in memory.[20]

For most of March, Frank remained in Galveston engaged in computing and work on the records. While the quality and quantity of his work always seemed to please his superiors, he tended to be critical of himself: "I find that one great defect in myself is the inaccuracy of my computation arising from too much haste—It is a source of much embarrassment to me and I am going to try and rid myself of the habit (for it is nothing else) by going over every computation twice." For a very young man, Blake possessed an enormous capacity for work. He began at 8:15 A.M. and continued steadily until 4:15 P.M., stopping only for a half-hour lunch. In six hours he read four chronograph sheets containing forty-two stars and prepared most of the forms for reading clock signals.[21]

The last leg of the Texas campaign took place in April at Port Lavaca, where Goodfellow set Frank to work on a list of stars for the zenith telescope. He compiled the list from the *British Association Catalogue*, "the slowest, dullest, most tiresome work I have ever done." He then carried out the same type of operations previously performed at Galveston, but without a telegraphic connection. Blake loved his work but advised readers of the *Boston Transcript*, in one of his first publications, that Port Lavaca was a wind-blown "collection of huts!" He had an equally low opinion of the local inhabitants: "Much more might be said in regard to the lawlessness of the people, but for the present I will refrain." He bid farewell to Texas on May 2 and a week later boarded a train for home. Blake's confidence grew as his colleagues at the Survey came to fully appreciate his abilities. When a colleague requested that Blake be assigned to another routine expedition, an official at the Washington office replied: "Damn it, we're not going to bury Blake in a hydrographic party."[22]

Endnotes

1. George S. Blake, Diary, May 28–30, 1866, (1866–1867), MHS; May 1866, Blake Diary, FBP.
2. For information about the US Coast Survey see: *Centennial Celebration of the United States Coast and Geodetic Survey* (Washington, D.C., 1916); Gustavus Weber, *The Coast and Geodetic Survey, Its History, Activities and Organization* (Baltimore, 1923); Hugh Richard Slotten, *Patronage, Practice, and the Culture of American Science: Alexander Dallas Bache and the U.S. Coast Survey* (Cambridge, Eng., 1994).
3. Blake, Diary, June 1866, FBP; Francis Blake, Sr. to Francis Blake, Jr., June 5, 1866, FBP.
4. Blake, Diary, June 3–8, 1866, FBP.
5. Francis Blake, Sr. to Francis Blake, Jr., June 16, 1866, FBP.
6. For a history of the Naval Observatory, see Gustavus Weber, *The Naval Observatory, Its History, Activities and Organization* (Baltimore, 1926) and William I. Milham, *Early American Observatories* (Williamstown, Mass., 1938); Stewart Sifakis, ed., *Who Was Who in the Civil War* (New York, 1988), 170.
7. Obituary, *Boston Herald*, May 8, 1891; *Centennial Celebration of the United States Coast and Geodetic Survey.*
8. Blake, Diary, June 11–12, 1866, FBP.

9. Georg Freiherr von Vega, *Logarithmic tables of numbers and trigonometrical functions*, Tr. from the 43d or Dr. Bremiker's . . . edition, by W. L. F. Fischer (Berlin, New York, 1859).

10. Blake, Diary, June 18–19, 23, July 9, 14, 1866, FBP; George S. Blake to Francis Blake, July 8, 1866, FBP.

11. George S. Blake, Diary, Dec. 17, 1866, (1866–1867), MHS.

12. *Boston Transcript*, Aug. 2, 1870.

13. Blake, Diary, Feb. 26, Mar. 15, 20, Apr. 7, 1867, FBP.

14. United States Coast Survey, *Report for* 1867 (Washington, D.C., 1867), 32.

15. Blake, Diary, July 27, Aug. 7–8, 1867, FBP; William Cranch Bond, *History and Description of the Astronomical Observatory of Harvard College* (Cambridge, Mass., 1856).

16. Blake's own copy of the second edition is in his reference collection at the Massachusetts Historical Society; Dumas Malone et al., eds., *Dictionary of American Biography* 17 vols (New York, 1936–1988), 4:447.

17. The Boston Athenæum's copy of *Spherical and Practical Astronomy* contains pen corrections to some of Chauvenet's computations in the unmistakable handwriting of Francis Blake. They may be found in vol. II.

18. Blake, Diary, Jan. 16–20, 1868, FBP.

19. Blake, Diary, Jan. 28, Feb. 7, 1868, FBP.

20. Blake, Diary, Feb. 13, 17, 1868, FBP.

21. Blake, Diary, Feb. 25, March 10, 26, 1868, FBP.

22. *Boston Transcript*, May 1, 1868; Blake, Diary, May 3, 1868, FBP.

CHAPTER 3

THE WIDE, WIDE WORLD

DURING THE NEXT THREE YEARS, Blake matured personally and professionally and saw more of the world than most people twice his age. Self-reliant and disciplined, he increasingly grew impatient with those who weren't, including his own family. Blake's Coast Survey work interested him deeply, but it hardly taxed his abilities. In a six-hour burst he could solve difficult calculations that took others three days to complete. With speed and genius that allowed him much time to do as he pleased—and in time a salary to make that possible—Blake indulged himself, a habit that would later define his character as he acquired real wealth. He collected scientific instruments—his sextant had been on an 1836 exploration of Hudson's Bay—and bought countless books—scientific treatises, literary works, and popular fiction. He read voraciously, taking full advantage of the Boston Athenæum's fine library, and frequented the theater in Boston, or in whatever city he visited. He bought a hot-bath tub, a set of twenty-pound dumbbells for his exercise regimen, and enlisted trainer John B. Bailey to give him boxing lessons. No surprise, he indulged his fascination for attractive young ladies.[1]

In the summer of 1868, Blake's sister Lisa married Charles Welles. The Blakes held a reception for the couple at their Longwood home, inviting twenty or thirty friends. Frank, short of cash due to a delayed paycheck, set about buying proper clothes and a wedding present at the last minute. Luck again fell Frank's way when he managed to find a tailor who could deliver trousers and a vest on one day's notice. A comb, brush, tooth and nail brush, sponge, and a bottle of cologne constituted his sister's gift, all he could afford on his current Coast Survey pay.[2]

Brother Charlie proved a humiliation to all, perhaps especially to the commodore who had arranged for him to enter the Naval Academy. He neglected his studies, and threats to expel him only led to drunkenness. When Charlie refused to swear off drink, the academy dismissed him. He passed time idly at the family house, refusing to do much of anything except drink, borrow money from his father—who had little to spare—and quarrel with the family. Frank's wizardry and success at the Coast Survey swelled his parent's pride, but only caused Charlie to resent him. Any comparison between the two siblings by their parents inflamed mounting tensions. One day Frank's father gave him a ticket to the Boston Museum. When Charlie learned of it, he "called me a d—ned puppy and told me to go to h—l &c &c." Several days later, Frank provoked his brother, commenting that he had spent yet another day loafing about the house. In response, Charlie excused his indolence with the claim that he had no shoes to wear. Upon hearing this, his father gave him $9.00, which Charlie immediately squandered. When Frank declined to lend his brother twenty cents, he broke Frank's hand magnifying glass.

Charlie's bullheaded conduct continued, even threatening his father's attempts to improve the family's chronically uncertain finances. Francis Blake, Sr., who had briefly worked as a leather merchant, decided to manufacture and sell boot blacking, "Dumont's Liquid Blacking or Parisian Polish." By mid-August, he had secured commercial space on or near Harvard Street and proudly produced his first batch. When 1,000 "Dumont" labels arrived from an engraver, he asked his troubled son to help bottle the polish. But Charlie could not be bothered with a task as pointless as bottling polish and only half-filled the containers. Francis sent his son home.

As the year passed, Charlie's behavior worsened. Unemployed and uncooperative, he even refused to help with household chores. Then came news that he had contracted venereal disease. Following this, in October, Francis, Sr., suffered a paralytic stroke, causing him to lose muscle control over the left side of his face. Family matters came to a dramatic head the first week of December when the furnace was shut down for a routine cleaning. A fire was built in Frank's room so he would be warm enough to do his Coast Survey work. Charlie's mother asked him to cut wood, but he refused. He then attacked Frank, and the two went at one another with the fireplace tongs. While Frank easily subdued his wayward older brother, their mother stood by in tears.[3]

Despite troubles at home, Frank managed to read omnivorously and began writing occasional letters for a Boston newspaper under the nom de plume, "Petit Trianon." He published letters about earthquakes, the Boston theater scene, the United States exploration expedition to the Dead Sea, and the activities of the Coast Survey. He also began what grew into a lifelong fascination with family genealogy. But the crisis over his brother had filled the Blake home with tension. It was not a place to study or write, much less perform calculations for the Survey. Frank would be working soon for the Survey at the Harvard Observatory, and on January 13, 1869, he seized the opportunity to move into the boarding house of a Mrs. Richardson on Mellen Street in Cambridge.[4]

At the Harvard Observatory, Blake helped establish longitudinal lines between Cambridge and San Francisco; using two wires from San Francisco, Frank and his colleagues measured the length of time it took a telegraphic signal to complete a circuit of over 7,000 miles. Blake made several sets of observations with the transit for time, corrected and calibrated his instruments, made the required duplicate records, and performed other duties of an astronomical party aid. He taught himself to use the telegraph and erected his own small system to practice with a friend. His work earned the praise of experienced observers and a welcomed pay raise.[5]

In June, the Survey sent Blake to New Jersey to gather more recordings and then in July to Shelbyville, Kentucky, where Winlock had attended college, to view the century's last observable solar eclipse in the United States. As Blake wrote under his pen name in the *Boston Transcript*, a "very valuable contribution to science may safely be predicted from a party under the direction of so distinguished an astronomer."[6] The eclipse would be visible along a track about 140 miles wide, stretching across the continent from the Bering Straits to North Carolina. The Survey engaged the legendary Boston photographer Joseph A. Whipple to record the event. Blake registered the precise time of the exterior and interior contacts, the occultation of sunspots, and, marking his astounding maturity and skill, wrote the Coast Survey's official report of its observations.[7]

Blake's youth and dazzling performance caught many eyes. Promotions, pay raises, and exciting new travel opportunities came his way, which likely eased his shock upon learning that his family no longer could afford their Longwood home. Throughout the year, his father's faltering business ventures had put the family on the skids; one man quit Blake's boot polish business in disgust. As early as January, the superintendent of the gas company had arrived to shut off the gas. "I turned it on with little difficulty," Blake wrote. His father rented out the house for $70 a month and moved with his wife to Pemberton Square in Boston. "Poor Dukie! What will become of him?" Frank sadly wondered. He packed up any of his possessions remaining in the house, leaving behind two trunks and his egg collection, and moved into a boarding house with his cousin George Lincoln at Mount Vernon Place. Irrepressible, Francis, Sr., celebrated their last day at Longwood with a final dinner and a bottle of champagne.[8]

In early October 1869, Blake's Coast Survey supervisor Julius Hilgard privately informed him that he would be returning to Washington and receiving orders to proceed west to help determine the longitude and latitude at St. Louis, Missouri, and Cedar Falls, Iowa. "It is my intention," wrote Hilgard, "to leave the execution of the work to you, aided by persons in the respective localities, where there are those both willing and able to assist you. I have an understanding with the Supt. that the successful accomplishment of the work will be considered grounds for your promotion." Blake gathered up his instruments in Washington and immediately departed for Cedar Falls and St. Louis. He arrived in St. Louis at the end of October. As he began setting up his observatory, Blake received orders to report to Assistant G. W. Dean and proceed with him to Brest, France, to take part in a vital project using the Atlantic cable to determine transatlantic longitude. Blake was likely the youngest employee ever to take part in so important a scientific venture. Family problems began to shrink in significance with such delightful news. Frank departed immediately for Boston.[9]

In some senses, a different Frank Blake returned east. Not yet nineteen years old, he had come to possess confidence in his intellectual abilities and believed that he could accomplish whatever professional goal he aspired to. With Hilgard's praise much on his mind, Frank spoke with W. W. Cooper on November 5 and learned that he would not receive his promotion and pay raise until the following January. Impatient and sure of himself, Blake advised Cooper, "I wanted it now." Cooper obligingly drafted a letter to the secretary of the Treasury for Superintendent Peirce's signature recommending that Blake be promoted at once to the rank of sub assistant at $800 per year. Reluctant to lose a good man, Professor Winlock offered Blake a position at the Harvard College Observatory for $2,500 per year. But Blake's loyalty to the Coast Survey, the connections that it afforded, and the Survey's long-term career opportunities induced him to decline Winlock's offer. Moreover, for an eighteen-year-old boy, the independence, recognition, and fascinating work that the Coast Survey offered could not be equaled.[10]

After saying goodbye to family and friends, Frank set out on November 10 for New York. Finding Admiral Davis and his family on the train delighted Frank considerably, but the sight of the admiral's daughter Nanny stirred his heart, and she occupied his thoughts as he proceeded to New York by boat the following night. In New York, Frank checked in at the Astor House. A colleague arrived with $700 of Survey funds that Frank took to Blake Brothers, an international banking firm owned by a cousin, and changed the money to francs. The day's mail brought detailed instructions, a letter of introduction, and news from Hilgard that his promotion had been confirmed. Frank sailed on the *Ville de Paris* on November 13, casting off on a sea as smooth as a millpond. But by breakfast the following morning, the rolling ocean had sent many passengers to their berths, and before the day was out, Frank turned in as well, "jolly sick."[11]

Two days later, Frank had recovered sufficiently to return to the deck. There he found the Burnhams of Longwood, Massachusetts, especially young Marie. The unfortunate Burnhams had also spent a wretched two days below deck but were now beginning to acquire their sea legs. Frank took an immediate liking to them: "I have never met a family with whom I have fallen so much in love with as this one. Mr. Burnham is a splendid specimen of a man. One of the most beautiful traits in his character is the perfect control which he exercises over his temper." In contrast to his father's unpredictable anger, Frank found Burnham's patience and self-control quite inviting. But the true focus of Frank's attention soon arrived on deck. After a day in Marie Burnham's company, Frank had convinced himself that he had fallen in love. He desperately read Shakespeare when she remained below deck and composed a poem—"To Marie"—that captured his latest fascination. "Now that the hour is drawing near / When we must surely part / I pray you speak some words of cheer / To sooth my breaking heart. . . ." He slept with Marie's photograph tucked under his pillow, and when they disembarked at Brest, she gave Frank a little book of devotions, *Daily Food for Christians*. He should have taken the gift as a warning, but he promised to read it every day. In return, he gave her his lead pencil, and they agreed to meet in Paris the following Friday.

On November 28, Frank dined with the Burnhams. The evening left him in raptures over Marie: "One of the happiest days of my life," he wrote in his diary. But the following evening he found his Marie in the company of a George Merritt and himself "perfectly snubbed." He returned to his room and spent an hour marking eclipse photographs for the American legation, trying as best he could to bury his bitter disappointment. "My first impulse was to swear & curse, but then I couldn't help loving Marie, and I ended by reading my 'daily food' & praying to God for help to bear my affliction." Now he recorded in his diary, "One of the most unhappy days of my life."[12]

Over the next several days, Frank visited the Louvre, Notre Dame, the famed Paris morgue—with a fresh cadaver—the Hotel de Cluny, and the Luxembourg Palace. He toured the Hotel Meunie and Napoleon's tomb, and spent an hour viewing the city from the top of the Eiffel tower. He also began visiting the Crosby family, who had been aboard the *Ville de Paris*, and managed to get an introduction to Lou, one of the five Crosby daughters. Lou diverted his attention from his recent disappointment, and he became "very much interested in her. I think she cares just a little for me." In early December, he tried to win her affections with a bottle of Jocky Club perfume. "How full of life she is! and how I enjoyed myself," Frank registered happily in his diary. But he could not forget his Marie, "I shall always look at her photograph and read 'Daily Food' every night and morning." And so he did for a time, often praying for her happiness at the end of his day. On Sunday, December 5, he went to the Episcopal Church and sat one row behind the Burnhams. He drew a diagram of the pews in his diary, identifying his own seat with an "x" and that of Marie with a heart.

Frank left Paris and his Marie the next day, and returned to Brest to re-sume his Coast Survey duties. He engaged a carpenter to build an obser-vatory and then, with his colleagues, experimented on the Atlantic cable. They set their chronometer, installed the transit stand, connected the bat-teries, and mounted the chronograph. By Christmas day, Frank's nine-teenth birthday, they began observations. The day after, they contacted the Coast Survey station by telegraph at Duxbury, Massachusetts, over the cable. The work went quickly and left Frank plenty of time to pine for Marie Burnham and to read the Bible, which he did straight through for the first time in his life. He wrote that on December 31, he spent the last minutes of 1869 thinking about Marie. "At about five minutes of twelve, I opened my photograph album to the first page and began to look at Marie's picture which was the last thing I saw in the year 1869."[13]

On January 2, 1870, Frank completed the telegraph circuit at his temporary observatory and received the circuit breaks from the chrono-meter. But in order to exchange time signals with the Duxbury station, the weather had to be clear at both locations, permitting accurate observations. As per a special arrangement with the cable company, at a predetermined time they connected the cable from the observatory to the Atlantic cable, made their observations, and exchanged time signals. By January 20 they had managed six exchanges with Duxbury—two of which produced usable data. By the second week of February, Blake and his colleagues had completed their work, packed their instruments, and delivered them to the wharf for shipment home. As he had hoped, Superintendent Peirce granted Blake a six-week leave. Upon receiving the news, Frank immediately boarded a train for Paris. He revisited Notre Dame, the Louvre, the morgue, and the tombs of Napoleon, Voltaire, and Rousseau. He encountered an American acquaintance, Johnny Welch, and together they went to the theater to see Offenbach's "Les Brigands," followed by a visit to the Luxembourg Museum and the Sorbonne, "where is Richelieu's head and a magnificent monument to his memory." They luxuriated with cigars at the Grand Cafe and in the evening saw the Champs Élysées illuminated by gaslight.[14]

Sunday morning February 20, Frank stepped onto the 11:00 train to Marseille, where he would board the steamer *Pausilippe* for Civita Vecchia, Italy. Two days later, Frank settled on the steamer, where he enjoyed a breathtaking view of the Snow Mountains on Corsica before arriving at Civita Vecchia. A handsome boat bearing a reception committee composed of the former queen of Naples, several royal household members, and the Abbey of Civita Vecchia floated alongside to receive the Prince Imperial of Spain, then a boy of twelve, who was also aboard with his entourage. Frank then proceeded by rail to Rome, where he took a room at the Hotel Molano in the Via Gregoriano and found the Crosbys. There he learned that the Burnhams had checked into a nearby hotel: "It seems like a providential thing—my coming to this hotel," Frank recorded in his diary.

He quickly found his way to the Burnhams, especially "Marie who looked and appeared more beautiful than ever—not a trace of her former coolness. Staid there for as much as two hours and came away feeling happier than I have for many & many a day." Frank made the most of having the Crosbys and the Burnhams in convenient proximity and visited with both Lou and Marie. In one meeting on the Burnham's balcony, young Frank was astonished to hear Marie complain that he had neglected her and had left Paris without so much as a goodbye. One can almost see her fluttering eyelashes as Marie expressed her wish that they "should be good good friends forevermore." But Frank's fickle ardor had cooled and he spent more time with Lou Crosby than his once-precious Marie. He enjoyed two exciting weeks in Rome attending parties and taking daily excursions to the Colosseum, the Catacombs of Calixtus, St. Paul's, and the Appian Way.[15]

Frank returned to Paris on March 17 and spent about two weeks before returning to American waters, arriving back in Boston on April 6. Significantly, he did not immediately visit his parents' residence, but instead checked into a room at the Tremont House. He later boarded alone in a room on the first floor at No. 3 Mount Vernon Place, where his parents and his cousin Russell Sullivan occupied separate rooms two flights up. His European adventure had considerably elevated his standing in the Coast Survey and earned him yet another pay raise. More important, the adventure had introduced Blake to some of the greatest artwork in western Europe, and in developing his aesthetic sensibility, had awakened him to the wider world. Although only nineteen years old, Frank returned from Europe with greater maturity and a good deal more independence.[16]

The summer passed rapidly and happily for Frank, who remained preoccupied with both his Coast Survey work and a number of young women. In August, Frank set out for Bar Harbor, Maine, in company with Russell Sullivan. On the 27th, Frank recorded in his diary in the most matter-of-fact way that he "was introduced at an Eagle Lake party to the two Miss Hubbards." Lovely Lizzie and Lottie Hubbard were the daughters of the successful Boston merchant, Charles T. Hubbard. For the rest of their stay, the Hubbard girls received almost daily mention in Blake's diary, but always casually and without the lovesick entries of his transatlantic affair with the coy Marie. A Miss May Whitwell also vacationed at

Bar Harbor and had the misfortune of engaging Frank on the subject of women's rights. Annoyed by Whitwell's strong position, Frank declared that, "no class of persons should be allowed to vote who cannot take part in enforcing the laws which they may make—or who will not be subjected to the results of those laws." Whitwell "acknowledged her inability to deny the truth of my statement"—the irony of which seemed not completely lost on poor Frank. "She is very bright, intelligent, and pleasant," Frank acknowledged, "but very very much too strong minded for my taste."[17]

In late September, Blake conducted another routine astronomical trip to Harpers Ferry, West Virginia—interrupted by a severe earthquake—and on November 22, received an assignment from Secretary of the Treasury George S. Boutwell to accompany the Darien Expedition to Central America in search of a likely route for an interoceanic canal and to make astronomical observations. Other observations also danced in Frank's mind. One of the Hubbard daughters had made an impression on Frank, and he confided to his diary that "Somehow or other I have taken a very strong liking to Lizzie Hubbard & I will have her photograph some day." On November 27, he called on the Hubbards at Woodlands, their country estate in Weston, and then caught the New York train to report for duty with the Darien Expedition.[18]

A Central American canal had figured in American diplomacy since the 1840s, with the seizure of California and western territories from Mexico. A transisthmian railroad built by the New York capitalist William Aspinwall relieved some of the pressure for a canal, but it did not altogether quash interest in the project. The concept of an interoceanic canal so captivated President Grant that he persuaded Congress to appropriate funds for an expedition. Because the engineering of the day could not overcome the barriers to cutting a canal in Nicaragua, engineers sought a route further to the south at Darien, at what is now on the gulf side of Panama. But Americans scarcely knew anything about the area. Thomas O. Selfridge, Jr., an 1854 graduate of the United States Naval Academy, had survived the sinking of three vessels during the Civil War. Having demonstrated great courage and ability, Selfridge received command of the survey party of the Isthmus of Darien to ascertain the best point for a canal connecting the Atlantic and Pacific Oceans.[19]

Selfridge's account of the expedition is testimony to the courageous willingness of nineteenth-century explorers to endure scorching sun, "torrential rains, floods, raging currents, swamps, dense vegetation, poisonous snakes, bloodsucking bats, tarantulas, scorpions, hornets, wildcats, sand flies, and mosquitoes so thick that I have seen them put out a lighted candle with their burnt bodies." Certainly, as he concluded, Darien posed a challenge great enough to keep knowledge of the area "locked up for hundreds of years."[20]

On the evening of November 27, Blake picked up a copy of the *British Association Catalogue*, a list of stars and their coordinates, and two almanacs and boarded the night train for New York. The following morning he proceeded to the Brooklyn Navy Yard to report aboard the U.S.S. *Guard*; "and a dismal sight it was," Blake sadly discovered. After inspecting his "stateroom," he went to the Fulton Market for oysters and returned to the vessel with a fearful cold. One night aboard the *Guard* sent him packing to the Astor House. Blake spent the next few days preparing his instruments, focusing on his Negus sidereal chronometer. On December 3, the harbor pilot came aboard and a Navy tug pulled them away from the pier. With its top gallant sails and flying jib unfurled, the *Guard* reached the speed of eight knots by midnight. During the voyage, Blake occupied his time by reading Thackery, smoking, playing whist and cribbage, checking his solar chronometers, and standing his watch. At the end of December, after a ten-day call at Cartagena, Colombia, where the party recruited machetteros, men possessing the skill and stamina to cut trails and sight lines through dense tropical vegetation, the *Guard* reached the Atrato River in the Gulf of Darien, near the Isle de los Muertos.[21]

Blake found the harbor bleak and murky, "one of the most desolate, dreary spots I have ever seen. The country around it consists of two swampy tracts of land formed from the deposit of the Atrato & cut up into islands by the many mouths of that river." The appropriately named Isle de los Muertos proved to be low, wet, and covered with mangroves, so the expedition proceeded to a barren island to the north where they found firmer soil. Blake then spent New Year's Day 1871 writing an article for the *New York Tribune* which described his vessel's call at Cartagena and Selfridge's plans to investigate a canal route suggested by a guide who had spent his life harvesting rubber along the Atrato River and its tributaries.[22]

By January 23, Blake had obtained sufficient observations to establish longitude with the transit instrument, enabling him to remove it and mount the zenith telescope and begin his observations for latitude. A hydrographic party surveyed the harbor, and John Moran busied himself photographing the area; meanwhile, Selfridge tramped through the jungle. Eventually, six days overdue, Selfridge arrived on a steam launch and "came tottering over the gangway pretty well used up." He could scarcely walk to his cabin, where the expedition's physician found him suffering from fever. Blake recounted Selfridge's reconnaissance up the Atrato, Cacarica, and Barial rivers in another letter to the *Tribune*. On February 7, having seen enough of Darien, Selfridge pressed Blake to wind up his observations. But poor weather prevented Frank from finishing, which vexed Selfridge considerably. Not even twenty years old, Blake stood up to the Civil War hero: "I wasn't the clerk of the weather," he retorted. The weather soon broke, allowing Blake to finish his work and the party to depart. On February 11, Blake and his colleagues boarded the 7:00 A.M. train for the city of Panama, a four-hour ride that Frank found very interesting. Because the exact longitudinal positioning of Panama had not been established, Blake set up his observatory and, through the courtesy of the Panama Railroad, was able to make a telegraphic connection with Aspinwall for the comparison of time.[23]

The USS *Resaca* transported the party to the mouth of the Tuyre River, about 120 miles to the southeast of Panama, and anchored about six miles below Chipigana. Selfridge ordered a hesitant Blake to go to Pinogana, an Indian village of seventy-five bamboo huts about thirty-five miles upriver, to observe for longitude and latitude. The river proved too shallow for the *Resaca*, so the party transferred their gear to a steam launch. On February 23, Blake went ashore to begin his work, and Selfridge continued up the Tuyre. Blake mounted the zenith telescope and spent an afternoon making a list of eleven pairs of stars in preparation for the night's observations. He had the good luck to locate all his stars that night, determining the latitude of Pinogana to be 8° 7' 24.87". Five days later, having completed his observations, Blake dismantled his observatory and rejoined the main party. He concluded that "this is just the place for a canal."[24]

With this stage of their work competed, the party attempted an early departure but repeatedly ran aground. March 2 found them still struggling, and just before 3:00 A.M. an ebbing tide left them high and dry on a sandy flat five or six hundred feet wide. Not expecting a lengthy run, the five men had brought few provisions, and what now remained were ten bananas, a box of sardines, and some crumbs in the bottom of a hardtack keg. Before long, Blake and his colleagues began to show the effects of their hardship. They grew pale and gaunt, and one of the men shook with feverish chills. Large black rings, which appeared to be covered with barnacles, circled one man's eyes. After rowing intermittently for twenty-eight hours back to the *Resaca*, Blake's hands were blistered and he felt giddy and faint.

Blake quickly recovered and on March 8 set up his observatory for the last time on the Isthmus of Darien. Two days later, Selfridge directed him to return to New York and gave him a copy of a letter he had sent to Superintendent Peirce. "Upon the close of Mr. Blake's connection with the Expedition under my command," Selfridge wrote, "it gives me great pleasure to bear witness to the zeal, ability and ingenuity with which he has labored, and to recommend him to your favorable consideration." Blake happily packed his gear and four days of provisions and headed for Panama aboard the schooner *Tuyra*. Safely arriving in Panama, he checked in at the Grand Hotel, had his instruments stored, booked passage for New York aboard the *Ocean Queen*, and purchased 1,000 cigars. In his third letter to the *Tribune*, Blake affirmed the feasibility of a canal across Darien. In 1873, Selfridge returned to the Isthmus in search of an even better route, following the Atrato River to the Napipi and then connecting with the Doguado River down to Chiri Chiri Bay on the Pacific. His estimation of the canal's cost, which included a three-mile tunnel large enough for ships to pass through a mountain, was $123,958,117.50. It would not be unreasonable to conclude that Blake's role proved the most successful and useful part of the Darien expedition.[25]

Endnotes

1. Blake, Diary, June 22, 1868, FBP.
2. Blake, Diary, Aug. 10–11, 1868, FBP.
3. Charles Blake, Diary, May 16, June 6, Aug. 17, Sept. 14, 1868, FBP; Blake, Diary, June–Sept., Dec. 5, 1868, FBP.
4. *Boston Transcript*, Oct. 10, Nov. 10, 1868, Jan. 9, 1869; Blake, Diary, Oct. 20, 1868, FBP; Blake's father collected most of the family genealogical material, and it is contained in vol. 31 of the FBP. Also see, chapter 1, note 1.
5. Blake, Diary, Sept. 14, Nov. 24, 1868, Jan.–Mar., 1869, FBP.
6. *Boston Transcript*, Apr. 20, 1869.
7. United States Coast Survey, *Annual Report* (Washington, D.C, 1869); *Harper's Weekly*, Aug. 28, 1869, printed a front-page account of the eclipse with an engraving showing the arrangement of the instruments the Coast Survey used.
8. A. J. Moseman to Benjamin Peirce, Mar. 25, 1869, FBP; Caroline Blake to Francis Blake, June 13, 1869, FBP; Blake, Diary, Jan. 11, 27, Sept. 30, Oct. 3, 1869, FBP.
9. Julius E. Hilgard to Francis Blake, Oct. 4, 1869, FBP; Benjamin F. Peirce to Blake, Oct. 15, 1869, FBP.
10. Blake, Diary, November 5, 10, 1869, FBP; Benjamin Peirce to George S. Boutwell, Nov. 5, 1869, copy in FBP.
11. Blake, Diary, Nov. 10–14, 1869, FBP.
12. Blake, Diary, Nov. 16–29, 1869, FBP.
13. Blake, Diary, Dec. 3–31, 1869, FBP.
14. G. W. Dean to Blake, Feb. 12, 1870, conveys the superintendent's leave approval, FBP; Blake Diary, Jan. 2–Feb. 12, 15–19, 1870, FBP.

15. Blake, Diary, Feb. 20 to Mar. 16, 1870, FBP.

16. Benjamin Peirce to Francis Blake, July 27, 1870, FBP. Peirce advised Blake of a salary increase to $900 per year.

17. Blake, Diary, Aug. 27, Sept. 15, 18, 1870, FBP.

18. Blake, Diary, Sept. 20–Nov. 8, 1870, FBP, for a description of Blake's work in Maryland and West Virginia; Thomas A. Selfridge to Julius E. Hilgard, Nov. 25, 1870, FBP; George S. Boutwell to Benjamin Peirce, Nov. 22, 1870, copies in FBP.

19. Secretary of the Navy George M. Robeson to Thomas A. Selfridge, Jan. 10, 1870, in Thomas Oliver Selfridge, *Reports of Explorations and Surveys to Ascertain the Practicability of a Ship-canal between the Atlantic and Pacific Oceans by the Way of the Isthmus of Darien* (Washington, D.C., 1874).

20. Thomas O. Selfridge, Jr., *Memoirs of Thomas O. Selfridge, Jr., Rear Admiral, U. S. N.* (New York and London: 1924), 160.

21. Blake, Diary, Nov. 27–Dec. 28, 1870, FBP.

22. Blake, Diary, Dec. 29, 1870, FBP; undated clipping, Blake scrapbook, vol. 42, FBP.

23. Blake, Diary, Dec. 29, 1870–Feb. 11, 1871, FBP.

24. Blake, Diary, Feb. 14–28, 1871, FBP.

25. Thomas A. Selfridge to Benjamin Peirce, Mar. 9, 1871, copy in Blake papers, MHS; clipping with the dateline Mar. 19, Blake scrapbook, vol. 42, FBP; Selfridge, *Memoirs*, 199; Selfridge, *Reports of Explorations*, 66, 195–221.

CHAPTER 4

THE COURTSHIP OF LIZZIE HUBBARD

WITHIN FORTY-EIGHT HOURS of his return from Panama, Frank visited Charles T. Hubbard's home at Louisburg Square on Beacon Hill; that "stunning Miss Lizzie H." preoccupied his thoughts. The Hubbards appeared to approve of young Blake and invited him to tea and the theater the following day. More importantly, Lizzie approved and repeatedly invited her suitor to play billiards and attend her many parties. Frank eagerly accepted her invitations: "I can refuse no opportunity to be near her."[1] An invitation to a formal party on April 25 left poor Frank in a dither. Anxious and callow, he nervously ordered a new suit for $65, a handsome sum for someone earning $900 a year. Frank's suit arrived at 6:15 P.M. the day of the party. He then scurried through a drizzling rain and reached the Hubbard's door at 7:30 P.M. There he found Lizzie wearing the pair of gloves that he had given her. "Lizzie (God bless her) was very, very kind," Frank recorded in his diary. He watched her dance and found her as graceful as she was attractive. Sensing his anxiety, Lizzie did what she could to make Frank feel at ease among the well-to-do guests he found at her home.[2]

Given his modest family background, Frank found the Hubbards' respectability and material success intimidating. Still, this was just the kind of family he had hoped to find and, eventually, emulate. Lizzie's grandfather Benjamin Sewall, who had come to Boston from Hallowell, Maine,

37

about 1830, made his start in the grocery business and soon diversified into shipping, manufacturing, banking, and insurance. His only child, Louisa Bowman Sewall, married Charles T. Hubbard and had three daughters, Elizabeth (Lizzie), Louisa, and Charlotte. Lizzie's father had entered the business world with Sewall, Day & Co., cordage manufacturers, and by the 1840s was trading in cotton, coffee, tobacco, and pig iron. He conducted business with some of Boston's elite families: Weld, Forbes, and Minot. Hubbard also became treasurer of the Boston Flax Mills and the Ludlow Manufacturing Company. A handsome townhouse on Louisburg Square, then as now a very fashionable neighborhood, served as the family's principal residence. They also owned a country residence covering about 445 idyllic acres in the lovely southern part of Weston near the Charles River.[3]

Frank understood the advantages of wealth and focused his attention on young Lizzie, calling on her nearly every day. They spent time shopping together, went to plays and teas, and attended church together. Impatient, Frank boldly asked if he could "throw aside the cold, formal Miss Hubbard, and call her Eliza," a name that Lizzie had once told him she liked. The prudent Miss Hubbard replied that she did not know if he could, but would tell him next time they met. Twenty-four hours later, Frank was calling her Lizzie. No one could miss the growing intimacy between the two. Mr. Hubbard certainly noticed the frequency of Frank's visits, and worried over the sparkle in his daughter's eye. One evening, as Frank and Lizzie first spent time gazing at the stars and then playing billiards, a concerned Mr. Hubbard burst into the billiard room, an act that later sent Frank grumbling to his diary. After friends inquired whether Lizzie and Frank were engaged, Mr. Hubbard began checking into Frank's background. This included asking Frank's cousin Charlotte many questions about the young man and his character.

By mid-May, the level of Frank's boldness had surpassed his considerable anxiety. On the 15th, following a morning's work at the Athenæum, he met Lizzie at the Boston and Albany railroad depot and noted that she "really seemed a little pleased at seeing me." After completing a few er-

Francis Blake, Jr., at age 20. By Alexander Bassano, 1872. #39.30

rands, they crossed the Common together and walked up Beacon Hill to the Hubbards' Louisburg Square home. The family was out at their country estate, but a servant admitted them. Frank found the darkened parlor as inviting and pleasant as ever, "in fact more pleasant because we were alone." Lizzie asked him for a sample of his penmanship, and Frank wrote on a piece of note paper, "Si vous aimez ce que j'aime / Vous vous-aimez vous-meme / Frank." She blushed, but still smiled.

Elizabeth Hubbard Blake. By Warren & Heald (Boston, Mass.),
ca. 1872-1874. #57.842

Frank again raised the subject of using first names. This time Lizzie replied that he must not call her anything but "Miss Hubbard." She considered it improper for him to address her by any name that he could not use in the presence of others. Feeling rebuked, Frank sulked horribly. Lizzie did her best to cheer him up and reassured him that she had not intended to hurt his feelings. But even her lively piano music could not elicit a smile from Frank's melancholy face. Overcome by a sense of rejection, he suddenly recognized the depth of his affections. Frank confessed that until now "I had never realized how much I liked her & that now I saw & knew that I liked her more & better than I had any right to & so perhaps it would be better if we never met again." Taken aback and hurt by Frank's grave words, Lizzie responded that "she was very angry at herself for having said what she did & asked me to forget all about it & call her what I pleased." They shook hands in the doorway and, as Frank sadly noted in his diary, "went out of the house together—perhaps for the last time!"[4]

Several days later, Frank again met Lizzie and, noting his sullen expression, she invited him to spend the day with her. Wishing to speak with her privately, he accompanied her on the train out to Woodlands. Perplexed by his own emotions and still intimidated by Lizzie and by the Hubbard family wealth, Frank began to pour out his heart. "I spoke as freely as I dared to one whom I had ever looked on as an angel far far above me in every way." Upon their arrival at Woodlands, he wanted to extend his visit, but believed that it would be best for both of them if he did not. Overwrought, Frank cheerlessly advised Lizzie that "I ought rather to go away & give . . . [you] a chance to forget all about me." He had confessed too much affection for her already—"much more than I had any right to"— and seeing Lizzie in "her bright rich home" only made Frank feel more "unworthy of her." On equally uncertain terrain, Lizzie simply replied, "I can't say anything more now, Mr. Blake, but you'd better come out."[5]

The momentary crisis passed and over the next few days the two continued their fragile ballet. Frank managed to wring from Lizzie her consent to let him "love her just as much as I wanted to." They grew increasingly intimate and Lizzie allowed her suitor to hold her hand "& let me pour out my heart's feelings as well as I could. . . ." She would not, however, confess her love for Frank—"she hadn't known me long enough to do that but she'd 'try'—that last word gave me hope. . . ." Frank left Lizzie with a bundle of flowers and went back to his room to ponder what he had done. "It seemed as if I had been so wicked in trying to win the love of one so pure & beautiful as she is—My only excuse is this— 'I love her!' God help me to do that which is right & bless her!"[6]

Frank spent a restless day pondering his next move. He decided to force the issue and tell Lizzie that if she still did not love him he would accept a Coast Survey assignment in California and end their relationship. "I shall think it is God's will for me to go to California & I feel that I shall have the strength to do anything for her sake." He went to bed early that night with confidence in his new plan. But when his train pulled up to Rice's Crossing in Weston the next morning and Lizzie came running, looking as "fresh & pretty as a rose," his resolve melted. Her striped pink and white skirt, with a white waistband, and a straw hat trimmed with a black feather and apple blossoms only made him think more about how much he loved her. They set off from the house toward a forty-acre rolling valley on the Hubbards' vast estate, and Frank marveled at how the sun caught her gold rings, earrings, and a diamond. They found a comfortable spot to sit on a hillside, and Lizzie asked him to tell her a story. But Frank could think only about his love for Lizzie. "I told her the story of my love—how I had asked God to be with me today—how I had made up my mind to tell her I was going away for three years and how impossible it was for me to do so." Eagerly hoping to prove his sincerity, he confessed that he was not twenty-one years old as he had claimed, and would not be twenty-one until Christmas. Although Frank did not hear the words he longed for, he felt that Lizzie loved him, "& so I went back to dinner the happiest fellow in the world." For the remainder of the day, the two rode in Lizzie's phaeton out to Newton Lower Falls, past the house where Frank was born. They held hands and spoke about their religious faith; Frank felt closer to her than ever before.[7]

Frank returned to his work and struggled to complete his computations for the Coast Survey and write his final report on the Darien expedition. But Lizzie's reluctance to declare her love to him consumed Frank. "Wrote a little on my Darien report this morning," he confided to his diary, "but I am so much taken with thoughts of my darling Lizzie that I find it impossible to apply myself to anything serious."[8] On Memorial Day, Lizzie invited Frank to spend another day with her at Woodlands. Despite the unrelenting heat, they had a pleasant time together. After dinner they wandered off alone. Frank became overwhelmed by his anxiety, and, as he later admitted, "acted like a perfect boy." He demanded Lizzie tell him whether she loved him; if not, he would go to California for three years. Lizzie didn't know how to respond; she "thought a long time" about what Frank had asked, "but couldn't answer." Later, after supper, the two went for a calming row on the Charles River. On their return to Woodlands, Frank was again unsuccessful in wrestling a declaration of love from poor Lizzie. As the evening wore on, they sat on the piazza under the moonlight. Clearly worried over what Frank might do, Lizzie addressed him by his first name and walked him to the site of their earlier confrontation. As "we stood on the summit of a little ridge looking down on 'Happy Valley' she told me that she loved me & I kissed her once—only once for though I told her I was happy—I really was not." He understood that the words he so desperately sought had been forced from his young love's lips. So the two "walked back hand in hand but not heart in heart." Unable to relent, Frank "asked if I might get a ring now but a shake of the head & request that I should meet her at Louisburg Square tomorrow morning at half after eleven made me feel sure that there was yet a great gulf between us." Abashed at his own petulant behavior, Frank asked Lizzie to forget all that had been said. "She thanked me and said I was very generous." They returned to the house, where they visited with Mr. Hubbard, and at 10:00 that night Frank caught the train back to Boston.[9]

The following morning dawned gloomy and threatening, mirroring Frank's heart as he returned again to Louisburg Square. Mr. Hubbard, not Lizzie, answered the door. Her father asked Frank to sit beside him on a small sofa in the drawing room. "I felt that something fearful was going to happen." He eased the young man into conversation and then told Frank that he "didn't know anything about love." Mr. Hubbard advised the nervous suitor, "I never should have asked . . . [Lizzie] to give me an answer so soon. That I couldn't expect to make her love me all at once." Just when Frank thought he would be politely dismissed, the conversation took an unexpected turn. Lizzie's father "went on to say that he thought I was a pretty good sort of a fellow, that he liked scientific men—that he should like to have a scientific man in the family, & that he didn't see any reason why he shouldn't learn to love me. As regards my pecuniary condition he doesn't care anything—he wants me to try to get a good name & position among scientific men & that's all." Hubbard's exceptional tact and patience put Frank at ease and calmed his anxious soul, while permitting his sensible daughter the time she needed to consider her future with a brilliant but impatient young man. Frank left Louisburg Square confident and filled with respect for the man that likely would soon be his father-in-law. Later that afternoon, Frank met Lizzie and again apologized for his immature behavior.[10]

Despite the assurances he received from Lizzie and her father, Frank spent a nervous summer waiting for a definitive expression of love. Concentrating on his Coast Survey work proved difficult. Even the death of Commodore Blake in June did not long divert Frank's attention from his thoughts of Lizzie. If a day passed without word from her, Frank felt hollow and low. Ever sensitive to Lizzie's variations in mood, any drop in her expression of affection sent Frank sulking. A particular letter he received from Lizzie in July kept him up "most of the night" because it seemed barren of even "the slightest spark of heart-feeling in it." When he attended a July Fourth picnic at Woodlands, Lizzie asked him to keep some distance and not be overly attentive, which upset him. But a few days later he received a "dear kind note from my 'loving Lizzie'," which put the sun back in his smile.[11]

On July 10, during one of his regular excursions to Woodlands, Frank and Lizzie strolled off by themselves. Frank again expressed his desire to be formally engaged. "She laid her head on my shoulder & let me tell her of my love once more. I felt happier when I went away than ever before." But the response he sought continued to elude him. Back at her home two days later, Frank began to receive the sort of assurances he needed. "I saw a change in my darling at once & knew that at last she loved me." She put her head on his shoulder and they kissed. After dark, as they sat together on the steps of the piazza, Lizzie told Frank that he could now consider them as engaged to be married. That warm July day, Frank joyously wrote in his diary, became the "very happiest day" in his life.[12]

But in less than a week, the Coast Survey interrupted Frank's by then blissful summer. On July 16, Blake departed for Washington and the next day proceeded to Clark's Mountain, Virginia, and later to Bull Run. Secure in the knowledge that he was formally engaged, Frank's life appeared to fall into place. When he arrived in Virginia, he received word that his pay had been raised to $1,100 per year. He could now think seriously about beginning married life.

The work in Virginia immediately fell into the normal routine of longitude work: preparing star lists, making observations at night, and computing by day. On Sundays, Frank would go off alone and read the Episcopal service during the hour that Lizzie would be in church. He wrote her every day, but was disappointed to find that his nine letters to her had sparked only three in return. Then came the shock of a letter "full of cruel, hard words" from Lizzie's father. Not only did he disapprove of the volume of mail pouring into his home, he was angry to learn that his daughter considered herself as good as engaged. Mr. Hubbard's thoughtful drawing room conversation with Frank clearly had been a little too diplomatic. He did not oppose the attention that Frank lavished on his daughter, but he believed that Frank was too young for marriage and that even an engagement was unwise at this time. Regrettably, Frank's reply has not survived, but it is not difficult to imagine his anger and disappointment.[13]

The incident put Frank in a poor frame of mind. Although Lizzie continued to assure him that her feelings remained unchanged, Frank proved difficult to convince. Jealously erupted with little provocation. With Frank away on Coast Survey work, the Hubbards vacationed at Bar Harbor, Maine, still a favorite resort for New Englanders. Despite her father's reservations about the correspondence, Lizzie continued to write Frank often. One letter innocently detailed her many lighthearted activities for Frank's amusement. But the "cold, heartless letter" made him "perfectly miserable." To Frank, the missive seemed a twelve-page catalog of provocative flirtations with a Roland Lincoln and Ned Lyon. When

Lizzie appeared to discourage him from visiting her in Maine, Frank could hardly contain himself. He remained up until 2:00 A.M. trying to craft a response; and the next day he tried to be more cheerful, but utterly failed. "It makes me almost crazy to think of Lizzie—cold, cruel & heartless as she has proved to be," Frank groused. Lizzie continued to write and referred to "My darling Frank," but the letters couldn't console his wounded pride or end the misery caused by her "cruel words." Frank returned to Boston for a short break at the end of August. He immediately called on Mr. Hubbard at his Commercial Street office to settle matters in a "square talk." Frank left no record of the meeting, but the results clearly satisfied both men. He accompanied Lizzie's father on the noon train to Woodlands and after dinner sat with Mr. Hubbard out on the familiar piazza to conclude their conversation.[14]

Blake returned to Virginia at the end of September to complete his Coast Survey work, which he did with speed and astounding precision. One of his supervisors praised his work, exclaiming that it had "never been excelled in the Coast Survey. The Results do you great credit & I shall take very great pleasure in reporting upon them to the Sup't." Some hint of the acclaim Frank had received must have reached Mr. Hubbard's ear. He dropped his objections to their relationship, and when Frank returned to Boston later that fall, Mr. Hubbard told him that he should consider himself invited to tea every evening at Louisburg Square. By Christmas, the Hubbards were treating Frank as a family member, although Mr. Hubbard kept a father's watchful eye on the young man. Lizzie presented Frank, now twenty-one years of age, with a beautiful Russian leather smoking set, complete with a cigar cup, ash holder, and match box with salver.[15] Frank could not recall ever having felt as secure or happy.

The winter passed pleasantly, with Frank spending most of his free time at the Hubbard's home or accompanying them to the theater, concerts, or the opera. Lizzie's father reacted to the ever-present Frank with both kindness and suspicion, wanting to like the earnest young man, but finding it difficult to watch his daughter slip away into adulthood. When Frank declined an invitation to dinner right after New Year's, Mr. Hubbard hand-delivered a note from his daughter requesting him to appear. Frank bolted from his bed and arrived at Louisburg Square just before the Hubbard's late dinner. The Hubbards enjoyed Frank's company and hardly a day passed without a visit from him. But with the new year, Frank's activities with the Coast Survey increased. Hilgard twice summoned Frank to Washington for consultations and advised him that he would again be heading to Europe on another longitudinal survey. Frank spent the evening prior to his last trip to Washington sitting with Lizzie— whom he affectionately called "Monkey"—in a small room in the Hubbard home. Eventually, he bid the family goodbye. As the two lingered at the front door, Lizzie's father "burst upon us with an angry look & throwing a heavy shawl upon her said, 'Here Lizzie if you want to stay out there take this.'" Frank made a tactical retreat, "feeling much hurt" by Mr. Hubbard's unexpected eruption. Lizzie slipped out a back door and ran after Frank to soothe his feelings and give him a final goodbye. Nevertheless, Frank returned to his room "feeling very, very sad."[16]

Frank returned to Boston for a short visit on April 13 and, of course, immediately went to the Hubbards' home at Louisburg Square. Preparations for his voyage to France left him with little free time. On April 17, Frank and Lizzie exchanged parting gifts. She gave him a beautiful traveling ink stand, and he presented her with a pair of tortoise shell earrings and a locket. Lizzie found the time to sew buttonholes on four of his shirts, and then slipped some beautiful candlesticks into the flannel shirts he had packed away in his trunk. Frank left Boston on April 22, excited by his new adventure for the Coast Survey and confident of Lizzie's love for him and of his own future.[17]

Endnotes

1. Frank Hubbard to Francis Blake, Nov. 13, 1870, FBP.
2. Blake, Diary, April 25, 1871, FBP.
3. *New England Historical and Genealogical Register* 34 (1880):327; Account Book of Charles T. Hubbard, vol. 38, FBP.
4. Blake, Diary, May 15, 1871, FBP.

5. Blake, Diary, May 19, 1871, FBP.
6. Blake, Diary, May 22, 1871, FBP.
7. Blake, Diary, May 23, 24, 187l, FBP.
8. Blake, Diary, May 25, 1871, FBP.
9. Blake, Diary, May 30, 1871, FBP.
10. Blake, Diary, May 31, 1871, FBP.
11. Blake, Diary, June 25, 1871, FBP; Frank Blake, Jr., *Memoir of George Smith Blake, Commodore, U. S. N.* (Cambridge, Mass., 1871).
12. Blake, Diary, July 10, 12, 1871, FBP.
13. Blake, Diary, July 31, 1871, FBP.
14. Blake, Diary, August 19, 22, 23, 30, 1871, FBP.
15. Charles O. Boutelle to Blake, Nov. 2, 1871, FBP; Blake, Diary, Nov. 1, Dec. 25, 1871, FBP.
16. Blake, Diary, March 22, 1872, FBP.
17. Blake, Diary, April 17, 19, 22, 1872, FBP.

CHAPTER 5

TRANSITIONS

B LAKE RECEIVED A LETTER from his Coast Survey supervisor Julius E. Hilgard on February 5, 1872, advising him to return to Europe in the spring to finalize the transatlantic longitude. Since 1848, the Survey had been steadily improving the accuracy of this work, particularly as technology improved. When Blake participated in the 1870 venture, the last link in the Atlantic cable network, a connection between Brest, France, and Greenwich, England, had not been established. With that cable now in place, the Survey went back to work. Hilgard assigned Blake a number of preliminary tasks, including the examination of a new circuit-breaking chronometer and a visit to Duxbury, Massachusetts, to determine if the French Atlantic cable remained in sufficiently good repair to make the measurements possible. Blake quickly completed his assignments and arrived in Washington on March 5 to meet with Hilgard at an evening reception in the Japanese Embassy. Hilgard invited Blake to stay at his home during his visit, but Blake preferred a hotel to the company of Hilgard's wife, whom he considered "a hard case, a most insufferable gossip and back-biter." Blake walked to the Hilgards' for breakfast the following morning and the two men went over the details of the new longitude campaign, the most elaborate up to that time, with observations at Cambridge and Duxbury, Massachusetts; St. Pierre, Newfoundland; Greenwich, England; and Paris and Brest, France. They would sail for Southampton, England, at the end of April on a German steamship.[1]

Back in Boston several days later, Blake continued his preparations, delivering the longitude records in his possession to the Harvard Observatory and to Sarah S. and Jane L. Lane, sisters and Cambridge mathematicians who periodically performed calculations for the Coast Survey. Hilgard came to town on March 15 to confer with Blake and to inspect the break-circuit chronometer and check on the status of the Atlantic cables with him. On March 21, Superintendent Peirce issued Blake his formal instructions to report to Hilgard at the Washington office without delay "for duty under his direction in determining the longitude between European and American observatories." Four days later Blake arrived in Washington and began preparing his instruments. He mounted the Krille clock and began overhauling the Survey's transit instrument No. 4, the apparatus he would be using during the trip. Blake mounted and spent several days experimenting with a Saxton register, another device that purported to record the precise time of transits. Blake had criticized the accuracy of the instrument which, according to Assistant George W. Dean, no one had ever used with any great success. He also met with Peirce in Cambridge to discuss various reforms of Coast Survey methods used in observations and computations. The Survey, always interested in increasing the precision of its work, encouraged such independent thinking.[2]

After the now familiar round of farewells, Blake left for Baltimore on April 22 and two days later departed on the steamship *Ohio*, passing by the famed Fort McHenry. On the second night of travel on the steamship, a despondent coal heaver jumped overboard, leaving behind a bundle of letters from his wife detailing problems with debt. Blake, no longer distracted by female passengers, spent most of his time on board reading, beginning with Dickens's *Bleak House*, and writing his precious Lizzie; as soon as he landed, Blake posted a fifty-page letter to her. He had the good fortune of meeting his cousin Russell Sullivan, who had been working in London for over a year. Blake spent the next two days shopping, sightseeing, and visiting his Aunt Mary Blake, the commodore's widow, who had moved to London following her husband's death.[3]

On May 9, Blake joined Hilgard at the Charing Cross Station and took the train to the Greenwich Observatory where he met Sir George M. Airy, one of the great astronomers and mathematicians of the nineteenth century. While Hilgard conferred with Airy, Blake toured the facility and viewed the collection of instruments prepared for the transit of Venus, which would take place December 8, 1874. Hilgard and Blake evidently made a favorable impression, for the next day they received an invitation from Airy to attend the dinner of the Royal Astronomical Society at Freemasons' Hall. Five days later, Blake proceeded to Paris with Russell Sullivan. Problems with the French Atlantic cable and the St. Pierre-to-Duxbury cable allowed added time for touring. When Hilgard arrived from London on May 23, Blake began preparations for construction of an observatory. He also took advantage of his time in the city, had his picture taken, and bought a little pocket "porte-portrait" for "the prettiest vignette of my darling little Monkey." Blake began his last morning in Paris with an early and most uncontinental breakfast of beefsteak, an omelette, Lyonnaise potatoes, and a bottle of pale ale, then headed off for Brest. At the end of a now familiar journey, he checked in at the Hotel Lequer, where he had stayed in 1870.[4]

After a meeting with Hilgard, Blake conducted a reconnaissance of the town beginning with the cable office, where he visited several of his old friends. At the maritime school he found the piers for the transit instrument just as he and Dean had left them two years earlier, and at the Place de Champ Bataille, he selected a site for his new observatory in front of the telegraph office. During the next few days, Blake met with telegraph and cable officials and electricians and erected the observatory, while Hilgard returned to Paris to work out details with the staff of the Paris Observatory. The Parisians proved surprisingly cooperative and agreed to adopt Hilgard's general plan. He wanted Blake to oversee the observations in Brest and Paris and arrange for time signals to be sent every night at 10:00, Paris time, for two minutes at ten-second intervals. Blake would then record these on the chronograph or compare them with his chronometer. Hilgard certainly won points with the Paris Observatory staff by stating that their star lists were superior to those of Greenwich. In working the final reductions, however, Hilgard thought it might be necessary to compare the Paris data with that of Greenwich. Largely as a diplomatic gesture, Hilgard sent Blake copies of the French bulletin of fundamental stars and the apparent locations of time-stars on their list, expressly selected for longitude operations. He also requested a copy of Blake's star list with mean places, which he wanted to forward to Airy at Greenwich.[5]

For the month of June, the observations went reasonably well, although the team endured the usual vexing problems with weather and instruments. At the beginning of July, Blake, who loved cigars, determined to give up smoking for a month. This temporary spasm of reform left him nervous, irritable, and depressed, although it did not much impair his concentration or hamper his ability to work. He continued through the month working the night shift in the observatory and exchanging signals when the earth's natural electrical current did not interfere with the telegraph. After completing his daily computations, he went for walks, associated with his friends in the cable office, and maintained his correspondence with Lizzie. On Bastille Day, which fell on a Sunday, Blake began reading the Episcopal service at exactly 10:30 A.M. Woodlands time, hoping that Lizzie would simultaneously be hearing the same comforting text.[6]

Blake completed his observations in Brest at the end of July and eagerly boarded the Paris train. Just as he finished putting all his instruments in order and making his wire connections to the telegraph office, he learned that Charles Eugene Delaunay, director of the Paris Observatory, had drowned. He immediately telegraphed the news to Hilgard, who worried that Delaunay's death might jeopardize the Survey's mission. But the work continued, and by August 21 Blake had completed his observations in Paris. He packed his instruments and arranged for their shipment to England. The end of his Paris assignment came just in time for Blake. Although he had worked hard and clearly assumed a central role in the mission, he had still found enough free time to spend himself into trouble.

He had again visited the city's architectural wonders and historical monuments, but had also frolicked in the evenings and indulged his taste for leather goods. In particular, his purchase of 162 pairs of gloves had put him on the verge of insolvency. Even the carefree Russell Sullivan remarked how, now that "we have gotten you away from Klein's repository of Russia leather articles there is some hope of saving you from utter ruin."[7]

Blake departed Paris for London August 23 and the next day again paid a visit to his Aunt Mary Blake. Four days later he began some preliminary observations. Paris and Greenwich enjoyed crystal-clear weather the following night. Both stations made excellent observations and successfully exchanged signals. Blake considered the results to be nothing short of "beautiful." Indeed, his work proved to be some of the best ever done for the Survey. Hilgard advised Superintendent Peirce that: "As Mr. Blake has borne all the brunt of the work here making the whole of the observations with great assiduity and perseverance, I beg leave to request that he may be placed in charge of his own operations in Cambridge so as to be entitled to the allowance of an Assistant in charge of a party while engaged in that work."[8] Blake had taken responsibility for the bulk of the Survey's work and did so with little or no supervision from Hilgard. But for now, Peirce preferred that Blake remain under Hilgard's immediate direction and do the reductions from the observations made at Brest, Paris, and Greenwich.

Blake arrived back in Boston on September 30, rented a room at Tremont Place, and resumed his daily visits to 2 Louisburg Square. While Blake steadily progressed on the reduction of his longitude work in Europe, the lack of communication from the French increasingly frustrated Hilgard. As a means of stirring them up, he wanted Blake to send the Paris Observatory some of his own results, but not enough to allow them to get the jump on Hilgard in publication of the Greenwich to Paris longitude. Blake complied promptly, and his results drew praise from Hilgard: "The accordance of the observations is admirable-a prob. error of only 0s.04. . . ." Blake's accomplishments had not gone unnoticed, and in February 1873 he received a promotion to assistant. The 1872 transatlantic longitude campaign was the culmination of Blake's career with the

Coast Survey and would be his most important assignment. While he continued officially to work under Hilgard's direction, the increasing independence his supervisors granted him eventually set Blake on a new course.[9]

A laconic entry appears in Blake's diary for June 24, 1873: "To church at 6, married & up to house again by 6:25. Off at 8:15 for Framingham." Not quite twenty-three years old, Blake already had become an accomplished professional. The embarrassments of his wayward brother and the economic uncertainties that always hovered over the household of his parents had receded into the distant past. From here on, Blake would know only security and success, enormous success. Blake married Elizabeth Livermore Hubbard at St. Mary's Church in Newton Lower Falls, and the ceremony was celebrated by the famous Episcopalian clergyman Phillips Brooks. It marked a profound turning point in his life, emotionally, spiritually, professionally, and materially. The absence of anxious entries in his diary testifies to his newfound sense of personal security and professional accomplishment. A letter from Hilgard further revealed the change in Blake's disposition. "Your letter of the 18th made a very pleasant impression upon me—as if you were feeling very good-natured and disposed to look on the bright side of things."[10]

As his confidence and domestic commitments increased, Blake began rejecting Coast Survey missions that previously he would have grasped eagerly. Simon Newcomb, director of the U.S. Naval Observatory, invited Blake to take an observing station in the southern hemisphere for the December 1874 transit of Venus, a very important assignment that promised to add significantly to Blake's professional stature. Despite having seen Sir George Airy's preparations at Greenwich and received a very complimentary recommendation from Peirce, Blake turned down the job. The rejection stunned Hilgard. "My dear Sir," he wrote Blake, "even if you had to go to the uttermost parts of the earth, you should not throw up that chance." Trying to be obliging, Hilgard proposed that Blake take a Coast Survey station that could accommodate his new wife.[11] Although Blake did not want long-term assignments that would take him far from Lizzie, traveling with her to do the work he enjoyed appealed to him. Immediately following their wedding reception, the Blakes boarded a train for connections west that would eventually take them to Madison, Wisconsin, where Blake would conduct astronomical and magnetic observations. They remained in the midwest for additional work at La Cross, Wisconsin, and at the University of Minnesota in Minneapolis, and began their long journey home on October 9, with an obligatory stop at Niagara Falls. They arrived back in Weston on October 14 and took up residence in Lizzie's father's home at Woodlands.[12]

A new house, not Coast Survey work, now preoccupied Blake's mind. Lizzie's father, who owned hundreds of acres in Weston, wanted to build a family compound and situate his three daughters and only son there in new, elegant homes.[13] Charles T. Hubbard first provided for his daughter Louisa and her husband John Jackson, who sent Blake copies of the floor plans for his new home. The Blakes would be the second to establish a new residence at "Woodlands," choosing a site some distance from the Hubbard house. The third daughter, Charlotte (Lottie), who married Benjamin Loring Young in September 1875, shortly afterward established residence at Woodlands, as did Hubbard's son, Charles W.[14]

Rolling hills dotted the countryside on Hubbard's estate along the Charles River. The area remained sparsely populated, settled with only a few scattered farmhouses along country roads. Blake chose a forested hilltop above the Boston and Albany railroad tracks as the site for his home, a location that offered a commanding, panoramic view down the meandering Charles River Valley. Conveniently close to the Hubbard and Jackson houses, the site offered room to grow and much privacy. Blake took on the job of building his new home in the same way that he approached all his work—with enormous energy and demanding standards. The architect that he employed met Blake's expectations as few others could. His cousin Russell Sullivan, who had returned from England in February 1873, told Blake about a home that a mutual friend, Joe Sargeant, was building in Worcester. It is "unique in every way, in fact, it is as handsome as any house I have ever seen," Sullivan told Blake. Blake's sister Louisa Wells did not share Sullivan's enthusiasm and described the structure as "very odd and irregular."[15] But Sullivan possessed prescient instincts, for Sargeant's architect was the youthful Charles Follen McKim, scion of the celebrated Pennsylvania abolitionist family, who would become one of the country's leading architects and help change the face of Boston.[16]

Blake clearly valued McKim's careful and meticulous work, and in return, McKim promised Blake that his new home "shall be a study with me to make the best house I can. Something good ought to go up in such a country." Within a month of returning from his working honeymoon, Blake had cleared the land and begun building the house.[17] The work proceeded swiftly—so fast, in fact, that McKim had to caution Blake against setting the foundation walls according to mere sketches he had provided, rather than completed architectural drawings. McKim worked with contractors and solicited bids to keep control over costs. Whatever Blake initially had in mind as the cost of his new home, the $15,200 estimate, exclusive of heating, plumbing, painting, stair building, and stonework, must have rattled him considerably.[18] McKim tried to appease Blake: "Now don't you be frightened! nor disappointed—these are only preliminary figures & altogether too high." Indeed, heating, plumbing, and painting would bring the estimate to $17,175, which still did not include the hardwood finish for the front hall, dining room, and library, nor the cost of the cistern, cess pool, and grading of the property. Nevertheless, whatever reservations Blake harbored, they did nothing to impede the progress of construction.[19]

Blake meticulously supervised the construction of his home, tracking every penny and brick—over 70,000 by completion of the first phase of construction. Indeed, Blake served as his own general contractor, and a huge amount of the material in the vast Blake papers at the Massachusetts Historical Society are receipts and records addressed to him for the construction and perpetual reconstruction of his home. His diary for 1874 is replete with entries detailing the number of men—nearly all local laborers—and horses that were on the job. Undoubtedly, the workers had their fill of Blake's detailed oversight, and in reaction the masons used an occasion when he complained about the cellar walls being six inches out of line, to avoid work for a solid week. For the most part, Blake paid by the day or $11 or $25 per thousand bricks depending on the quality of workmanship required. The relationship between Blake and the masons remained strained, and not until two years after completion of the work did Blake finally settle with the head mason, Francis E. Hamblin.[20]

McKim invested all his efforts in producing a magnificent home. The working drawings that he sent to Blake proved as carefully executed as they were exciting. McKim's lifelong insistence upon beauty and perfection of detail were realized in his plans for Blake's house. Although mindful of costs, he worked to convince Blake that the detail he admired, such as elegant hardwood in the hall, dining room, and library, would in the coming years prove worth the additional cost. "This is an important point," McKim insisted, and the wood could season while Blake went on a Coast Survey trip and be ready to install upon his return, thus "much time & swearing may be saved." McKim felt so strongly about building according to his design that "I would rather cut down on my commission than have you disappoint me in my library & dining room finish." Blake kept a careful eye on McKim's charges, but in most cases acquiesced to his architect's wishes. And why not? Blake's father-in-law, but especially his wife's grandfather, Benjamin Sewall, paid the bills, and they grew increasingly impatient as the design grew more elaborate. Early in January, Blake met both men at Hubbard's downtown office where "Mr. Sewall gave me a great blowing & check for $1182.71." Blake went home to Newton with Sewall where they continued discussions about the house. In the end, Blake got his house and Sewall paid the bills.[21]

By June, work began on interior portions of the house, with McKim either staying one or two steps ahead of the workmen or falling completely behind with his design plans. During a slowdown in the middle of the month, McKim's partner William Rutherford Mead explained that the delay resulted from the death of McKim's father. But by the 18th, McKim was back on schedule, and designs for the remainder of the house flowed in more regularly. McKim did his best to relieve any stress and maintain good relations with Blake and his "family banker." "I trust you haven't been saying "Damn?! lately when you have happened to think of me," McKim wrote Blake. He tried to assure Blake that despite the number of "hungry, growling, and unserved clients" lurking in his office, the house was getting his attention. When he could not keep to schedules, he wrote humorously apologetic letters to Blake to break the tension and admit fault. "You may blackguard me as much as you like & I won't answer back. Pile it on hot—to teach me 'business'—'the importance of promptness' 'the answering of letters' 'the keeping of promises'—& all the other virtuous attributes which I sometimes despair of owning—& which save a man from disgrace." He conscientiously discussed minute details with Blake and produced the sort of ornate and rich designs usually meant to flatter wealthy, established businessmen, not to please a twenty-four-year-old employee of the Coast Survey. McKim designed ornate chimneys, a carriage porch, "'whirligigs' for the Lib[rary]. chimney," a $250 windmill, original fireplace mantels, and an "intercom" system for thirteen of the house's rooms, which rapidly increased the cost. Workmen labored for over a year painting the house. But Grandfather Sewall dutifully paid the bills, $3,405 just for June.[22]

Blake's relationship with McKim concluded amicably, with each tolerating the other's idiosyncrasies. McKim cheerfully endured Blake's intense scrutiny of each bill he received, and Blake said little about the slow pace of construction or the tardy arrival of architectural drawings. Although Blake's was not the first home McKim had designed, it was one of his earliest, and he greatly appreciated the professional manner in which Blake had treated him. "The whole job has been one of great pleasure to me," he told Blake, "& if in any way it answers your expectations & Mrs. Blake's I shall be proud. . . . To design a house & have your client agree with you & let you alone is to know something about Paradise in advance."[23]

On January 13, 1875, Blake made another laconic entry in his diary: "Moved into new house. . . . Found two bottles of tasteless current wine & 1 bottle of good claret which came from Mr. Sewall." Blake's remark stood in marked contrast to the reality of the home he had built. Piazzas stood at each end of the house and a porte-cochére graced the main entrance. The home also included a hall, lavatories, a kitchen, storerooms, pantries, a servants' hall, dining room, a library with bay windows, a parlor, four bedrooms, and an elaborate main staircase leading to a sitting room with a bay window, along with a billiard room and servants' quarters. Such a home deserved a name, and Blake devoted himself to finding the right one. He asked friends and family, and even his boss Hilgard, for suggestions. By November, Blake had settled on "Keewaydin Towers." "Keewaydin," in the local Massachuset Indian language, referred to the northwest wind that occasionally swept over the hillside with considerable authority. The towers referred to the two octagonal structures, decorated with McKim's weather vanes, that lent the house much of its distinctive style. Before long, everyone simply called the estate Keewaydin.[24]

Keewaydin as originally constructed. By Francis Blake, ca. 1875-1880. #57.382

In designing the Blake house, McKim contributed to the creation of a new architectural style. One of the earliest and finest examples of the "shingle style," the structure possessed characteristic piazzas, corbeled chimneys, scalloped shingles above clapboards, and towers. The Blake house and the shingle style in general descended from the work of Richard Norman Shaw, whose "Queen Anne" form H. H. Richardson greatly admired and passed along to McKim when he apprenticed in Richardson's office. The great firm of McKim, Mead, and White, and scores of architects around the country, employed the style in countless homes over the next decade, and many of its elements became common features of wood-frame homes into the early twentieth century.[25]

The financial independence that Blake gained through marriage inspired in him greater professional independence. Rather than continue reporting to Coast Survey Assistant George Dean, who had authority over the telegraphic longitude operations, Blake preferred to work directly for Hilgard and Superintendent Peirce. Although Blake had initially admired Dean, he now chafed under his direction. When Dean asked him for his standard reports, Blake told him that he could obtain them from Hilgard. And when Dean requested a financial report, Blake advised him that the information was none of his business. As tensions increased, Peirce unexpectedly resigned, leaving Blake's fate to the new superintendent, Captain Carlisle P. Patterson. Patterson quickly reaffirmed Dean's authority and directed Blake to comply with all his requests. Hilgard thoughtfully interceded, seeking to calm offended pride and restore order. He supported Blake's request to report directly to him, but advised the young mathematician that his blunt methods hurt him. While the new superintendent "has a very good perception of your ability and knowledge and knows how to compare them with the corresponding qualities in others," Hilgard admonished, "he was a little 'riled' by your telling him that you felt independent of the Coast Survey. If you had said at the same time, as I know you feel, that you liked and preferred the duty, and would regret being obliged to give it up by being forced into relations at variance with your self-respect, he would not probably have had his official feathers ruf-fled." Despite his undiplomatic conduct, Blake won exactly the arrange-ment he preferred, and in May Superintendent Patterson order him to report directly to Hilgard "for such duty as he may assign to you in con-nection with the preparation for publication of the results of transatlantic longitude work."[26]

Benjamin Sewall. By John Adams Whipple (Boston, Mass.) n.d. #57.893

For the next two years, Blake worked mostly from his home, writing reports for the Survey and checking texts and figures before their official publication. The family vacationed in the White Mountains, made improvements on the house and grounds of Keewaydin, and lived grandly, spending about 85 percent more than they received in income. When the bills again mounted, including the $600 Blake gave to his parents every year, he marched over to Grandfather Sewall's office for another subsidy. For someone as prideful as Blake, these pilgrimages may have been excruciating. But his diary reveals no tension and little information other than the family's constant need for additional resources. Perhaps by now Blake felt the support was due him.[27]

New Year's Day in 1876, springlike at 68 degrees, saw the Blake house filled with Lizzie's parents and other relatives, "Duff" the Scotch terrier, and no less than six servants. The following day broke equally warm, as Blake recorded in his diary, and at 5:00 A.M. Lizzie experienced "queer pains." Two hours later, she continued to suffer from what everyone believed was colic. At 9:45 A.M. the doctor arrived "and at once informed us that we would shortly have a baby in the house." About two hours later "Miss Agnes Blake came into the world." After two weeks, Lizzie finally sat up in bed, a reminder of how long some nineteenth-century women took to recuperate from childbirth. Frank took an active interest in the new baby and thought enough of his pediatric talents to prescribe ten drops of gin for what appeared to be a stomachache. Even Frank's mother offered advice, inquiring about Agnes's weight and whether the child received nourishment "in the natural way."[28]

The demands of his family life further strained Blake's relationship with the Coast Survey. On July 4, 1876, Hilgard summoned Blake to Philadelphia to discuss his future duties, especially plans for him to remove to Washington for a year. Blake instead wrote to Hilgard explaining that he could not be away from his home for so long a period and, therefore, must resign, take a leave of absence, or perform office work at reduced pay. He did not wish to resign and hoped Hilgard would tactfully explain his situation to the superintendent. Patterson, however, desired a corps of officers ready to go anywhere at any time and did not want to recognize exceptions to his rules. But with Hilgard's encouragement, Patterson extended to Blake the offer to remain at home, perform Coast Survey computations at the rate of $100 per month, and remain officially listed as an "assistant." Blake promptly accepted the offer.[29]

But in April of 1877, Patterson notified Blake that if Congress restored the appropriation for the geodetic survey lost during the prior session, he would be leading a telegraphic longitude party between the Mississippi River and the Sierra Nevada Mountains. He told Blake that he should therefore begin to estimate expenses and report in person to Washington the next month. Blake promptly submitted his resignation. He confessed to the "deep feeling of affection I have for the service which, during the last eleven years, has made me what I am." He hoped Patterson would reconsider his orders and "if my labors here can be of use to the Coast Survey, you will retain them at any price—however small—you may see fit to name." Conscious of Blake's importance to the Survey, Patterson promptly answered that "I must decline to accept your resignation, and you will please continue the work upon which you are for the time being engaged." In an accompanying private note, he also confessed that "I cannot think of letting you leave the Coast Survey and fully appreciate the motives and sentiment inducing you to offer your resignation." For the present, no change in Blake's relationship with the Survey would take place.[30]

Blake's next field assignment could hardly have been more convenient. Beginning in September, Blake would be on loan to the Board of Harbor Commissioners of Massachusetts to head up the resurvey of Boston Harbor. His meticulous work would support the commissioners in creating accurate maps designed to be easily revised to accommodate Boston's constantly changing waterfront. Blake completed his "very interesting and exhaustive report," as Superintendent Paterson called it, in March 1878.[31]

But completing this assignment only placed him back into the same situation he had been in the previous spring. At the end of the month, Patterson requested he take charge of a party scheduled to determine azimuths and base lines in Mississippi. Without Blake's assistance, Patterson warned, the work could not be done for another year. Blake declined the assignment, again believing that it would likely lead to his termination. He wanted to retain his connection to the Survey, but because he could not leave his family he could offer no satisfactory alternative to resignation. Patterson sympathized with Blake's predicament. "You possess so many qualities both moral and mental to ensure success professionally," Patterson wrote Blake, "that it is with the extremest reluctance I can bring myself to entertain the proposition to which you refer." Despite Blake's prickly personality, even the new superintendent perceived his enormous abilities and the terrible loss Blake's departure would create. "I cannot but mourn the necessity which constrains me," Patterson concluded. Moreover, because Congress had refused to approve any increase in the Survey's staffing, Patterson could not carry Blake's name on the staff list without preventing the advancement of other qualified employees. Blake pondered Patterson's letter and asked Benjamin Sewall what he should do. "He said resign," Blake recorded in his diary on April 5, and he submitted his resignation that day. Blake's association with the Coast Survey gradually tapered off. He completed work on the transatlantic longitude report, which Hilgard had arranged for him to do on a piecework basis. But his long association with the Coast Survey was over.[32]

The birth of Blake's second child, Benjamin Sewall Blake, on Valentine's Day 1877, was one of the few bright spots in a troubled period for the Blakes. Dependence upon the Hubbards and Grandfather Sewall, coupled with the loss of his position with the Coast Survey, left Frank irritable and ever more demanding. In January 1878, Blake received a letter from his grandmother Louisa Trumbull which included a letter she had written to his mother *three* years earlier. Louisa's letter explained how Blake's virtual abandonment of his family after marrying into the Hubbards had caused hurt and resentment. Grandmother Trumbull wrote to Blake that she had been reluctant to tell Blake's mother the reason the Trumbulls now avoided her son. "As a dear daughter affectionate and careful to avoid any thing that could trouble us," Trumbull wrote Frank, "how could I pain her if it could be avoided!!" Clearly, the Trumbulls had cause to be angry with Blake. Many Trumbull relatives, including his grandmother, who had been so kind to the Blake family during their difficult early days, had neither received an announcement of Frank's engagement nor been invited to his wedding. Moreover, he showed absolutely no interest in them and never offered any invitations to visit Keewaydin. The Trumbulls reached the unavoidable conclusion that, having become part of the wealthy Hubbard family, Frank was ashamed of his own. Blake assured his grandmother that the Trumbulls had misconstrued his actions and true sentiments. But his response lacked conviction and he could not explain away his failure to invite family members to his wedding.[33]

Having spoiled relations with his own family, Blake then took aim at the Hubbards. Prompted by an unspecified clumsiness by one of Mr. Hubbard's servants, Blake wrote an outrageous letter to Lizzie's father. Rather than simply walking over to Woodlands to explain the awkward situation, Blake chose to berate one of his benefactors in writing for not firing a servant who he felt had behaved in a disrespectful manner toward himself and his wife. In Frank's deliberate, insulting letter, he accused his father-in-law of being a derelict father and gentleman by failing to deal harshly with the insolent servant. Two days later Hubbard wrote Frank: "You have made two grievous errors in your note to me. First, in trying to make a mountain out of less than a mole hill, & then by addressing language to me that no circumstances whatever could justify." Hubbard wrote that he certainly did not need to be advised on how to defend the honor of his daughter, and he explained to his hotheaded son-in-law that as a rule he took no notice of squabbles among his servants. He advised Blake to do similarly. Unable to let a foolish incident pass, Blake aggravated the situation by arrogantly asserting that their differences clearly stemmed from a disagreement over the proper relationship between master and servant. Blake did not explain why he understood such relationships better than his father-in-law, and Hubbard did not bother to dignify the second letter with a response.[34]

The ugly family storms eventually passed and ironically helped heal some wounds among the Trumbulls and Blakes. Because Frank no longer had an income, he could not continue his monthly stipend to his parents. He explained his situation to Grandmother Trumbull and asked if, until he resumed work, she would take over the payments, which he would later reimburse with interest. Blake told her that he was doing his best to help his parents and had even invited them for a week's stay at Keewaydin. Louisa Trumbull felt relieved by Frank's show of maturity and responded enthusiastically with a long letter agreeing to the arrangement. She wished Frank happiness and success, congratulated him on his marriage, and recalled the kindness and self-sacrifice his own mother had always shown to all members of the family. Concerned about her daughter and pleased by Frank's display of responsibility, Grandmother Trumbull would do whatever she could "to smooth the remaining path of your dear mother's declining years." Blake and Trumbull also agreed to keep the arrangement a secret.[35]

If Blake worried about his career or sources of income, he showed no indication of it. Hospitality at Keewaydin increased, and Blake, Lincoln, and Hubbard family members made regular visits. Weston neighbors, such as the former consul at Hong Kong (1845–1853), Frederick T. Bush, began to visit as well. Bush moved to Weston in 1856 and for many years was one of the town's wealthiest residents; his granddaughter later married Blake's son.[36] Henry Silas Payson, Lizzie's cousin, and Frank's cousin Russell Sullivan, now an amateur playwright, also visited often. Russell's new work, "Hearts are Trumps," opened in April at the Boston Museum, and the Blakes turned out in full force. Frank also began attending Thursday Club meetings at Louisburg Square and became a stalwart member of that learned group. The Blakes began to vacation regularly at North Conway, New Hampshire, and spent considerable sums of cash on a pianoforte, dinnerware, Napoleon IV cups and saucers, and a custom-made Rushton canoe. Frank took particular delight in his canoe, and when it arrived he temporarily placed it in his library where he could contemplate its graceful lines and superior finish. A new canoe needed a landing, so Blake immediately set his carpenter to work on one. He spent much time on the river that summer, characteristically measuring distances between certain points along the way, and sometimes paddling over four miles. Charlie Wells and Frank Hubbard frequently joined him, with one or the other rowing a single shell. To finance his spending habits and his elaborate plans for landscaping Keewaydin, and perhaps embarrassed by constant trips to Grandfather Sewall's office, Blake took out a three-year mortgage for $10,000.[37]

Autumn fell heavily on the Blake household. Grandfather Sewall, Blake's great benefactor, died following a brief illness on October 12, 1878. Blake's own father spent the better part of a year in declining health, suffering from what one doctor described simply as brain and heart trouble. A form of dementia set in, causing the elder Blake to imagine that he had business at the Custom House, a position he had not held for years. On Christmas Eve, the Blakes received a postcard from Louisa Trumbull: Francis Blake, Sr., had died the previous night at 12:20 A.M. His body joined those of his ancestors in the family plot in Worcester, and Frank, the only financially solvent member of the family, bore the considerable cost of internment. Little more than a year later, Frank's mother Caroline Blake followed her husband to the grave.[38]

Endnotes

1. Julius E. Hilgard to Blake, Feb. 5, 1872, FBP; Blake, Diary, Mar. 6, 1872, FBP.
2. William A. Rogers to Blake, Mar. 28, 1872, FPB; George M. Dean to Blake, Apr. 4, 1872, FBP; Cambridge *City Directory*, 1867, 1874, 1879.
3. Blake, Diary, Apr. 22–May 6, 1872, FBP.
4. Blake Diary, May 9–June 3, 1872, FBP.
5. Julius E. Hilgard to Blake, June 12, 1872, FBP.
6. Blake, Diary, June 4, 15–30, July 1, 14, 1872, FBP.
7. List of expenditures, Blake, scrapbook, vol. 44, FBP; Russell Sullivan to Blake, Oct. 27, 1872, FBP.
8. Julius E. Hilgard to Benjamin Peirce, Sept. 13, 1872, a copy of the letter is in FBP.
9. Samuel Hein, General Disbursing Agent, to Blake, Feb. 24, 1873, FBP. Hein advised Blake that he had received his promotion and a raise to $1,400 per

year; Julius E. Hilgard to Blake, Feb. 17, March 2, 1873, FBP; Julius E. Hilgard, "Determination of Transatlantic Longitudes," in *Proceedings of the American Association for the Advancement of Science* (Aug. 20, 1873); A final report was published as appendix 18 in *the Report of the Superintendent, United States Coast Survey* (Washington, D.C., 1874).

10. Julius E. Hilgard to Blake, July 27, 1873, FBP.

11. Julius E. Hilgard to Blake, June 17, 1873, FBP, quoted: Julius E. Hilgard to Blake, July 5, 1873, FPB; Simon Newcomb to Blake, July 28, 1873, FBP.

12. An account of Blake's work may be found in the *Report of the Superintendent, United States Coast Survey* (Washington, D.C., 1874). The field records, in Blake's hand, are in the National Archives, Record Group 23.

13. Charles T. Hubbard's land purchases can be traced in the following: Middlesex County Registry of Deeds, Southern Division, Book 1009, page 2. While principally located in Weston, parts of this and another tract were located in what was at the time Needham, but became Wellesley in 1881; Middlesex County Registry of Deeds, Book 1008, page 101. When Hubbard conveyed a building lot to his daughter, Louisa Jackson, he specified that it was "part of the Slack place now occupied by me." Book 1283, page 20; Middlesex County Registry of Deeds, Book 1016, page 176; Book 1087, page 201; Book 1283, page 20.

14. John Jackson to Blake, Sept. 5, 1873, FBP.

15. Russell Sullivan to Blake, Mar. 17, May 1, 1873, FBP; Lisa Wells to Blake, July 29, 1872, FBP. An account of what little is known about the Sargeant house and its influence on Blake is given by Ann H. Schiller, "Charles F. McKim and His Francis Blake House," *Journal of the Society of Architectural Historians* 47 (1988):5–13.

16. For a well-illustrated history of Blake's home see: Pamela Fox, *Farm Town to Suburb: The History and Architecture of Weston, Massachusetts, 1830–1980* (Portsmouth, N.H., 2002), 521–542. On McKim, see Charles Moore, *The Life and Times of Charles Follen McKim* (Boston, New York, 1929); Richard Guy Wilson, *McKim, Mead, and White, Architects* (New York, 1983); Walter Muir Whitehill, "The Making of an Architectural Masterpiece: The Boston Public Library," *American Art Journal* 2 (1970):13–35.

17. Charles Follen McKim to Blake, Nov. 8, 1873, FBP.

18. James H. Crosby, the contractor, provided McKim with estimates in two letters, November 17, 19, 1873, FBP.

19. Charles Follen McKim to Blake, Nov. 21, 1873, FBP.

20. Blake, Diary, Jan. 5–13, 1874, and 1874 *passim*, FBP; bills and receipts for construction of Keewaydin, "Bills, Housebuilding, 1874–1875" series, FBP.

21. Charles Follen McKim to Blake, Jan. 13, 1874, FBP; Blake, Diary, Jan. 17–18, 1874, FBP.

22. William Rutherford Mead to Blake, June 13, 1874, FBP; Charles Follen McKim to Blake, June 18, July 28, Oct. 15, Nov. 11, 1874, FBP; Bill for Challenger Windmill, Aug. 4, 1874, FBP.

23. Charles Follen McKim to Blake, Feb. 4, 1875, FBP.

24. Blake, Diary, January 13, 1875, FBP; Julius E. Hilgard to Blake, Nov. 4, 1874, FBP. Blake even paid his master painter James Rae $4.50 to paint and gild a "Keewaydin" estate sign.

25. Richard Guy Wilson, "The Early Work of Charles F. McKim: Country House Commissions," *Winterthur Portfolio* 14 (1979):235–267.

26. Blake to George Dean, Feb. 25, 1874, FBP; Capt. Carlisle P. Patterson to Blake, Mar. 6, 1874, FBP; Julius E. Hilgard to Blake, May 10, 1874, Capt. Carlisle P. Patterson to Julius E. Hilgard, May 18, 1874, FBP.

27. Blake, Diary, Jan. 1, 1877 in FBP. The family budget for 1876 can be found in this entry. The Blake papers also contain mountains of bills for everything from milk and poultry, to ice and manure.

28. Blake, Diary, Jan. 2, 1876, FBP; Caroline Blake to Blake, Jan. 18, 1876, FBP. The Blake papers include receipts for a wet nurse.

29. Julius E. Hilgard to Blake, July 4, 24, 1876, FBP; Blake to Julius E. Hilgard, July 11, 1876, FPB; Capt. Carlisle P. Patterson to Blake, August 1, 1876, FBP.

30. Capt. Carlisle P. Patterson to Blake, Apr. 16, 24, 1877, FBP; Blake to Capt. Carlisle P. Paterson, Apr. 21, 1877, FBP.

31. Capt. Carlisle P. Patterson to Blake, Aug. 28, 1877, Apr. 2, 1878, FBP; Blake's report was published in the *Annual Report of the Board of Harbor Commissioners for the Year* 1878 (Boston, 1879), 31–43.

32. Capt. Carlisle P. Patterson to Blake, Mar. 26, Apr. 2, 9, 1878, FBP; Blake to Capt. Carlisle P. Patterson, Mar. 29, Apr. 5, 1878, FBP; Blake, Diary, Apr. 5, 1878, FBP; Blake's final work is in *Report of the Superintendent, United States Coast Survey* (Washington, D.C., 1878).

33. Louisa Trumbull to Caroline Blake, Feb. 15, 1878, FBP; Louisa Trumbull to Blake, Jan. [n.d.], 1878, FBP; Blake kept a copy of his Jan. 28, 1878, reply to Louisa Trumbull, FBP.

34. Blake to Charles T. Hubbard, Feb. 16, 1878, FBP; Charles T. Hubbard to Blake, Feb. 20, 1878, FBP; Blake to Charles T. Hubbard, Feb. 21, 1878, FBP.

35. Blake to Louisa Trumbull, Apr. 23, 1838, FBP (draft in Blake papers); Louisa Trumbull to Blake, May 1, 1878, FBP.

36. Fox, *Farm Town to Suburb*, 25, 51, 548.

37. The piano was a seven-octave upright, No.13482, made by G. S. Russell & Co. Invoice dated Apr. 13, 1878; Blake's canoeing data is in the back of his 1878 diary, FBP; Middlesex County Registry of Deeds, Vol. 1518, p. 345.

38. Caroline Blake to Lizzie Blake, Apr. 22, May 17, 1878, FBP; Louisa Trumbull to Mr. and Mrs. Blake, Dec. 24, 1878, FBP; Charlie Wells to Blake, Mar. 24, 28, 1880, telegrams, FBP.

CHAPTER 6

THE BLAKE TRANSMITTER
AND THE TELEPHONE

Blake's departure from the Coast Survey proved troubling to him at first. Although he would no longer travel on long expeditions far from home, his independence increased his considerable financial dependence upon his wife's family. Understandably, he desired personal income for his own expenses, particularly to continue supporting his extended family. Hubbard money came at a cost, and one that made Blake very uncomfortable. He cast about for suitable employment, but without success. Without work, he increasingly indulged his immense curiosity, especially in regard to the workings of instruments and tools. For more than a year, Blake had been tinkering with metalworking tools and had made several visits to a nearby instrument-making shop. His mysterious labors aroused the curiosity of family, friends, and neighbors, but Blake initially kept his activities private. He soon realized that any serious experimental work on his part required professional equipment. By August 1877, he had transformed his billiard room into a machine shop, complete with lathes. For many months, Blake toyed with the idea of refining Edison's phonograph, but he gradually transferred his energies to redesigning the telephone transmitter.[1]

Blake first learned of Alexander Graham Bell's invention from his Coast Survey supervisor, Julius E. Hilgard, who had been one of several judges that had awarded Bell a prize at the 1876 Centennial Exposition.

The telegraphic work Blake had done during his years at the Coast Survey had provided him with a highly sophisticated understanding of electricity. And perhaps the "intercom" system he had installed at Keewaydin had sparked some ideas about transmitters. Nevertheless, by late January 1878, Blake was devoting most of his time to applying his knowledge, as he noted in his diary, to "telephones, workshop, observatory & home." For the next several months, he worked feverishly on his telephone transmitter and phonograph and began inviting relatives and friends to Keewaydin to observe his handiwork.[2] On July 20, he asked his cousin John Hubbard to visit: "I want you to hear my phonograph, microphone, and improved telephone." Blake then dropped work on the phonograph and concentrated on the telephone. He read the latest professional literature on microphones, and after considerable experimentation succeeded in constructing a transmitter with "most satisfactory results."[3] In mid-October, Dr. Clarence J. Blake, the Boston physician who had supplied Bell with a cadaver's prepared ear for his aural experiments, tested Frank's transmitter, sparking local "interest in my description of your trial on my wire."[4]

On October 18, 1878, Blake took his transmitter to the Bell Telephone Company offices in Boston where it underwent thorough testing by Thomas Watson, Bell's famed assistant. The results left little doubt; Blake's transmitter was better than anything else available. Blake recalled that every word in that first test "was distinctly understood, while even a whisper was perfectly transmitted. I then became satisfied that I had discovered the broad principle of an important invention, and from that time on I devoted myself to a series of careful experiments to perfect the details and to discover the methods of adjustment of the parts necessary to produce the most nearly perfect results." At the office of Chauncy Smith, one of Bell's principal attorneys, Blake agreed to meet with Gardiner G. Hubbard, president of the Bell Telephone Company. Returning home that afternoon, Blake went right to work on a second transmitter, laboring from 7:00 P.M. until early the next morning, when he successfully completed tests on the new instrument. Bell Telephone needed Blake's transmitter and Blake knew just how much.[5]

Although it is nearly impossible for us to understand today, in the 1870s few people grasped the importance of Alexander Graham Bell's invention. For most, the telephone represented little more than a rich man's clever toy or merely an amusing technological curiosity. Bell Telephone Company could find few investors and almost sold out entirely to its main rival, Western Union. "We were very much disappointed," recalled Watson, "because the President of the Western Union Telegraph Co. had refused somewhat contemptuously Mr. Hubbard's offer to sell him all the Bell patents for the exorbitant sum of $100,000.[6]

Although Western Union passed up the Bell offer, its officials realized that one day the telephone would be an important commercial product. They entered the phone business through a subsidiary, the Gold and Stock Telegraph Company, and acquired all rights to a telephone created by Bell's competitors, especially Thomas A. Edison. Western Union organized the legally questionable—because of patent infringements—American Speaking Telephone Company in December 1877. Prior to Blake's intervention, a good phone transmitter did not exist. Edison's carbon button phone, a variable resistance instrument, proved better than Bell's patented phone, which used a magneto-driven, variable resistance transmitter. The inferior Bell phone, as Watson recalled, did "much to develop American voice and lungs, making them powerful but not melodious. . . . Edison's transmitter talked louder than the magnetos we were using and our agents began to clamor for them, and I had to work nights to get up something just as good. Fortunately for my constitution, Frank Blake came along with his transmitter. We bought it, and I got a little sleep for a few days."[7]

Although Blake's transmitter surpassed Edison's, this did not prevent Western Union from continuing to defy Bell's patent rights with their telephone business. On September 12, 1878, Western Union's persistence brought them to the Circuit Court of the United States, District of Massachusetts, for infringement of Bell's patents. Although they fought the suit, Western Union eventually admitted that the court would ultimately rule in Bell's favor and settled on November 10, 1879, acknowledging that

Bell had indeed invented the telephone.[8] The suit against Western Union ensured Bell's legal right to domination of the telephone industry in the years to come, but that would not amount to much unless the company could also maintain technical supremacy. Blake's timely intervention, both technologically and financially, made all the difference in the world.

As astonishing as we might find Blake's inventive genius, it was equaled by his skill as a negotiator. Given his rather careless spending habits with his in-laws' money, one would not have expected Blake to envision so clearly the business arrangement he would strike with Bell Telephone. Nevertheless, he convinced Benjamin Sewall to set aside the princely sum of $10,000 to invest in the phone company, should negotiations go according to Blake's plan. Unfortunately, a copy of the final agreement between Blake and Bell has not been found. But George L. Bradley, treasurer and general agent of the New England Telephone Company, outlined the major provisions to Bell Telephone president Gardiner Hubbard, Bell's father-in-law, on November 4. The Bell Telephone Company would pay Blake $1,000 at once and $1,000 when Blake received a patent on his new transmitter. One year after securing the patent, the company could secure full assignment of the patent by paying Blake $3,000. Bell Telephone Company would assume the cost of securing the patent and if the company encountered a court challenge it could contest or drop the matter. In return, Blake would invest $10,000 cash into the company and provide them his services for one year at a salary of $1,000. As Bradley informed Hubbard, "Mr. Blake says he is ready to put in $10,000 as soon as the matter can be definitely arranged."[9]

A contentious point not addressed in Bradley's original letter focused on Blake's insistence that his name be stamped on the front of each transmitter. Correspondence among the Bell officials early in November indicates that, while Gardiner Hubbard and George Bradley were ready to gratify Blake, Watson thought that Bell and inventor Emile Berliner should also be acknowledged. To avoid ill feelings, the company agreed to prominently place "Blake Transmitter" on the front of every transmitter, with the dates of all other relevant patents stamped onto the telephone's side.[10]

Rather than the $10,000 first discussed with Bell Telephone, Blake obtained two checks from Benjamin Sewall totaling $15,000 on November 6. With this money he bought 200 shares of Bell Telephone Company and 75 shares of New England Bell Company. Blake owned forty shares in the parent company and twenty of the regional Bell subsidiary, with the remaining majority of stock shares going to Sewall. The infusion of capital to the Bell Company likely saved it from serious disruption, if not bankruptcy. The arrangement also produced a great fortune for the Sewalls and Blake.[11]

Bell needed technical supremacy to survive, and Blake worked with top officials of Bell Telephone and its affiliates to improve his transmitter and operation of the Bell phone.[12] William A. Childs, head of Bell's New York affiliate, received a phone with a new transmitter from Blake. "Telephone received," Childs telegrammed. "It is better in every respect than Edison's latest and best. Accept congratulations. Adjustment not affected by journey." The new phone

Complete telephone set with receiver, Blake transmitter, and battery box. Unidentified clipping, Blake papers.

and transmitter would be exhibited on the floor of New York's Produce Exchange where the Gold and Stock Company displayed and sold their Edison instrument. Childs stressed the need for speed in order to compete with Edison. By the end of the year, an arrangement had been made with Charles Williams, who had manufactured Bell's first instruments, to produce transmitters at a cost of $3.10 each. By this time, the New York office had almost 200 subscribers.[13]

Bell also had to act swiftly to secure new patents, which greatly concerned Bell president Gardiner Hubbard. "I think it is of the greatest importance that you prepare at once your specifications for your Patent," he advised Blake, "& that you forward same to Washington to our Patent counsel A. Pollok Esq. that he may present it to the office as soon as it is rec'd." Receiving no response after two weeks, Hubbard again wrote Blake urging him to deliver the specifications to Pollok for filing. Blake replied that he had put the matter of specifications into the hands of Chauncy Smith, who "would doubtless have it well advanced were it not for the fact that experiments in progress promise to result in changes which it will be of the utmost importance to embody in the specifications." Hubbard reminded Blake that he had been instructed to forward the specifications to Pollok, who had charge of all patent office matters, not Smith. Despite the company's eagerness to get the new, patent-protected phones out to the public, three years passed before Bell finally secured full legal rights for the Blake Transmitter.[14]

With the patents pending, Bell Telephone energetically sought to put the new transmitter and phone in service. On December 20, 1878, the company announced "to our agents, customers, and to the public, that we are now ready to furnish a battery-transmitting Telephone, in addition to, and to use in connection with our ordinary Magneto Telephone." The new Blake battery telephone would be used in larger cities where the induced currents from telegraph or other wires might cause interference, or for long distance or other situations requiring a greater volume of sound.[15]

Although the Blake transmitter represented the best available technology, it required refinement, and Blake was in the Bell workshop every day, "testing, etc." But he disliked working at the Bell facility and probably abhorred the idea of anyone looking over his shoulder. Emile Berliner recalled that Blake had become so "hampered in his work by increasing nervousness" that "he soon afterwards retired to his country place near Newton, where he had fitted up a complete shop and laboratory for the pursuit of scientific research."[16] Blake continued his experiments at home and in January created a new transmitter with contacts made of a rubber tube filled with mercury. Edmund Wilson, a Bell employee who worked with Blake, suggested damping the diaphragm with a rubber ring, which resulted in clear and steady articulation. They also experimented with a hard rubber diaphragm that produced very loud and distinct articulation. Although Blake believed that he was responsible for the innovations, the application for a patent for the rubber band surrounding the diaphragm was made in Edmund Wilson's name.[17]

New problems arose when Bell began production and distribution. Thomas A. Watson, now serving as Bell's general superintendent, offered technical suggestions and expressed concern that the latest batch of transmitters emitted an annoying overtone. "Are you sure you are not unconsciously allowing them to deteriorate?" he queried. All concerned agreed that rough handling in transit also contributed to deterioration in the transmitters' performance. Even while resolving these problems, Watson urged Blake not to slacken up on production. Orders poured in every day, and the company could easily accommodate distribution of two hundred transmitters a week, but Watson considered himself lucky to receive half that number. While Blake fabricated the transmitter prototypes himself, Bell placed responsibility for commercial production in the hands of Charles Williams, Jr., in Boston. Blake provided close supervision, testing each instrument before it was shipped; yet problems persisted.[18]

In early February, Berliner, who had joined the company in New York the previous November, arrived in Boston to take up duties in Williams's shop. Bell expected him to perfect the Blake transmitter; the company, much to its dismay, had discovered that it could not make twelve good transmitters alike. The instrument tended to easily fall out of adjustment and "boom" during transmission if users did not speak with care. Berliner discovered that the transmitter's platinum electrode quickly dug a cavity into the carbon button, which immediately put the instrument out of adjustment. Placing a hard carbon button in the transmitter solved that problem and modifying the springs that held the diaphragm and electrodes eliminated the "booming." Berliner's work brought the Blake transmitter to perfection, and the company immediately went into production at the astonishing rate of two hundred per day.[19]

The Blake transmitter, an improvement on an existing invention rather than a wholly new one, did not permit Blake to obtain as broad a patent as Bell's original one. Negotiating the best specification and claim possible required a great deal of maneuvering around existing caveats, applications, and patents. Edison's patent rights proved the most difficult to negotiate around. Blake claimed that the double-spring element of his transmitter was his invention. But in May, Blake's patent attorney, William W. Swan, advised him that "January 3, 1879 is as far back as you can go with the double spring claim. . . . Edison has a double spring claim that will press you hard. Now, before Edison beats you in this, you ought to be fully satisfied that the two inventions are substantially the same." Blake rejected the idea that Edison had invented the two-spring device, claiming that Edison never produced one that worked nearly as well as his own. Swan wrote to Blake, then vacationing at his favorite resort in North Conway, that "It will be a pity if we can't get a good patent for you. Couldn't you come down? You need to point out why your instrument is infinitely better than any other."[20] Blake replied impatiently:

> Your letter of the 28th inst. is received. The reason why my instrument "is infinitely better than any which preceded it" is that the lengths and strengths of its springs, the weights of its electrodes and the proportions and arrangements of all its parts are such as were proved to be the best by six months of the hardest work I have ever done. . . . I have sacrificed my time and health for two years to the production of an instrument which the friends and foes of our company alike admit to be the connecting link between its failure and success. Beside this instrument no one has shown a similar one of previous construction and the failure of the Patent Office to recognize me as its inventor will be a severe blow to my personal feelings to say nothing of the pecuniary loss of at least $25,000 which it will entail.[21]

The double-spring patent controversy wore on for another year. On July 4, Swan advised Blake that certain elements of the double-spring device had been awarded to Edison and others to him. At the time of Blake's patent bid, scores of other applications for telephone inventions and improvements, both legitimate and fraudulent, poured into Washington. While the patent office appeared to have been extremely conscientious in rendering its judgments, the process could be very difficult and enormously time consuming. Suits over patents became a routine part of telephone company business for years to come. Even Blake proved a hindrance. Swan worked tirelessly to defend Blake's interests and secure his overseas patent rights.[22] But Blake preferred the role of inventor to that of businessman and often made himself scarce just when his attorney needed him the most. On at least one occasion, Swan pursued Blake all the way to the White Mountains to obtain his signature on a patent specification. Despite several claims that Blake's transmitter infringed upon existing patents, the patent office sustained most of Blake's claims. In the end, his transmitter received four separate patents, granted on November 29, 1881.[23]

In February 1879, Bell Telephone Company incorporated as the National Bell Telephone Company—soon changed to American Bell Telephone Company—to develop telephone service throughout the United States and around the world. All activities centered at the national office in Boston at 95 Milk Street with William Hathaway Forbes as president, Theodore N. Vail as general manager, Thomas A. Watson as general inspector, and Alexander Graham Bell and Francis Blake as electricians. Blake also served as a director and a member of the corporation's executive committee. The newly consolidated corporation not only achieved a stronger position to defend its patents against Western Union but also to protect its patent interests around the world.

Blake had sold only United States rights for his transmitter to the Bell company. Foreign patents generally went to the Bell affiliate in that country for a single lump-sum payment. But complications inevitably arose. Although the British patent on the Blake transmitter had been granted promptly, Edison's nephew had been dispatched to England to introduce Edison's telephone. Hubbard agreed to introduce the Blake transmitter to the British in return for one-half interest in the British patent, hoping to sell the rights for a round sum to the Telephone Company Limited. Upon arrival in England, however, Hubbard learned that Bell had been forced to disclaim some important parts of his patent because of earlier similar British work. The resulting complications raised the disturbing possibility that Edison might be able completely to prevent the introduction of the Bell telephone.[24] Despite the superior operation of the Blake transmitter, the Edison company began to discourage potential buyers of Bell telephones by claiming patent infringements. But after engaging three different agents, Blake obtained £5,000 from United Telephone Company for the rights to his transmitter throughout the United Kingdom.

Canadian matters went more smoothly. Blake corresponded with Charles Williams, who arranged the Canadian rights to manufacture the Blake transmitter under license from Blake and to sell each for $10 above cost. In this lucrative arrangement, Blake and Williams would divide the profits equally. On November 5, 1879, Williams sent Blake a check for $300, Blake's share in the first proceeds of Canadian sales. By March 1880, Blake's Canadian royalties totaled $3,139.50. The following year Blake sold his patent rights to the newly organized Canadian telephone company for $10,000.[25]

A subsequent transaction with the Bell Telephone Company of Canada proved that Blake did not always need sharp pencils and lawyers to do business. C. F. Sise, the Canadian Bell vice president, asked Blake about transmitter rights for Newfoundland. Pointing out that the number of units sold there would probably not exceed 200 and that Bell himself had given his telephone patent rights to the area, Sise asked Blake to make the same arrangement. In return, Sise promised to "send you down a Tandem Sleigh which will not only excite the envy of the Mill Dam but doubtless be the cause of divers other Damns." The delighted Blake agreed to the arrangement with a warning to Sise that, "When you select the tandem sleigh bear in mind that I shall insist upon taking you out on the road in it next winter; and that the eyes of all Boston will then be upon you; and judgment passed upon your selection."[26] Sise replied that the sleigh would be built at once and either shipped or held until autumn, as Blake preferred, but asked, "Is it your honest opinion that I am expected to risk my life for this company? This query is in reference to the last clause of your note, wherein you propose to drive me yourself in that Tandem sleigh."[27]

Bell also arranged profitable patent rights for Blake and itself in Spain, Portugal, Italy, Russia, and several South American countries, which they had purchased for $10,000 and later for Cuba, Mexico, and Asian markets.[28] When Blake secured foreign rights he was blunt, knowing that he could get exactly what he wanted. True to his typical fashion, he wrote:

> I am advised that you have in mind the organization of a company for the purpose of introducing and controlling the use of the speaking telephone in Mexico. Should you wish to secure my good-will and any right I may have in that country as the inventor of the form of speaking telephone known as the "Blake Transmitter" I shall be pleased to convey the same to your proposed company upon the receipt [of] one hundred shares of its stock.[29]

Seeking ways to show its respect for the temperamental Blake and recognize his importance to the company, National Bell Telephone provided him with a desk at its Boston offices. The company also had appointed him as an "electrician," a title shared only with Alexander Graham Bell, and named him editor of its new magazine, *The Telephone Journal.* National Bell conceived of the monthly *Journal* as the official organ of "telephonic interests," a source that would include the latest information about telephonic work, district systems, summaries of articles about telephones in scientific journals, original communications, and advertisements. As editor-in-chief, Blake had complete responsibility for it, and he set right to work accumulating material for the first issue.[30] Alexander

Graham Bell planned to submit something for the *Journal*, and Blake hoped to publish a portion of a paper he was preparing for the National Academy of Arts and Sciences. But the pressure of everyday work quickly caught up to Blake, who became ill and fell far behind. Lizzie told Bell vice president George L. Bradley that her husband's sickness would certainly not prevent him from completing work on the *Journal* at home. In early May, Blake believed he would be well enough to return to his Boston desk the following month. Bell president Forbes replied patiently, "We shall be heartily glad to see you when you feel like looking in." But patience and Blake's eventual recovery could not save the journal, which died quickly and quietly.[31]

Being chained to an office desk working as an editor soon became very unappealing to the independent-minded Blake. He was happiest in his own workshop, laboring on projects that he found challenging. Now that Bell had a perfected phone, other mechanical challenges arose to capture Blake's imagination. It took Blake and his colleagues little time to discover that when placing a call some sort of signal was needed to attract attention at the other end of the line. Pondering this problem, Blake developed a call system using a combination of voltaic and magneto electric currents. He discovered that an electric current could make an adjustable pendulum vibrate. He exhibited the apparatus he devised to his family and then sent a telegram to Forbes at 95 Milk Street declaring his call apparatus "a perfect success." The new instrument also impressed Watson, who immediately persuaded Vail to stop negotiations with other firms that had been working on an alternate scheme. After calling on Chauncy Smith and William Swan, his patent attorneys, Blake spent six long days producing a working model of his invention.[32]

Experienced in the patent process, Blake presented himself at Swan's Pemberton Square office in Boston to demonstrate the apparatus. At Blake's invitation, "Forbes, Bradley, Vail, and Watson came up at 2 o'-clock" to see his new design. He wanted it clear to all concerned that the device was of his own invention, quite independent of his connection to the Bell Company. But in January 1880, after signing the application for a patent on his pendulum call, he learned from Swan that a Canadian patent had been granted for a rival apparatus. The German patent office also rejected his application because of a similar pre-existing German patent. After expending precisely $961.75—Blake kept *all* his receipts—and much effort, the call device could not be used.[33]

Even before Blake learned of the failure of his patent applications, he set to work on another call bell. His revolving disk call apparatus would not only ring a bell at a particular station, but would also indicate to all stations that the line was in use. By January 8, 1880, he felt ready to demonstrate the call system to Bell representatives he had invited out to Keewaydin. In September, the patent office accepted Blake's application. While conveying the news to Blake, Swan urged him to file for an English patent immediately. The next step, of course, was to make them pay. Blake immediately began negotiations with the American Bell Telephone Company, which ended in assignment of the patent to Bell for $1,500 and royalties, which eventually earned Blake $10,317.55.[34]

As the number of telephone subscribers dramatically increased, Bell's rudimentary phone system came under escalating pressure. Telephone operators could handle only a few lines at once and soon became overwhelmed by the very success of Blake's inventions. Now Bell needed new call-switching technology. Charles Blake had earlier entered the phone business, and with a friend named Ellis Frost had been at work on a switchboard. He wrote Blake in February 1881 about some electrical matters and mentioned that he and Frost had an appointment to show their model to Theodore N. Vail, Bell general manager, at the company's Milk Street offices. Blake also had been working on a switchboard, one that would allow an operator to handle at least fifty lines, something Vail saw as Bell's minimum requirements.[35]

For the next month, Blake developed various ideas for a switchboard. As always, his enthusiasm ran high when confronted with a new technological problem, and he fully devoted himself to devising a solution to the switchboard challenge. After William Chaffee, one of Charles Williams's best workmen, visited Blake one evening at Keewaydin, Blake began working in his shop at 10:30 P.M., and at 2 A.M. had completed a working model. A week later Chaffee returned with a drawing of a switching device. Blake showed Chaffee his model, but he seemed to prefer something in Chaffee's drawing with "sliding line bars with only one contact point each." Chaffee asked for $200 as payment to "Abandon all claims and to assign any improvements he might add in working it up." Blake thought the idea was worth $500 and the two agreed on the higher fee.[36]

Little time could be wasted in developing the switchboard idea. Phone systems needed the device, in any reliable form, as soon as possible. The phone company in Providence, Rhode Island, for instance, heard about Blake's idea wanted to see it immediately.[37] By April, Blake had finished his work and applied for the first of eight patents for the switchboard. The patent office moved with uncharacteristic speed and granted the first two on June 21, 1881. William Swan handled Blake's new patent applications, including the international rights application, and assured Blake that this time little would stand in the way of securing his rights. "There is nothing in the office which resembles it in the least," he assured Blake, "and your claims as allowed will be very broad." He used his personal influence with a colleague at the patent office to encourage swift action, and the office issued Blake's patent on November 15, 1881, at least a month ahead of the normal schedule.[38]

Blake naturally offered the rights to the Bell Company, and after some discussion, Forbes directed that Blake be paid $4,000 for them. Prompted, perhaps, by the grant of his sixth switchboard patent in April 1883, Blake made an offer to transfer all his interests in the switching technology to the company. Vail sent a memorandum to Bell's executive committee on September 26, 1883, recommending that the company accept Blake's request for $15,000 to release the company of all obligation to pay royalties on those new patents.[39]

Blake seems to have given away too much, given the future growth of the telephone industry. But he continued to refine the switching technology and waited for what he saw as the right opportunity to seal a deal that would provide him with a steadier income. Blake secured his last patent for a switchboard on November 6, 1888. Two days later, the American Bell Telephone Company bought the rights together with all reissues and extensions for $1,000 and the obligation to cover all expenses involved in securing the patent. More important, the company agreed to pay Blake a royalty of twenty-five cents for each substation line connected to a central office by appliances based upon his invention. Assuming steady growth in the phone business, that agreement would have produced a staggering amount of income so long as Bell used Blake's ideas. But it did not. Indeed, for all the patents Blake secured none produced as much wealth for him as the simple rise in the value of Bell's stock price.[40]

As a practicing inventor, Blake held a unique position on the board of the American Bell Telephone Company. Although he understood the company's profit-driven needs, he could never fully reconcile his role as inventor with the requirements of business. For instance, when asked to help resolve a dispute between Bell and another inventor, he refused. Writing to Swan, Blake declined to become involved "for the reason that the Am'n. Bell side of it seems to me to be a very mean one—one not calculated to add to the reputation of the company for fair dealing with inventors."[41] His October 13, 1883, letter to fellow director Charles Bowditch provides great insight into Blake's understanding of the inventive process and of how companies could maximize benefit from a particular inventor. It also displays Blake's practical understanding of human nature and his usual prickliness, but little that a business would find appealing.

I am grateful to learn that my remarks about relations between our company and inventors have led you to ask for a more extended expression of my opinions on the subject. Premising that as I have had no business experience much of what I say may seem to be mere "twaddle" to business men, I will fire away at you as freely as if we were having an informal talk in your office at 95 Milk St.

I. I believe our company should so deal with inventors that we may have the reputation of being their friends and not their oppressors. Undoubtedly many of them come to us with very much exaggerated notions of the values of their inventions and while our interests demand that these notions should be upset there is a broad field for diplomacy in doing it.

An inventor is apt to be a man of extremely sensitive feeling and of unbusinesslike modes of thought so that our methods of "personal manipulation" must in many cases determine whether he assigns his patent feeling that he has been ground between upper and nether millstones driven by the engines of a great monopoly or that he has been kindly welcomed, considerately treated and paid a fair price for the results of his labor.

II. A stipulation that the purchase of a patent shall include any and all improvements which the patentee may subsequently make upon his invention, seems to me unwise. The practical effect of such a stipulation must be to discourage the inventor from applying his mind to the further improvement of his invention. On the other hand we must protect ourselves against dishonest inventors who may have in mind important improvements at the very time they assign their patents to us. This we can accomplish, I think, by stipulating that any and all improvements that they may make during a certain time—say the six months or year following the assignment, shall be ours. Or in cases where the necessity of further improvement is manifest, and the inventor of known honesty and ambition, we might encourage him at a fair salary to work upon his inventions for us.

III. I do not think we should derive benefits from salaries paid to inventors to cover their subsequent inventions. The hope of a large reward is what in most cases quickens the inventor's spirit; and to pay him a certain sum in advance reduces his labor to the level of what mechanics call "working for a dead horse." Many a mechanic has told me in substance that a final payment for work unfinished leads the recipient to regard every day he thereafter devotes to the work as so much out of his pocket.

Nor is this feeling confined to the lower ranks of life—the same confession has been made to me by one of the leading artists in

Boston. In this connection may well be cited the case of the poet Tennyson who, having been subsidized to the extent of £3,000 by one of the leading English magazines, produced but one short poem of doubtful merit during the period covered by his subsidy; but within two years thereafter published several long and brilliant poems to his own great gain.

IV. A wild bird caged you have in your power, but he won't sing. A wild bird fed from your library window will come round periodically and enliven the air with song. Metaphorically speaking it is just so with the inventor. Don't let us lock him up in our laboratory and dull his brains with salary or advance payment! Let him have the utmost freedom as to work and uncertainty as to gain. Let him at all times receive from us a kindly reception; let a ready ear be lent to his exposition of ideas; and sound judgment be passed upon his results. We shall then, I think, have no difficulty in securing his patents at a fair price.

V. Finally if an examination of our electrical budget shows that we have paid money to any person or persons on the assumption that they were going to give us valuable inventions and they have failed to do so we must console ourselves with the reflection that roosters cannot be made to lay eggs.

> Very sincerely yrs
> Francis Blake
> 13 October 1883

P. S. As to the numerous mechanics and others in our employ I think that while they should legally be obliged to assign their inventions to us, it should be distinctly understood that our policy is to encourage such inventions by giving gratuities therefor.

However unhappy Blake might have been with the treatment he received from his colleagues at Bell, he did not think to terminate the relationship and continued to research new ways to improve phone service. Long-distance communication was the next obvious step in development.

In March 1884, Blake learned of Bell's new phone line and participated in a call to the company's New York office. "I heard him perfectly with both Edison & Blake transmitters in circuit at his end. At our end the Blake only was used," Theodore N. Vail reported. "He got my whisper distinctly & I his in return." Although the Blake transmitter worked adequately, other inventors sought to improve transmitter performance, forcing Bell to keep pace or lose its competitive edge. Edison had invented a granular carbon electrode similar to an English model.[42] But neither worked perfectly, and in 1884 Blake began to apply himself to designing a "new long distance transmitter."[43] He worked steadily on the problem, and by mid-December had completed a prototype. On Monday, December 15, he took his new transmitter to 95 Milk Street and conducted successful tests between New York and Providence, Rhode Island, "the operator at Providence saying it was the best transmitter he had ever heard." But Blake continued to tinker with the design, and his diary for December 22, 1884, bears the heading, "Eureka!" It includes a sketch of the transmitter and a description of a diaphragm made of a sieve with meshes large enough to allow carbon particles to pass through. He went to work on it at once and at 7:15 P.M. tested it with his wife. He then called his brother-in-law Charles Wells, who declared the signal to be five times as loud as the original Blake transmitter.[44]

During January 1885, Blake continued testing his new device, achieving positive results. He displayed his "New Blake Transmitter" to Bell officials and to his lawyer, Swan. He applied for a patent the following month, and the patent office granted it on March 24. Blake immediately proposed to Bell that he assign the new patent to the company for $25,000 with the condition that each be marked "New Blake Transmitter," with no other inventor's name appearing on the product without Blake's consent. He also sought a fifty-cent royalty for each transmitter sold, equal sharing of all profits on foreign sales, and agreement that at the end of one year the company would pay him $25,000 to continue manufacturing the instruments. Finally, Blake insisted on the right to exhibit the transmitter at fairs and keep any awards it earned.[45]

Bell balked at Blake's list of demands. In July, Blake renewed the offer but modified the terms by proposing that the arrangement be extended to include all other telephone inventions he might produce during his lifetime. This time Blake overplayed his hand. Bell had been testing the "New Blake Transmitter" and determined that other equipment already available without patent complications actually proved superior to Blake's. In fact, four other transmitters produced better results.[46] Familiar with Blake's explosive temper, Charles Bowditch tactfully suggested to Blake that, given the new transmitter's performance, he develop it further and then allow Bell the opportunity to buy it. Blake swiftly replied that he would keep the invention under his control, and predicted that soon the company would be buying it at a considerably higher price.[47]

Despite his disappointment, Blake continued to work closely with Bell. Bell's executive committee believed that Blake's new transmitter was "all that I could wish for" and beyond what the average "poor inventor" could ever have attained. But because he was no closer to convincing the company to take on his invention, he recommended that Bowditch speak with Charles Wells, cashier of the New England Telephone and Telegraph Company, who had been using the new transmitter successfully for over three months. Somehow Blake had convinced himself that Bell would accept the testimony of his brother-in-law as unbiased. He further stated, with more credibility, that commercial use proved a far more reliable test of the durability and clarity of Blake's new instrument than any results achieved in a mere laboratory.[48]

Bowditch acknowledged that Wells had made a very fair statement of his experience with the transmitter. "I was much impressed with his views as to its advantages for long distance work." But he declined to offer encouragement and only stated that "for reasons that I will explain to you later," Bell would decline to make any decision for a few weeks.[49] On July 30, Theodore Vail informed Blake that Emile Berliner would test the new transmitter and seek to modify and improve it and asked him to fully cooperate with Berliner. Through August and September, Blake and Berliner corresponded and met to fully analyze the transmitter. Then their contact tapered off, although Blake continued experimenting with his new device well into 1886.[50]

Berliner had little reason to renew contact with Blake about the new transmitter. His work and the analysis by the company's laboratory made it abundantly clear that there was little "new" in the new transmitter. In a lengthy letter to John Hudson, who had recently succeeded Vail as Bell general manager, James J. Storrow, one of the company's patent attorneys, described the problems with Blake's claims. Storrow determined that the sieve electrode was really what Blake had contributed to an existing class of instruments that already contained granular conducting material. Such as it is, he wrote, Blake had a very narrow claim to originality and his patent did not cover various other forms of the instrument. Dismayed by Storrow's ruling, Blake attempted to resign from Bell's executive board on June 9, 1886. Reiterating the views expressed in his lengthy October 13, 1883, letter about the plight of the inventor, Blake complained about the unjust and ungenerous treatment he had received over his new transmitter. Fortunately, Charles Bowditch read the letter in William Hathaway Forbes's absence and persuaded Blake to let the matter lie until the next executive board meeting.[51]

Patent analysis remains a hairsplitting task. Inventors often find themselves carrying on parallel research, producing very similar results sometimes simultaneously. Companies, in Blake's time and today, have to guard against spurious claims of original invention or patents that amounted to worthless modifications of another's invention. While Bell had no reason to suspect Blake's motives, it had to evaluate carefully all inventions and decide which had meritorious patent rights, regardless of the inventor's claims. In the case of Blake's "new" transmitter, Bell treated the sensitive inventor with complete fairness, especially considering the large sums he demanded and the special conditions he wished to impose. In the end, no grounds existed for the company to close a deal with Blake for what largely amounted to pre-existing technology. But more lay behind Bell's reluctance to recognize Blake's work.

Blake remained convinced that he could significantly improve telephone service and continued experimenting with electrodes during the summer and fall of 1886, eventually filing two new patent applications for transmitter improvements.[52] But on July 16, he spoke with Chauncy Smith about his application for a patent covering gold-plated electrodes. In the course of their conversation, Smith remarked that Hudson had confessed the previous day that Bell really did not want a better transmitter. Replacing all their transmitters would be enormously expensive because users did not own but leased their telephones. The company, barring competition from another manufacturer, had no incentive to improve the performance of individual telephones. Not one penny of additional revenue would result, and the entire cost of the change would be borne by the company. The news must have frustrated Blake and increased his cynicism about business motives. Nevertheless, before the end of the year Blake and Bell came to terms on his inventions. Blake offered to assign or sell six patents and inventions to Bell, requesting that his name continue to be affixed to all Bell phones produced under his patents. Although John Hudson assured Blake that Bell would happily comply with this request, he believed that it could pose a problem for other inventors who might have made far greater contributions. Although Blake wished to make his request a condition of the sale, he knew the leverage now had shifted entirely to the company, and he assured Hudson that this was simply a request, not a demand. He "purposely left the Company free to do that which its sense of justice would prompt it to do in the matter."[53] On November 12, Hudson signed Bell's agreement with Blake and paid him $10,000—while not the large sum he had hoped for, it certainly represented a substantial payment. Bowditch had been right to encourage Blake to cool off rather than resign from the company's executive board in a blaze of self-defeating glory. Eventually, Bell manufactured three different models of Blake granular-carbon transmitters, amounting to only about 13,000 units. As this represented only a token replacement of transmitters, the settlement proved more valuable to Blake than to the company.[54]

Blake continued to tinker with telephones after the mid-1880s, but made no further important innovations. He remained active in the affairs of the company, clearly valued as a member of the Bell community. He even once received the unenviable assignment of discharging the company's "expert" accountant for dereliction of duty. During the 1890s, Blake chaired the company's audit committee, and when Bell considered another reorganization in 1895, Bell officials spent nearly four hours with Blake reviewing the plans. Blake freely spoke his mind to company directors and believed that he had "Stirred them up on the importance of a scheme for reorganization and when each Director was asked to express his opinion my views were unanimously sustained outside of the Ex. Com. & Hudson & Forbes were evidently with me." Blake formed a close relationship with Hudson, who sometimes called on him to discuss candidates for the board of directors. When Hudson passed away in 1900, Blake wrote his memoir for the American Antiquarian Society. After his days as a telephone inventor had passed, Blake remained an important voice in the company, continuing his contribution to the history of the telephone.[55]

Endnotes

1. Blake to Julius E. Hilgard, Aug. 24, 1877, FBP. For the history of the telephone, see: John Brooks, *Telephone: The First Hundred Years* (New York, 1976), and Frederick L. Rhodes, *Beginnings of Telephony* (New York and London, 1929).
2. Blake, Diary, Jan. to July, 1878, *passim*, FBP.
3. Blake to John Hubbard, July 12, 1878, FBP; "Man Who Enjoys Life," [article on Blake] *Boston Globe*, Dec. 15, 1895, copy in Blake scrapbook, vol. 41, FBP.
4. Clarence J. Blake to Francis Blake, Oct. 17, 1878, FBP.
5. Blake, Diary, Oct. 18–19, 1878, FBP.
6. Rhodes, *Beginnings of Telephony*, 51; Herbert N. Casson, *History of the Telephone* (Chicago, 1910), 33. Bell was assigned United States patent number 174,465. Thomas A. Watson, *Birth and Babyhood of the Telephone . . .* (An address delivered before the third annual convention of the Telephone Pioneers

of America at Chicago, Oct. 17, 1913) (New York reprinted from *The Telephone Review* by A.T.& T., 1936), 24.

7. Rhodes, *Beginnings of Telephony*, 51; Watson, *Birth and Babyhood of the Telephone,* p. 36.

8. Rhodes, *Beginnings of Telephony*, 52. The final decree in the case was handed down on Apr. 4, 1881. Bell claimed that Western Union had violated patents numbers 174,465 and 186,787.

9. George L. Bradley to Gardiner Hubbard, Nov. 1, 4, 1878, A.T.&T. Co. Archives, Warren, N.J., Box 1194. Blake's attorney, William W. Swan to American Bell Telephone Co., Feb. 2, 1882, A. T.& T. Archives, Box 1060. Swan wrote to transmit four deeds of assignment for the patents Blake eventually received and seeking payment under the terms of the contract, giving the date of the original document. A.T.&T. Archives, box 1060.

10. George L. Bradley to Thomas A. Watson, Jan. 15, 1897, A.T.&T. Archives, Box 1194; Thomas A. Watson to George L. Bradley, Jan. 16, 1879 (copy), A.T.&T. Archives, Box 1194.

11. Blake, Diary, Nov. 6, 1878, FBP.

12. Blake to William A. Childs, Nov. 9, 1878, copy in FBP.

13. Thomas A. Watson to Blake, Dec. 31, 1878, FBP.

14. Gardiner Hubbard to Blake, Nov. 25, 1878, FBP; Blake to Gardiner Hubbard, Dec. 10, 1878, FBP.

15. A copy of the Bell circular is in A.T.&T. Co. Archives, Box 1194.

16. Charles Williams to R. W. Devonshire, Nov. 14, 1878, A.T.&T. Co. Archives, Box 1194; Emile Berliner, "The Final Development of the Blake Transmitter," speech given July 31, 1923, typescript in A.T.&T. Co. Archives, Box 1076.

17. Blake, Diary, Jan. 4, 1879, FBP; William W. Swan to Blake, May 16, 1879, FBP; Blake to William W. Swan, May 18, 1879 [copy], FBP.

18. Thomas Watson to Blake, Jan. 4, 9, 10, 1879, FBP.

19. Berliner, "The Final Development of the Blake Transmitter."

20. William W. Swan to Blake, May 27, 1880, FBP.

21. Blake to William W. Swan, May 30, 1880, FBP.

22. By the time Blake received his United States patent, the following countries had already granted rights: England: Jan. 20, 1879; Canada: May 28, 1879; Italy: May 20, 1880; New South Wales: July 20, 1880; Cape of Good Hope: Aug. 30, 1880; Natal: Sept. 6, 1880; Spain: Nov. 5, 1880; Portugal: Nov. 10, 1880; and British Guiana: Mar. 23, 1881.

23. Patent numbers 250,126 through 250,129.

24. Gardiner Hubbard to Blake, Apr. 11, July 24, 1879, FBP.

25. James Cowherd to Blake, Apr. 28, 1879, FBP; Saunders to Blake, Mar. 2, 22, 1880, FPB; Gardiner Hubbard to Theodore Vail, Mar. 6, 1880, FBP.

26. C. F. Sise to Blake, Apr. 2, 1883, FBP, Blake to C. F. Sise, undated draft reply, FBP.

27. C. F. Sise to Blake, Apr. 12, 1883, FBP.

28. Blake, Diary, Nov. 1, 1879, FBP.

29. Blake to Sydney A. Williams, Sept. 13, 1880, FBP.

30. Broadside announcing publication of the journal, Box 48, FBP.

31. Alexander Graham Bell to Blake, Apr. 1, 1879, FBP; Elizabeth Blake to George L. Bradley, Apr. 6, 1879, FBP; William H. Forbes to Blake, May 13, 1879, FBP.

32. Blake Diary, Mar. 11–12, Oct. 7, 11, 13, 1879, FBP.

33. Blake, Diary, Oct. 22, 1879, FBP; William W. Swan to Blake, Jan. 20, 1880; Hazeltine & Lake to William W. Swan, Feb. 27, 1880, FBP; Blake ledger, vol. 40, p. 52, FBP.

34. Patent no. 232,442, Sept. 21, 1880; Blake, Diary, Jan. 8, 1880, FBP; William W. Swan to Blake, Sept. 23, 1880; Blake ledger, vol. 40, p. 53, vol. 41, Oct. 11, 1883, FBP.

35. Charles Blake to Blake, Feb. 19, 1881, FBP; Theodore N. Vail to Blake, Feb. 22, 24, 1881, FBP.

36. Blake, Diary, Mar. 19,1881, FBP. In Blake's ledger, vol. 40, p. 62, there is an expense item concerning the switchboard of $500 paid to William Chaffee, Mar. 26, 1881, FBP.

37. Theodore N. Vail to Blake, Mar. 23, 1881, FBP; patent nos. 243,100 and 243,101, A.T.&T. Company Archives, Box 1060.

38. William Swan to Blake, Oct. 21, 1881, FBP.

39. Blake's ledger, vol. 40, p. 53; vol. 41 Oct. 11, 1883, FBP. A letter from John Hudson to Blake of May 6, 1886 refers to an indenture of May 5, 1881 and the assignment of patent No. 232442.

40. Theodore N. Vail to Blake, Mar. 23, 24, 1881, FBP.

41. William W. Swan to Blake, Feb. 3, 18, 1882, FBP; Blake to William W. Swan, June 3, 1886, FBP.

42. Memorandum from Theodore N. Vail to the Executive Committee, American Bell Telephone Co., Sept. 26, 1883, A.T.&T. Archives, Box 1037.

43. Blake, Diary, Dec. 9, 1884, FBP.

44. Blake, Diary, Dec. 9–22, 1884, FBP.

45. Blake's memorandum of the agreement is in A.T.&T.Co. Archives, Box 1037.

46. Lockwood to Theodore N. Vail, July 1, 1885, A.T.&T.Co. Archives, Box 1037.

47. Charles Bowditch to Blake, July 2, 1885, FBP; Blake to Charles Bowditch, July 3, 1885, FBP.

48. Blake to Charles Bowditch, July 8, 1885, FBP.

49. Charles Bowditch to Blake, July 10, 1885, FBP.

50. Theodore N. Vail to Blake, July 30, 1885, FBP; Blake, Diary, July 9, 26, Aug. 4, 5, 1886, FBP.

51. James J. Storrow to John Hudson, May 27, 1886, copy in Blake's hand, FBP; Blake to William H. Forbes, June 9, 1886 (copy), FBP; Blake, Diary, June 9, 1886, FBP.

52. Copies of the patent applications are in A.T.&.T. Co. Archives, Box 1037.

53. John Hudson to Blake, Oct. 29, 1886, FBP; acknowledging Blake's letter of Oct. 20, Blake to John Hudson, Nov. 4, 1886 (copy in Blake's hand), FBP.

54. John Hudson to Blake, Nov. 12, 1886, FBP; M. D. Fagen, ed., *A History of Engineering and Science in the Bell System* (New York, 1975, 1985), 74.

55. Blake, Diary, Dec. 17, 1885, July 15, 1896, Dec. 20, 1897, Oct. 21, 1898, FBP; *Proceedings of the American Antiquarian Society*, new ser., 14 (1902):31–36.

CHAPTER 7

RE-INVENTIONS

By 1880, Blake had inherited a substantial share of Grandfather Sewall's wealth and had begun accruing even more from his telephone inventions and stock investments. Increased means fueled greater aspirations. But Blake did not wish to become a swaggering captain of industry, nor did he seek self-aggrandizing political power and personal influence. While the scale of his ambitions became grand, the scope proved exceedingly narrow. Blake sought power, but only the power to do as he pleased. He wanted recognition, but simply the recognition of his name on telephone transmitters. He demanded influence, but only over the domain of Keewaydin and its inhabitants. From the start, Blake's dominance over his Weston estate rivaled that of any medieval lord over his manor. Blake made and remade his estate, a fabulously picturesque and efficient compound, complete with its own water supply and distribution system. In the end, the creation of Keewaydin paralleled the trajectory of Blake's own self-made life, where family connections, a smart marriage, and intellectual brilliance allowed a boy of modest means to become an ingenious inventor, and—unattainable to previous generations of Blakes —a country gentleman.

Next to the forging of his professional career, only Keewaydin absorbed so much of Blake's energy and interest. With his financial future secure, he lost no time in summoning architects and engineers to begin four major projects at Keewaydin, any one of which would have been sufficient to consume the average individual. He greatly expanded and altered the main house, inside and out. He created a complex of buildings on the property known as "The Cottage" that contained stables, a cow barn, servants' quarters, and a gymnasium. The Blake waterworks included a massive well, steam pump, and pump house that supplied a 250,000-gallon reservoir situated atop the estate's highest hill. Blake also created a distribution system that supplied water to Keewaydin and several other nearby households. Finally, through an extensive program of land acquisition, road building, landscape architecture, horticulture, and arboriculture, Blake transformed the very appearance of the terrain.

Two growing children, an increasingly elaborate social life, and the demands of Blake's scientific work made the original house obsolete almost as soon as the workmen rested their hammers. Blake then immediately went back to Charles Follen McKim for an expansive redesign. But the firm of McKim, Meade, & White now had a national reputation and all the work they could handle. Blake then met with William R. Meade, who had worked on the original house, and Ernest W. Bowditch, Blake's landscape architect and engineer as well as a participant on a Darien expedition for the Coast Survey. But McKim, ill and overworked, could find little time to meet with Blake; "for reasons good & bad I have allowed it [Keewaydin] to remain pigeon holed." He praised Blake's patience and charity and exhorted him not to lose faith in his firm.[1] Although McKim visited Boston on March 5, 1880, he failed to see Blake and Bowditch; the three did not meet until March 12. Bowditch developed and submitted to McKim a topographical survey and ideas that McKim would need for the additions to the house, and McKim hoped that Bowditch's plans would arrive in Boston when he and Mead would be there. They planned to lunch with Meade's sister Elinor, William Dean Howells's wife, before going on to Keewaydin. Blake's connection with Meade led to a friendship with Howells, who became a frequent visitor at Keewaydin. Howells, who would begin publishing his most famous novel, *The Rise of Silas Lapham*, in 1884, might have seen in Blake the same kind of aspiring man who sought a place for himself in Brahmin Boston.[2]

After their March meeting, Blake's relationship with McKim crumbled. Stanford White wrote to Blake on April 9 to explain that McKim, upon his return from Boston, "was prostrated by a severe attack of congestion of the brain and has been confined to his bed until within a few days." McKim did his best to begin work on the Blake project, but could not. Three days later, Blake wrote to McKim, Mead, & White wishing McKim a speedy recovery but complaining that his builder had no architectural plans. Because of McKim's uncertain health, Blake decided to ask the Boston firm of Cabot & Chandler to draw up studies and plans, "provided, however, that I shall be free to accept them or not if yours [McKim's] come to hand in time for me to exercise a choice." McKim never submitted any plans, so Blake hired Cabot & Chandler.[3]

Edward Clark Cabot (1818–1901) was the son of Samuel Cabot, active in the old China trade, and grandson of the great merchant prince Thomas Handasyd Perkins. After a financially disastrous effort at sheep farming, Cabot, with no professional training, submitted a drawing that won the 1845 competition for the new Boston Athenæum building. He joined with George M. Dexter, a civil engineer, to complete the Athenæum project and remained with him long enough to learn the architectural trade and open his own office. In 1875, he formed a partnership with Frank W. Chandler, who later became professor of architecture at the Massachusetts Institute of Technology.[4]

Cabot & Chandler pushed right ahead with Blake's project, advising him on April 15 that they already had developed plans for the redesign of his house. Within two weeks, Blake had a workman tearing up the piazza to make way for the extension of the dining room and the new conservatory. Before the end of June, Cabot & Chandler's final plans for the house were completed.[5] Photographs of the original structure shortly after its completion, preserved in the Blake papers, reveal the ground sloping off to the south, with the piazzas raised considerably above the ground, allowing light to enter the cellar through windows. The plan to level the lawn for a hundred feet from the front of the house on the south side required construction of a retaining wall of truly impressive proportions, about three hundred feet long and sixteen feet high. Braced by six buttresses three feet thick along the front, the wall held the entrance to a tunnel that led beneath the lawn to the kitchen and allowed the servants discreet passage to and from the gardens below the wall. The new lawn, bordered by a terra cotta balustrade atop the retaining wall, offered a panoramic view of the Charles River Valley and the Boston and Albany Railroad, which became the setting for Blake's most memorable photograph.

Cabot & Chandler added a new wing to the northeast corner of the house, extending the east piazza and dining room, and placing a conservatory adjacent to it. These additions required a shortening of the porch, which had previously extended almost the full length of the house. To provide headroom for the extension of the main staircase to the third floor, builders enlarged the dormer in what had been the servants' room, now replaced with a new flight of stairs. Blake also made numerous interior changes. The kitchen moved to the basement in place of the laundry, which now had its own new building. The new kitchen had access to the dining room via a dumbwaiter to the butler's pantry, which accommodated the elaborate scale of entertaining that Blake had in mind.

Removal of the heating plant to the stable complex produced a good deal of space in the existing cellar, which Blake enhanced by excavating under the extension to the dining room and conservatory. This new portion of the cellar contained a wonderfully arched brick ceiling to support the tile floor of the conservatory. An exterior door led into a depressed passageway around the kitchen, beneath the piazza, past the servants' hall, and exited by the driveway. The passageway afforded light and ventilation to the kitchen and servants' hall and provided access to the terraced kitchen vegetable garden on the slope down by the railroad tracks through a tunnel, mentioned above, roofed with enormous slabs of granite, which allowed staff to pass from the kitchen to the garden without crossing the splendid new lawn.

Interior changes left the home barely recognizable from its original McKim appearance. The entry hall was enlarged and turned to the left, past the stairs occupying space that had been the servants' hall. The main staircase's first landing disappeared, with the first steps moved one quarter turn counter-clockwise. The enlarged dining room was reoriented along a north-south axis. While the dining room fireplace retained its original location, it now occupied a niche in a corner at one end of the room and

Front hall of Keewaydin. By Francis Blake, stereoview, n.d. #57.930

out of sight of many seats at the dinner table. In the room that previously held the kitchen, Cabot & Chandler placed a new billiard room with a large, handsome, fireplace adorned by a stone mantel bearing the Blake arms. The entrance to the new wing, off to the left in the billiard room, was shut off by a door with a stained glass window to advise visitors of the private space beyond. There, Blake placed his private library arrestingly complemented by another fireplace and a view of the sunken garden.

A staircase led to the second floor of the new wing, which held a schoolroom for the two Blake children and their cousins. Other changes to the second floor included a piazza off the master bedroom. The "Hubbard room," the principal guest room, possessed its own bath, and an extension to the second-floor hall led to a balcony overlooking the oval landscaping and a pond. The northwest wall cantilevered out five and one-half feet and, supported by five enormous brackets, allowed for five additional rooms. The one-room nursery was expanded into a suite with two smaller rooms in the adjacent wing, one furnished with a fireplace. Beyond the central chimney of the wing lay three servants' chambers, with no access to the nursery, all reached only by a staircase from the ground floor of the wing. On the third floor, the old billiard room, which included the tower, had become the laboratory and machine shop where Blake developed the transmitter and performed his other work. Even after the completion of the Cottage complex with its magnificently equipped machine shop, Blake continued to use the room for experimentation, and later generations always referred to the space as "the telephone room."

Blake possessed a clear vision of the alterations and, as usual, closely oversaw the work.[6] Perhaps reflecting the scale and complexity of the construction, Blake also had a number of supervisors to assist him. Cabot & Chandler provided Warren A. Rodman, who oversaw the workmen and reported on progress to the architects.[7] Blake also employed as many relatives as he could, perhaps returning the favors he enjoyed as a young man with the Coast Survey. His brother-in-law, Charles Wells, who had returned east from Omaha to work for the telephone company, looked after the estate in the Blakes' absence. On July 29, he reported to Blake, then at Portsmouth, New Hampshire, on the progress of construction. At the time, no work had started on the extension to the dining room or the conservatory, but the materials, including window frames, lay on the ground ready to go up. He suggested that Blake and his family might want to remain away another week, "The noise is deafening of hammering and sawing." His brother Charlie, no longer in the phone business, now worked as contractor for the waterworks and also kept Frank apprised of progress around the estate.[8]

With Christmas passed and the new year under way, work continued. Blake's standard of elegance fed upon itself, growing to new heights. The servants' dining hall had to be tiled, and the chimney for the new wing contained five fireplaces. Keewaydin's heating system proved a complex undertaking with radiators and hot-air ducts. Blake spared little expense, and anything not readily procured locally came from the best available suppliers wherever they could be found. Installers went to Tuttle & Bailey in New York, for instance, to procure specially made brass registers in a "Persian Pattern."[9] Frank Hill Smith, a Boston artist and interior designer, handled much of the interior finish, including the few rooms not altered by Cabot & Chandler. Smith seemed intent on lightening McKim's heavy, masculine finish. "I do not fancy Black walnut, & I would like to know whether you have any objection to my having the Bookcases painted, & rubbed down. This can be done by going over the work with several coats, of varnish or shellac, and have them rubbed down so as to show no gloss. I can then get a better effect in the entire mass, and make a far more handsome room, than by retaining the Black walnut color. . . ."[10]

Smith's letter of August 27, 1881, to Blake provides invaluable insight into the expectations of new wealth at the turn of the century:

I find that, to do the Dado, bookcases, cornices in both rooms, ceiling, & change in the same, mantel, fire place marble facing, iron back tile hearth, will cost about $2,350. There will be a saving in dado abt. $2.50 per foot, but there is more in quantity than in my former estimate. The book case will cost less, but there is the item of cornice which in the two rooms proves quite an item., & I find that it will require more wall paper than we had at first allowed. I propose to run mahogany in a large member of the cornice all round the room, and to have the panels of that also. The color will be kept in tone with the black walnut, and will prove a very agreeable addition to the color of the rooms. Taking all things into account you will have a very handsome room, rich & full in tone, and not out of the way in price when you take into consideration the rich wall with the dado, Mantel, Ceiling &C. &C.—in fact I consider this quite moderate in comparison with other rooms.[11]

Frank Hill Smith's services to Blake eventually ended, although he must have been a fixture at the house for nearly two years. Blake's interim settlement with him, $4,977.62, testifies to the depth of the relationship. The charge included all of Smith's work, commissions on subcontractor's work, the superintending of exterior painting, selections of tile, carpet designs, wine labels, and other miscellaneous items.[12] During the fall of 1882, various interior decorators continued with additional details, but Blake still relied largely upon Smith. Smith found Blake a carpet for his library and arranged for the installation of portiers for the doorways between the hall and dining room, hall and parlor, library and dining room, and various rooms on the second floor.

In May 1883, Blake finally settled on plush dining room curtains and he scrutinized samples of cretonnes for the portiere in the guest room and blue plush for library furniture. The bill for curtains in the library, dining room, and Hubbard room exceeded $3,000.[13] He hired a fresco painter, Louis Rinn, to add gold lines on the parlor ceiling and touch up the mantel shelf in the library. But Smith remained at the center of the interior work, even selecting the stays for the dining room curtains and the billiard counters. Between January and June 1884, Blake expended $3,596.89 to decorate his private office in the new wing adjacent to the billiard room.[14] Smith also planned the decoration of Blake's den in an "Indian style," incorporating Indian panels, pilasters, hangings, and ceiling work.

He completed the den in mid April 1883, laying twenty-nine and two-thirds yards of Axminster carpet at $5 per yard, plus sewing, fitting, and lining. For these services Smith charged $2,151.57, which also included painting vases, a brass frame for the hearth, fireplace equipment, and commissions.[15]

During the Blakes' trip abroad in 1881–1882, they bought countless furnishings, including china, glass, meteorological instruments, clocks, and objets d'art. Upon returning to the United States they made additional purchases. From a Mr. F. Barbedienne of a firm called Bronze D'art, Blake obtained a replica of the Venus de Milo and a number of other statues which he placed strategically around the interior of the house. A stream of correspondence with customhouse brokers, bills of lading, and invoices from abroad, recorded the volume of Blake's imports.[16]

The accumulated bills, carefully preserved in the Blake papers, renders somewhat absurd the guilt Blake's friend William Dean Howells once suffered over the purchase of a fur coat: one table for $240; three plush ottomans for $73; a sofa for $275; one English chair for $67.50; two gilt chairs for $160; an easy chair for $147; an ash washstand for $55.[17] For furniture re-upholstered in plush, a Morris chair, two chairs, an Astor chair, a reclining chair, and a slip seat, $210.95; a mahogany bedstead, spring, and mattress for $158; two mahogany chairs for $35; two brass towel racks for $30; two ash chairs for $10.42; and a mahogany desk for $120. Blake also accumulated a considerable amount of less formal furniture. The Wakefield Rattan Company supplied chairs, cribs, tables, crickets, trunks, and baskets.[18] By the time most of the reconstruction and decoration of the main house at Keewaydin ended in July 1884, Blake had spent $88,573.23, at least $4 million in modern values.[19]

The "Cottage" carried the basic functions of a country estate to new levels. Blake set the requirements for the various buildings he wanted and Cabot & Chandler produced the designs, with no detail too small for his attention. Situated at a convenient distance from the main house and below eye-level from the estate's main road, it included a horse stable, hayloft, oat storage, cow barn, manure pit, carriage shed, courtyard, laundry, gas room, heating plant, coal bins, and apartments for servants and grounds keepers. The Cottage also held Blake's photographic laboratory, machine shop, a garden tool room, a theater, and two bowling alleys. As with everything in Blake's life, the Cottage had to be on a grand scale, meticulously planned, and fully equipped with the best that money could buy. And when the best that money could buy was not good enough, Blake instructed the manufacturer on how to improve his product, or modified the item himself in his machine shop.[20]

The Cottage was built as a group of contiguous buildings around a courtyard, the largest structure being a three-story building for animals, their feed, and related equipment.[21] The ground floor, one level below the courtyard, housed the cow and horse stalls with mangers and pens for calves. The second story, at the courtyard level, contained the carriage house, measuring forty by forty-five feet with sheathed walls and ceilings, the stable, and the harness room. The harness room adjoined the south end of the carriage house and contained glazed cabinets, a bathroom, a stairway to the loft, and three grain chutes. The southeast portion of the building housed the stable, with two large box stalls and seven smaller stalls arranged on both sides of a central corridor which led to a large ventilator. The stables had separate access to the courtyard through a sliding door. Heavy trusses supported the roof, which was attached to tie rods for holding the loft floor, leaving a relatively open room for fodder and bedding. Bins stored oats, which Blake bought from the midwest by the train-car load, and chutes conducted supplies to the lower levels.

The southwest portion of the building at the courtyard level accommodated various estate employees. A servants' hall with a fireplace stood near the stable. The kitchen adjoined the servants' hall, connected to a corridor with entrances from both the outside and the courtyard and with stairways to the basement and second floor. The servants' living room, with a fireplace, was next to the entrance and stair corridor and looked out over a porch. The remaining room, located between the servants' living room and the courtyard entrance, served as Blake's photographic laboratory. Six bedrooms with windows completed the upper floor. The rooms varied in size and were occupied mostly by unmarried employees, principally males, who worked the grounds and the stable complex as grooms, gardeners, and a fireman.

At one side of the courtyard, on the first level, stood the machine shop. The level below housed the heating plant: two horizontal boilers built by the Walworth Manufacturing Company of Boston. "We hope to give you the prettiest pair of fronts of the size in this country," Arthur Walworth advised Blake. They offered him a choice of polished brass work, "Kept bright by hand, naval fashion," or nickel-plated brightwork. The heating plant supplied steam to the stable and the house through underground pipes that left an open path of green grass through the snows all winter. Two additional sections of the complex projected from the north side. At the front next to the boiler room sat the gymnasium, which Blake quickly converted into a ninety-seat theater. A lean-to extending back along the north wall beyond the theater held two bowling alleys. By the close of 1882, Blake had expended $37,158.94 on the Cottage complex.[22]

Blake spent considerably more in his effort to transform Keewaydin's landscape and build his own waterworks. Few estates in New England could rival Blake's vision. Keewaydin graced a six-acre hilltop overlooking the sleepy Charles River Valley and the Boston and Albany Railroad. Although relatively small originally, it always gave the appearance of grandeur because it adjoined 200 acres of Charles Hubbard's Woodlands estate. As with the house, Blake's property would not remain modest for long. As early as 1879, Blake began surveying the area, including land he would buy from the Boston and Albany Railroad (headed by his cousin, D. Waldo Lincoln) and obtain from his father-in-law.[23] Soon after Blake acquired the railroad property, Hubbard conveyed several acres to Lizzie, including the remaining parts of a pond he owned that straddled their property. Two years later, he gave her additional acreage near the railroad parcel. In March 1881, Blake purchased a nearby farm from his head gardener, Alfred Wattez, that included a farmhouse and buildings on about sixteen acres of land. Blake, who never missed the smallest detail, added a

Keewaydin and cottage complex. View from Woodlands, the Hubbard estate.
Photographer unknown, n.d. #39.412

special clause to the sale agreement so that "all manure now situated upon either of the parcels hereby conveyed or in any building thereon is to pass by this deed to the said Francis Blake and to become his property." By the time Blake halted his land purchases, Keewaydin had expanded to about eighty-three acres.[24]

Ernest W. Bowditch, grandson of the famed Nathaniel Bowditch—author of the *American Practical Navigator*—had responsibility for landscaping, road construction and general development of Keewaydin's grounds. Trained as an engineer at the Massachusetts Institute of Technology, Bowditch eventually established a large practice with offices in

Boston, New York, and Cleveland, and employed a team of engineers and foresters who executed 2,500 projects between 1870 and 1910.[25] Bowditch built the main avenue to the estate and laid out a formal sunken garden east of the house, inspired by a garden at Hampton Court. The sloping ground required considerable earth-moving to achieve the sunken effect and support a curved retaining wall around the north side between the garden and the stable complex. The rectangular garden, reached by a broad herringbone brick path across the lawn, measured approximately 160 by 120 feet and was surrounded by a broad gravel path, four steps below the level of the lawn.

The summer of 1881 brought Blake and Bowditch unexpected trouble. In July, Bowditch inspected the property and discovered that the subcontractor, Patrick Tracy, had deliberately failed to hire enough men to do the work. Bowditch believed the job required no less than fifty men working at once, but because of rising labor costs Tracy sought to recoup his losses with fewer men. If all went well, Bowditch advised Tracy, Blake would pay the extra labor costs. But in August, relations deteriorated further with Tracy, who, Bowditch sadly discovered, "has been off the work two whole days this week and the larger part of a third. As he appeared very seedy on his return I opine that he is not given to strictly temperance habits. . . ."[26] Moreover, Bowditch discovered that Tracy had not been paying any of his men. Blake's lawyer, the great civil rights attorney Moorfield Storey, advised him to withhold all payment until Tracy completed the job. By the beginning of September, relations continued to decline, and Bowditch threatened to look elsewhere for a contract if Tracy did not pay his men. "I don't think he believes it," Bowditch informed Blake, "so I anticipate an explosion."[27] By mid-September, on Storey's advice and with Blake vacationing in the White Mountains, Bowditch used $2,500 of his own money to pay Tracy's men, as "the men are in positively pitiful condition." When Blake returned from vacation he fired Tracy, but put his men back to work to complete the job.[28]

Ernest W. Bowditch also bore prime responsibility for designing and constructing the self-contained waterworks for Keewaydin. This extraor-

dinary system, complete with reservoir, pump house, and underground
piping system that linked the reservoir to nearby homes, made Keewaydin one of the most unusual estates in New England. When Blake first discussed the idea of a water system in 1879, Bowditch believed that one
could be constructed for $10,000. After three year's work, Blake had spent
almost $49,000 on it. He hired his house architects Cabot & Chandler to
design the necessary buildings, recruited a small army of laborers to do the
work, and even employed his wayward brother, who desperately needed
employment, to serve as hydraulic engineer.[29]

Charlie proposed a plan for the waterworks that included a filter basin,
a pump well, 1,400 feet of four-inch pipe, 800 feet of six-inch pipe, and a
reservoir. A steam engine and pump cleared the excavation site of water as
digging progressed, at one point yielding 150,000 gallons in twenty-four
hours. Charlie regularly reported on the progress of construction and expected to finish excavation and commence stoning within two days. By
mid-June a forty-eight-inch pipe had been installed at the bottom of the
well, producing "more water than you and your neighbors could ever
use."[30] D. W. Pratt, Bowditch's superintendent, prepared a pipe system of
about 2,200 feet to connect the well, reservoir, and Blake's home, as well
as additional lines to Woodlands and to the house of Blake's sister-in-law,
Louisa Jackson.[31]

To obtain maximum water pressure, the reservoir had to be located at
the highest elevation possible. While Blake's father-in-law owned a hillside at the northwest corner of the Keewaydin property, the crest belonged
to a neighbor, Benjamin F. Cutter. During the summer, Blake and Hubbard bought Cutter's land and exchanged about five acres of other parcels
so that Blake could build his reservoir. Blake constructed the reservoir by
scooping out the top of the hill in a large, dish-shaped rectangular earth-
work with a wet clay and stone lining and loamed outer slopes. Workmen
then seeded the slopes to prevent erosion and cut down all trees to the east
and west to create a scenic view.[32]

Charlie monitored the quality of the water by sending a sample to
William Ripley Nichols of the Massachusetts Institute of Technology

Chemical Laboratory for analysis.[33] Although the water proved uncontaminated and trouble-free, the system did not. In November, Blake wrote a prickly letter to Daniel H. Johnson, the Boston representative of the Henry R. Worthington Company, expressing dissatisfaction with the pumps and boiler it had supplied. He asked Johnson to inspect the pump and determine if it represented a "fair specimen of Mr. H. R. Worthington's celebrated pumps." If Johnson found no fault with the pump, Blake advised him that he intended to sell it and buy or make another of acceptable quality.[34] Surprised by the tone of the inquiry, Johnson had his brother inspect the pump. He then informed Blake that he had been running the pump at twice the prescribed speed, and it was in shocking order, shaken to pieces by Blake's men who ran it beyond specifications. Convinced of the accuracy of his calculations, Blake argued that the pump would have to operate at 257 strokes per minute to deliver the 75,000 gallons of water in ten hours as promised in his contract with Worthington. But Johnson pointed out that Blake had made a mistake in his calculations, using the wrong figure for the volume of water contained in one stroke of the pump. Blake then changed his tone and, while decrying the "shocking condition" of the pump, he admitted that Worthington pumps were the best available. They resolved the problems and the pumps sustained Worthington's reputation by operating efficiently until January 1904. The system proved enduring. Although electric pumps eventually replaced the steam-powered Worthington, the works remained in operation until the mid-1960s and the end of Keewaydin.[35]

Charlie Blake also assumed responsibility for laying gas pipes to the house and its adjoining buildings and for outside illumination. Blake wished to connect his estate to the Newton and Watertown Gas Light Company. He asked the company to cover the cost of laying the pipe, in return for the volume of gas he would consume. But the gas company agreed to accept only half of the cost, and Blake agreed to pay $2,559 for the line to Keewaydin. The work progressed at a painfully slow rate. Jurisdictional and legal issues surrounding rights to bridge the Charles

River, as will as legal issues with the town of Weston, delayed progress, and the gas did not begin to flow until October.[36]

No surprise, phone service proved easier to establish at Keewaydin. Undaunted by the distance to the nearest telephone line, Blake wrote the Central Massachusetts Telephone Company in December 1880 expressing his desire to connect with the district telephone office in Boston. He proposed that the company attach an additional wire to the Boston-to-Worcester line at the corner of Concord and Washington streets in Newton Lower Falls. From that point they could build a pole line to his house. Blake demanded the finest workmanship and material, which he would purchase, as well as a reasonable profit for the company. Thereafter, the company could at any time purchase the line from him at market value. Blake paid $887.50 for the service line and an annual rental of $4 per mile for twelve miles.[37]

Blake also added an abundant collection of trees, flowers, and plants to form a border and cover a distant hillside, and gardens to provide cut flowers for the house and vegetables for the table. He delegated large-scale procurement of nursery stock to James H. Bowditch, Ernest Bowditch's brother and business partner. The first major delivery on November 15, 1880, included twenty-nine varieties of flowering plants and about a hundred different species of bushes, shrubs and trees, barberry, deutzia, spirea, weigelia, forsythia, dogwood, hydrangea, flowering plum, Japanese quince, euonymous, snowberry, lilac, and hibiscus. The 1,238 plants and 1,470 pounds of trees, which came from Geneva, New York, testified to Blake's dedication.[38] With no more patience for growing trees than for germinating grass, Blake cruised his neighbor's property for likely mature trees that he could buy and move to Keewaydin. Bowditch drew Blake's attention to "quite a pretty elm" he had noticed on his way back to the railroad station. Although modest in size, it had good spread and balance. Bowditch offered to negotiate with the neighbors on Blake's behalf to secure any desired trees. A beech went to the west end of the piazza and he placed a Norway spruce near the estate's main road. The elm that caught

Bowditch's eye turned out "frightfully expensive" to move; "dare say it will have cost you on that tree alone $175."[39]

Although Blake and his father-in-law bickered frequently, Hubbard complimented his son-in-law for his development of Keewaydin and even for his wisdom in buying mature trees. "The elm & other trees you mention will give your place an entirely different look & improve it immensely," he wrote Blake from France in February 1881. "You showed good judgment in taking trees 25 years old instead of waiting for them to grow 25 years on your land. There is no difficulty in transplanting even much larger ones with care & money. Money indeed is as near a lever to raise the world as will ever be found & I rejoice that you & Liz have enough of it."[40]

These changes, though, hardly indicated the end of Blake's physical transformation of Keewaydin. Just before the start of spring, Bowditch found in New York and Pennsylvania "some very handsome evergreen stock that will enliven the house surrounding considerably."[41] Soon, 994 trees and bushes comprising 92 species of fir and pine, and many flowering bushes including azaleas, rhododendrons, wisteria, viburnum, and others materialized at Blake's estate. A year later, Blake increased his arboretum with 199 deciduous trees of 41 species ordered from Mount Hope Nurseries of Rochester, New York. He also purchased 60 fruit trees, including 14 varieties of pear, 4 different peaches, 21 kinds of apple, and 2 different quinces. In the spring of 1883, he added another 492 evergreens, spruce, pine, and balsam.[42]

The major Keewaydin projects had been completed by the fall of 1883, and Blake turned to the task of stocking his array of buildings with the finest equipment. His need for carriages and other hauling vehicles knew no bounds. Although he had acquired two carriages early in 1880, he quickly obtained three more, plus a coupe carryall for $400, an elegant booby hut—an original Boston vehicle consisting of an enclosed carriage body suspended by leather braces on sleigh runners—for $225, and a double sleigh for $125. After the first of the year, he bought a light sleigh for $160 and in early March a "light Bayley Patent" for $160, with the Blake crest on its doors. With spring, he sought more style in his vehicles and obtained a "Fine Partition Rockaway no. 3120 with pole & shafts" for $650 and a "Top Wilson Wagon no. #3004" for $225. In April he parted with one carriage, but then bought a "Goddard Top Buggy" for $450.[43]

In 1882, Blake acquired a Brewster & Co. "box top wagon, no. 5784," for $450. Nothing, however, could equal the elegant omnibus he specially ordered in London with the carriage manufactory of Laurie & Marner. The "handsome New Omnibus" held 6 people inside "& 3 or 4 on the roof behind the driving seat." The builders painted the Blake crest on the doors and assured him that, "the whole shall receive the best attention." According to Laurie & Marner it was:

> a fashionable new omnibus with framed & panelled head & solid front. Painted & lined green, globe lamps, silver plated furniture & polished plate glasses to body. Hung on elliptic & side springs & patent axles. Driving seat, 2 half cushions & box. Roof seat, cushion, foot board. Luggage rail to roof painted black & Japanned. Packing the whole in strong deal case. . . . Painting crest on hind door rail. Reading lamp to inside fore end of body. Patent lever break and India rubber block.

At £220.12—$1,045.55 in American currency, with an additional $436.95 for transatlantic shipment—it must have been a work of art.[44] But it was not the last carriage purchase. In 1883, Blake added several more, a two-seat open wagon for $115, a Brewster & Co. "T. Cart no., 549" for $825, and a depot wagon for $275.[45] Blake also invested an equal amount of time and resources on the purchase of horses, cows, and livery and by the end of 1883, he had expended another $8,276 on livestock. Based on the wages of one professional painter, Blake spent more on his stable in one year than would be earned by eleven skilled tradesmen.[46]

Blake took particular care in building his machine shop, a single room about sixteen by twenty-eight feet with a high ceiling. The chimney—which had an arched niche above the mantel with a statue of a benevolent-looking angel—had three separate flues: one for the fireplace, one for

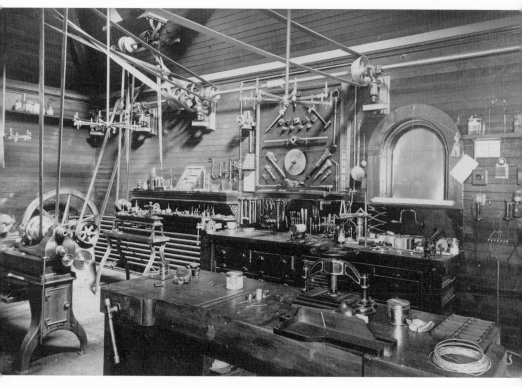

Machine shop. By Francis Blake, ca. 1875-1880. #57.397

the forge, and another for the boilers. Along the north wall stood several rows of drawers and shelves for tools. A panel on the north wall held a collection of machinist's tools arranged to suggest an armor display in an English country house. In addition to natural light, a row of eight-armed gas lighting fixtures suspended from the ceiling provided illumination for Blake's long nights. In the earliest photographs of the shop, taken by Blake himself, everything is in meticulous order, conveying the feeling of elegance and efficiency that Blake always demanded.

Using the machinery he had purchased, Blake could fabricate virtually anything he needed. A stationary one-cylinder, two-horse-power Otto gas engine drove all the machinery with a system of overhead shafts and countershafts which drove each machine.[47] In May 1883, Hill, Clarke & Co.

sent a representative to Keewaydin to ascertain Blake's requirements for the shafts, pulleys, collars, hangers, belting, and lacing for the power system. When the material arrived early in June, Blake found it substandard. A brief exchange of correspondence produced satisfactory results, and with an additional $837 Blake had the shop's power system in place.[48]

Blake then obtained a Brown & Sharpe sixteen-inch engine lathe, but not before traveling to the manufacturing plant in Providence, Rhode Island, to explain the special modifications he wanted. He then obtained a universal milling machine, not an amateur's toy. Clearly, Blake contemplated extensive machine work. The milling machine's rotary cutters could plane, shape, bore, drill, and cut gears and spirals. The *American Machinist* described it as "Peculiarly American in its design and construction," a great attraction at the 1867 Paris Exhibition that did more to stimulate a demand for American machinery in Europe than any other product.[49] By the time Blake finished stocking his facility, he had built one of the finest machine shops in New England. H. C. Littlefield, a Boston manufacturer of fishing tackle and a Blake acquaintance, told Blake about his own shop, which fumbled along without the "Brown & Sharpe lathes" that Blake owned. "Envy is a bad thing," Littlefield confessed, "but I often think of the perfect machines in your shop."[50]

Endnotes

1. Charles Follen McKim to Blake, Feb. 17, 1880, FBP.

2. Ernest W. Bowditch to Blake, Mar. 8, 1880, FBP; Telegram from Bowditch to Blake, Mar. 11, 1880, FBP; Charles Follen McKim to Blake, Mar. 21, 1880, FBP; on Howells and the issue of Boston see, Augusta Rohrback, "'You're a Natural-Born Literary Man': Becoming William Dean Howells, Culture Maker and Cultural Marker," *The New England Quarterly* 73 (2000):625–653 and Kenneth S. Lynn, *William Dean Howells: An American Life* (New York, 1971).

3. Blake to McKim, Mead, & White, Apr. 12, 1880, FBP.

4. Dumas Malone et al., eds., *Dictionary of American Biography* (New York, 1958), 2:394.

5. Blake Diary, April 30, 1880, FBP; Cabot & Chandler to Blake, May 20, 1880, FBP; C. A. Wellington to Blake, May 28, 1881, FBP. Cabot & Chandler's

elevations, plans, framing plans, and sections for the alterations are preserved in a large album Blake assembled.

6. See, for instance, the diary entry for Mar. 8, 1880, where Blake mentioned arrival of a stone shipment.

7. Cabot & Chandler to Blake, May 20, 1880, FBP.

8. Charles Welles to Blake, July 29, 1880, FBP.

9. A. G. Walworth to Blake, Aug. 18, 1881, FBP.

10. Frank Hill Smith to Blake, July 6, 1881, FBP.

11. Frank Hill Smith to Blake, Aug. 27, 1881, FBP.

12. Blake bound account books, "memorandum of account with Smith," vol. 5, pp. 61, 138, FBP; Blake ledger, vol. 40, p. 65, FBP.

13. Bills for the many purchases between Nov. 28, 1882 and Mar. 22, 1883 are in the Blake papers, especially see: vol. 5, pp. 194, 249, FBP.

14. Frank Hill Smith to Blake, Mar. 17, 1883, FBP; Rinn bills are in vol. 5, p. 299, vol. 6, pp. 22, 23, FBP; vol. 40, House Plant, FBP.

15. Frank Hill Smith to Blake, Oct. 25, 1883, FBP; Smith's bill's for extra work are in vol. 6, p. 142, FBP.

16. Bills from the Blake family's European trip are in vol. 4, FBP.

17. Bills for work from Apr. 4 to June 2, including $2,999 worth of furniture, upholstery, and drapery, are in vol. 5, FBP.

18. Bills for these items are in vol. 6, FBP.

19. See John J. McCusker, "How Much is that in Real Money? A Historical Price Index for Use as a Deflator of Money Values in the Economy of the United States," *Proceedings of the American Antiquarian Society* 101 (1991):297–360, and the addenda, 106 (1996):327–334. Given the real estate boom of 2001, the value could easily approach $8 million or more.

20. A bill for Mar. 9, 1880 from Isburgh & Co., Boston auctioneers and dealers in carriages, harnesses, saddles, &c. included two gray horses, a bay horse, harness, a dog cart, and a landaulet, is in vol. 2, FBP.

21. Cabot & Chandler to Blake, June 22, 1880, FBP.

22. Arthur Walworth to Blake, Apr. 11, 1880, FBP.

23. Blake, Diary, Oct.–Dec. 1879, FBP; land plant account, vol. 40, p. 34, FBP; Middlesex County Registry of Deeds, vol. 1536, p. 464.

24. Middlesex County Registry of Deeds, vol. 1552, p. 421; vol. 1578, p. 268; vol. 1562, p. 417; vol. 1607, p. 358; vol. 1789, p. 481; vol. 1792, p. 438; vol. 1936, p. 84; vol. 2163, p. 244.

25. Kevin D. Murphy, "Ernest W. Bowditch and the Practice of Landscape Architecture," *Essex Institute Historical Collections* 125 (1989):162–176.

26. Ernest Bowditch to Blake, July 23, Aug. 20, 1881, FBP.

27. Ernest Bowditch to Blake, Sept. 4, 1881, FBP.

28. Ernest Bowditch to Blake, Sept. 14, 15, 1881, FBP.

29. Blake, Diary, Nov. 14, 1879, FBP.

30. Charles Blake to Blake, Apr. 14, May 30, June 8, June 14 [quoted], 1880, FBP.

31. Charles Blake to Blake, June 9, 1880, FBP; Ernest Bowditch to Blake, June 14, 1880, FBP.

32. Middlesex County Registry of Deeds, vol. 1562, p. 414; vol. 1578, pp. 265, 267; Charles Blake to Blake, Aug. 26, Sept. 3, 1880, FBP.

33. Charles Blake to Blake, Aug. 26, 1880, FBP; William R. Nichols to Charles Blake, Aug. 21, 1880, FBP.

34. Blake to Daniel H. Johnson, Nov. 11, 1880, FBP; Henry Worthington to Charles Blake, July 2, 1880. On a leaflet describing the pump, Blake noted the pump's number as 11589, FBP.

35. Daniel H. Johnson to Blake, Nov. 16, 1880, FBP; Blake to Daniel H. Johnson, November 11, 13, 17, 1880, FBP; Charles Blake's table of the reservoir's capacity at various depths, FBP.

36. Charles Blake to Blake, Aug. 20, 1880, FBP; Newton and Watertown Gas Light Company to Blake, July 12, 1880, FBP; Charles Blake to Blake, July 20, 1880, FBP; Blake, Diary, July to Oct., 1880, FBP.

37. Blake to Central Massachusetts Telephone Company, Dec. 11, 1880 (copy), FBP; bill from Central Massachusetts Telephone Company, Dec. 30, 1880 is in vol. 3, p. 653, FBP.

38. Bill is in vol. 3, p. 633, FBP.

39. James Bowditch to Blake, Dec. 18, 1880, Jan. 3, 27, 1881, FBP. One group of maple trees cost $488.

40. Charles T. Hubbard to Blake, Feb. [?] 1881, FBP. The first page of this lengthy letter is missing.

41. James Bowditch to Blake, Mar. 4, 1881, FBP.

42. Bills for nursery stock from James Bowditch, May 26, 1881, are in vol. 3, pp. 719, 722, FBP; Mount Hope Nursery bills, May 22, 1882, are in vol. 4, pp. 346, 347; Reading Nursery bills, June 1, 1883, are in vol. 5, p. 318, FBP.

43. The bills for Blake's carriage purchases are in vol. 3, FBP.

44. The bills for the London carriage are in vol. 4, FBP.

45. Additional carriage bills are in box 4 and box 6, FBP; Francis B. Rice to Blake, May 21, June 5, 1881, FBP; Josiah Stickney to Blake, May 31, 1881, FBP.

46. Animal and livery bills are in vol. 6, FBP.

47. Bills for Blake's machinery are in vol. 6, FBP.

48. Hill, Clarke & Co. to Blake, June 7, 1883, FBP; bills enumerating the work performed in Blake's machine shop are in vol. 6, FBP.

49. *American Machinist* (April 1879), quoted in, *A Treatise on the Construction and Use of Universal Milling Machines* (Providence, R.I., 1882, reprint, Bradley, Il., 1991), 1.

50. H. C. Littlefield to Blake, Mar. 1, 1888, FBP.

CHAPTER 8

THE WORLD OF
KEEWAYDIN

BLAKE CONSTRUCTED A SAFE, secure, and lavish world for his
family. He desired insularity so that life's necessities, pleasures, and en-
tertainments, even the early education of his children, would be found in a
place he had created and he controlled. He belonged to many professional
and private organizations, as many as sixty, but he attended few if any of
their meetings beyond Boston, although he sometimes offered his own estate as a gathering place for his favored gentlemen's clubs. Friends such as
William Dean Howells came for dinner, but most visitors were members
of his extended family. Blake spent a great deal of time and money helping
his own family, including brother Charles, who did not possess great ability or good fortune. Although intolerant and demanding by nature, Blake
displayed an extraordinary amount of patience with Charles, whose troubled life would have tested anyone. Such intense intimacy, almost tribal-
ism, created tense relationships, and Blake often found himself bickering
with Lizzie's family over matters large and small. He possessed enormous
confidence in his own judgment and the smallest point could easily mush-
room into a matter of principle. Although conflicts could be severe,
most—except those with his father-in-law—proved short-lived. In the
end, Blake seemed resistant (although not unwilling) to alienate permanently any relatives. He had not forgotten that his professional success
came about through the timely influence of family members.

Having invested so many resources and so much effort into creating his estate, Blake understandably was reluctant to leave it for long. The Blakes' longest absence from Keewaydin occurred in 1881 when the constant din of hammers and saws, the clouds of dirt and dust, and the small army of laborers at their estate drove them to vacation in France. In other years, when they left Keewaydin at all it was usually to visit North Conway, New Hampshire, where the family became a regular fixture, or to visit the Adirondacks to escape the summer humidity and seek relief from allergies. It took two years of badgering by Henry Silas Payson, "Uncle Sy," perhaps Frank's favorite of Lizzie's cousins, to convince Blake to visit the Payson farm in Mossville, Illinois. Still in good health, Blake could have traveled the world, but instead he chose familiar paths year in and year out. Lizzie's uncertain health may have dissuaded Frank from taking adventurous cruises, or perhaps his youthful travels to Europe and Central America had satisfied his wanderlust. More likely, Blake simply wished to enjoy the world he had built.

The chaos of construction coupled with concerns over Lizzie's health put the Blake family on Cunard's S.S. *Gallia* in November, 1881, for an extended stay in Menton, in southeastern France.[1] The Blake entourage included their two children, Ben and Agnes, a nurse, and the seemingly ever-present Uncle Sy. Their leisurely vacation began in London, where they spent four days touring, shopping, and relaxing. It was from here that they ordered their luxurious omnibus from Laurie and Marner. On November 14, they traveled to Paris, remaining for a week before proceeding to Menton, where they stayed at the Grand Hôtel du Louvre et de la Paix until April 13, 1882. When the Blakes returned to Paris on April 15, they checked into the Hotel Continental. With more than a month to roam Parisian streets, the Blakes waged a grand shopping campaign. Elizabeth secured enough hats, dresses, blouses, gloves, shoes, and other attire to clothe a small town. Frank bought books and timepieces, including a gold watch with a one-minute repeater, and a complex clock with a perpetual calendar and dials for sunrise and sunset, zodiac, and equinoctial time. For Charles T. Hubbard, Charles B. Wells, and Richard

Sewall, Blake bought gold watches. He obtained a clock with Westminster chimes for his sister Lisa Wells, and for cousin Russell Sullivan he purchased a deluxe edition of the works of Molière. When Sullivan received the books he exclaimed, "The Molière has come. For pure, unadulterated luxe you, certainly, have taken the cake!"[2] When the Blakes returned to London on May 22, Frank bought clothes and some scientific instruments, including a gold pocket compass, a watch aneroid,

Blake family and Henry Silas Payson on the grass tennis courts at Keewaydin.
Unknown photographer, n.d. #57.140

and thermometers from Louis P. Casella. They also bought stationery embossed with the Blake crest, table linens, household furnishings, clothes and toys for the children, and several trunks in which to transport their possessions. Although Lizzie did not fully recover her health while on their long European sojourn, the Blakes may have found some compensation in the relaxing atmosphere and the bow-breaking number of items they stowed below decks for the voyage home on May 27. Including the omnibus ordered in London, the Blakes expended $23,341.26 on their vacation.[3]

Travel on the railroad line that passed near Keewaydin, more convenient and comfortable than a modern-day commute, made Boston's businesses and best tradesmen readily accessible to the Blakes. Even Blake's Boston barber made house calls to Keewaydin. Sometimes Blake arranged for trains to make a stop at Keewaydin just for him, and occasionally, in the case of a large social gathering, he would arrange for a special train car or an extra train to run for the convenience of his party. Blake expected the service, paid well for it, and thought nothing of negotiating with the division superintendent of the Boston and Albany Railroad to obtain what he sought. Blake usually got his way. Proximity to the railroad also made the prompt delivery of goods and special services possible. Blake, for instance, arranged with the Boston and Albany Railroad baggage master to have bread and newspapers thrown off an early train from Boston as it passed Keewaydin. One representative of the railroad, when acknowledging receipt of a $10 payment, assured Blake that he would "endeavor here after as here to fore to use the utmost care in throwing off any package that you choose to send on my train."[4] To the end of Keewaydin's days a well-worn trail from the edge of the sunken garden to the tracks, "the paper path," marked the butler's daily route to retrieve the newspaper.

Keewaydin offered more diversions and recreational activities than did most towns. In addition to his technical library, Blake had accumulated an extensive collection of French and English literature. He could also interest visitors with his extensive stamp collection, or a small group might play whist or listen to a sonata on his piano. Lizzie took drawing lessons for a time, and in addition to his copious scientific work and hobbies, Frank carried on an extensive correspondence with scores of people around the country. For light activity, one could retire to the billiards room or stroll to the bowling alleys in the stable complex, and depending upon the season, the Blakes and their guests could engage in many outdoor activities. In winter, guests could go for a sleigh ride or sled, and if snow covered ice on the estate pond, the staff promptly cleared it away for skating. In other seasons, one could go horse-riding, play tennis on the wonderfully equipped grass courts, or use Frank's gear for archery, fly-fishing, or shooting. Blake also erected a boathouse on the Charles, fully stocked with canoes and rowboats.

Although he originally built a gymnasium, Blake soon turned the room at the northwest corner of the stable complex into a ninety-seat theater, complete with gas lighting and a drop curtain.[5] Lizzie noted the titles of two plays performed there, "A Timid Pair" and the musical, "Cox & Box." One of Blake's first productions, "A Very Odd Trick" by J. C. Robinson, used a whist club as its setting, with Blake friends and neighbors as the actors. A local newspaper reported:

> The charming operetta "A Very Odd Trick" was repeated last Wednesday evening at the cosy little theatre attached to Mr. Francis Blake's elegant residence at Weston. The audience, which was composed of many notables from Boston and vicinity, expressed unqualified admiration for the work and the talent that ably carried out the ideas of both composer and author. It is not often that so fine an amateur performance is given in private or public, and the event with its brilliant social surroundings marks the gay season with a white stone.

The white stone, a symbol of the season's start, did not reflect upon the actors' abilities. The reviewer gave much individual credit to the author and the players, and expressed the desire that "A Very Odd Trick" would speedily find its way to Boston so that many more people could see

"What their friends pronounce to be the best musical performance of the amateur stage."[6]

In the summer, the Blakes held sumptuous parties. They celebrated the 4th of July, the Blake wedding anniversary, and special events such as Louise Jackson's (Lizzie's sister) return home from Paris in August 1883. Guests would find Keewaydin's grand terrace illuminated by dozens of electric "owl lamps," provided by The Chemical Electric Light and Power Company, and would hear music by the Germania Band or an orchestra from Boston, while enjoying bountiful catering by Woodland Farms Park of Newton. The New England Fire Works Laboratory, which for many years put on the annual 4th of July display on Boston Common, provided impressive pyrotechnics. For his 1883 party, Blake decorated his estate with four varieties of balloons and set off eighteen different kinds of fireworks.[7]

Blake entertained lavishly; in addition to plays, fireworks, and fine food, he owned one of the most extensive private wine collections in the area. From his youth, Frank had an interest in wines, a taste acquired with the encouragement of his father. Keewaydin housed a small wine cellar at first, but during his extended stay in France, Blake developed a connoisseurship. Beginning in May 1882, he kept a wine scrapbook in which he saved correspondence with wine merchants as well as collections of wine lists and labels.[8] A cask of Chateau Leoville followed Blake home from France in 1882, and from there his interest in wine grew. The fall of that year Blake had his interior designer make up a personal wine label and printed 2,300 copies.[9]

Not surprisingly, Blake approached his wine cellar with the determination and vigor with which he approached everything. He received five barriques of wine in November: three Chateau Margaux, one Chateau Larose, and one Chateau Pichon Longueville. The following year, he bought eight barriques of Chateau Margaux, 1875. In November 1883, he purchased corking and capping machines, wine ventilators, and needles used in bottling. Characteristically, Blake suggested to the manufacturer how he might improve his needles, and his idea won acceptance. "Your idea of beveling the needle, we think a good one," businessman John Power replied, "& hope you will give it a practical trial." Blake, Power, and several assistants began bottling at the end of the month. The first day they filled 303 quart bottles; the following day Blake's gardener, Wattez, four of his crew, and one of Power's assistants bottled two barriques into pints. On November 30, they filled 860 bottles. By the time they had completed their initial bottling venture, Blake and his assistants had filled or recorked 1,760 bottles.[10]

By 1885, Blake had laid down a prodigious quantity of wine in his cellar. To one correspondent he revealed the extent of his collection. "I have in my cellar nearly 5,000 bottles of Chateau Margaux 1878; 500 Chateau Pichon-Longuille 1875; and 500 Chateau Larose 1875 which together make a stock sufficient for my ordinary consumption for some years to come." But Blake did not find this supply entirely satisfactory. These wines, he said, "do not have that finesse which would prompt me to offer them as rarities on special occasions." So he searched for more. Whenever traveling, he kept a sharp eye for a wine bargain, such as when he passed through Trenton Falls, New York, in 1888, and bought twelve bottles of sixty-year-old Madeira.[11]

During the 1880s, Blake's two children, Agnes and Benjamin, grew into their teens. With its beautiful gardens, rolling hills, farm, livestock, and many servants, Keewaydin proved a marvelous place for children. Judging from the many invoices found among Blake's papers, Ben and Agnes possessed all the toys they could want, and Richard Schwartz, proprietor of a Boston toy store, received all the business he could possibly wish for, particularly at Christmas. The Keewaydin Christmas of 1885 probably typified most. Lizzie recorded in her diary that "Uncle Sy came. Christmas morning presents in stockings at home. More on the tree in the afternoon at Grandpapa's. Benjamin was presented with a mechanical toy, a man in a cart with a donkey. Each child had a silver watch. Agnes a doll's bureau. Ben a workbench especially made for him. Ben had a knitting machine on which he made gifts."[12]

Ben and Agnes's early education took place at Keewaydin in the second-floor school room Blake had added during the expansion of the house. Charlotte Young, Lizzie's sister, also educated her two children in the "Blake School." In her diary, Charlotte left a brief description of one class. "Our little school for this winter began day before yesterday," she wrote in October 1883. "The teacher is my cousin, Miss Munroe from Cambridge. The school room Mrs. Blake has fitted up in her house. The scholars are my two children, Agnes & Ben, Joe & Horace Field, Jessie & Carrie Mirriam. They are all delighted with it thus far, but I think they imagine it is more a getting together for play than anything else." The home education continued successfully with several different teachers until 1889, at which time Ben began to attend the Williams School in Newton.[13]

Lizzie devoted herself to raising her children, and they remained the focus of her attention for all of Agnes's and Ben's childhood. Her diary, begun in 1885, is a paean to her children's amiable traits, their progress, amusements, and ailments. Informed by her doctor in 1885 that her tonsillitis was contagious, Lizzie "was careful that the children did not take my breath." Although normally she slept in her mother's chambers, Agnes was temporarily relegated to sleeping "in the sitting room which she thought was very sad." Lizzie hovered over her children like a guardian angel, always nearby and rarely out of their sight. "I seldom leave the children and I & they dislike it & make great objections even for a few hours & they seem as thankful to have me back again as I am to get to them." No evidence exists suggesting that the children resented the level of attention they received from their mother, and without question Frank preferred this arrangement.[14] Perhaps following a pattern set by his own father, or enacting his view of the appropriate manner of great men of business and the professions, Blake took little daily interest in his children.

One is hard pressed to envision Blake, with his relentless pursuit of precision and order and absorbed by his own pursuits, taking time to play with Ben and Agnes. The activities he shared with them, such as reading to them in the evening, was largely on his own terms.[15] To compensate for his lack

Agnes and Benjamin Sewall Blake in the conservatory at Keewaydin,
April 26, 1887. By Francis Blake. #57.132

of attention, he provided them with splendid recreational facilities. During the summer of 1886, Agnes and Benjamin learned to row and Benjamin learned to play tennis with Uncle Sy Payson. Far more relaxed and jovial than Blake, Payson likely proved an entertaining surrogate father whenever he came to visit. For a man once so vigorous, Lizzie noted that "Papa cares little for out-of-door sports. He spends much time & labor in photography & does splendid work." The surprising admission that her husband had little interest in physical activity, with or without his children, Lizzie justified by noting the importance of what her husband accomplished. Such conduct certainly falls far short of modern expectations of fatherhood, but neither does it fully reveal the character of Francis Blake.[16]

Because of his wealth, siblings, relatives, friends, and strangers constantly turned to Frank for help. While strangers never knew what to expect from Blake—some received a gift or loan, others went away empty-handed—family members could generally count on his assistance. His sister Lisa and her husband Charles Wells lived in the west for several years and returned to Massachusetts in 1879. Frank found Charles a minor position with the National Bell Telephone Company. The job paid poorly and the Wellses sometimes asked Blake for financial aid. Their requests, however, came infrequently and generally they sought loans rather than outright gifts. In 1882, for instance, Blake agreed to lend them $2,000 to rent and furnish an apartment on Pinckney Street in Boston. In return, Charlie, as Frank liked to call him, proved helpful in overseeing construction at Keewaydin, taking care of Blake's accounts and forwarding mail and news to Frank when he was away on vacation. When Charlie became ill in 1888, Frank paid for his travel to the famed Karlsbad water cure in the present-day Czech Republic, provided him with substantial financial support, and ensured that the New England Telephone Company kept his job open for him until he could return to work.[17]

Winslow Lincoln, one of Blake's many Worcester relatives, assisted Frank in acquiring livestock for his estate, for which Blake rewarded him generously. After smoothing over relations with his grandmother in 1880, Blake remained a respectful and thoughtful grandson, as he had been a dutiful son in providing for his parents. He also made sure that Christmas for his grandmother and Worcester relations was joyous. "With many thanks and wishes for a 'Happy New Year,'" his grandmother Trumbull once wrote Frank, "which can hardly fail to be such to you, who delight in making others happy."[18] His grandmother still lived in the old family house in Worcester, a haven to generations of Trumbulls. In the early 1880s, two unmarried daughters lived with her in the house, and her advancing years raised concern for their welfare. Writing to Frank in the spring of 1883, Louise Trumbull explained that a recent illness had confined her to her room and caused her tremendous anxiety about the future of her daughters, "who value their home tenderly and would be dreadfully troubled by the necessity which would tear them from the place of their birth. . . ."[19] She asked Frank to take possession of the house to guarantee that his aunts would have a familiar place to live out their lives. Although not wealthy, she had saved enough to pay him rent, and believed that rising property values would protect Blake from any loss. Frank conferred with his uncle William Lincoln and agreed to do whatever he could to comfort his grandmother and ensure that his aunts' future would be secure. Frank advised his uncle that he was "anxious to do what I can toward realizing her wishes with reference to the ultimate disposition of the homestead estate." Grandmother Trumbull died on December 8, 1885, confident that because of Frank her daughters would never have to leave their home.[20]

Charles Blake—Charlie as he had been called since childhood—never enjoyed success in life. His dismal performance at the Naval Academy and his conflicts at home sadly foretold the future. During the 1870s, he managed to acquire some engineering experience and briefly worked in Maine before moving to Pawtucket, Rhode Island, where he lived with his wife Margie and his son Willie and tried to break into the phone business. But he soon found himself without a job. Frank did all he could to help his brother, including loaning him money and hiring him to oversee construction of Keewaydin's waterworks. After completion of that project, Charlie again faced unemployment, but this time with the addition of another son, also named Charlie. Back in Pawtucket, Charlie made an effort to revive the old family boot-blacking business. But although he showed more interest in this project than he had displayed in his father's business, it went nowhere. He hoped that with his engineering experience, he could find employment on the Cape Cod Canal, but nothing came of that. Without means of support, Charlie and his family lived on a monthly check from Frank.[21]

During the summer of 1881, Frank moved his brother and family to a farm in Providence. Just before the beginning of fall, Charlie informed Frank he had been offered a job on the Mexican Central Railroad and would soon leave the country. Naturally he needed travel money and assured Frank that this would be his last request for funds. As the months went by, Margie heard little from her husband and received no money. Frank had to step in. Between 1880 and 1882, Frank—not including Charlie's employment on the water works—had given his brother $1,778.03.[22]

Early in 1883, Charlie found himself again without a job and returned home to what must have been a chilly reception. Employment continued to elude him. Against the wishes of his wife and the advice of his brother, he returned to Mexico in hopes of establishing himself as a civil engineer. Charlie drifted in and out of work complaining of health problems, and offered excuses, but sent no money home. Given his temperament, it is amazing that Frank stood by his brother for so long. But by January 1884, in response to yet another request from Charlie for money, Frank reached the limit of his patience.

I have today telegraphed you at Silao "I shall do nothing." I have done this after careful consideration of your telegram and letter to Margie and letter to myself. As you well know your going to Mexico was in direct opposition to my advice and wishes; and with a full understanding that $100. per month was the maximum sum that I could or would contribute toward the support of yourself and family. It is therefore a most unwelcome surprise to have you call upon me for a cash advance of $350 and a further advancement of $75 per month. You say $350 would pay your debts and your passage home. As the latter from the

City of Mexico via Vera Cruz and New York is but $125 I infer that you are indebted to the extent of $225 or three month's @ $75 per month.

If you have sat still at Silao for three months and allowed this debt to accumulate I think you have done a most unwise thing; and I do not think it manly for you [to] call on me to foot your bills. I have to suggest that you seek employment professionally from the Mexican Central R. R. engineers who endorsed you so highly at the close of your previous service with them. In the meantime you need give no thought as to the welfare of your family as they will be amply provided for by the $100 per month which I send to Margie.[23]

This stern message from Frank held Charlie at bay until Christmas of 1884—Frank's birthday—when he wrote Margie lamenting that he had nothing to eat and was about to be evicted from his hotel. Suspicious, Frank inquired into Charlie activities, his standing with his associates, and whether or not he had descended back into his earlier habits of drinking and licentiousness. Whatever Frank learned from his investigation into his brother's life could not have been good and he decided to end his financial assistance permanently, although he promised to help if Charlie became ill or destitute.[24]

Charlie's family, of course, suffered the most from his escapades. Wisely, and with little alternative, Margie realized that Charlie would never become a responsible husband and father and sought a divorce. Her lawyer, J. S. Thurston of Providence, advised Frank in January 1888 that his firm had succeeded in obtaining an absolute divorce for Mrs. Blake. "As the last act," Thurston wrote Blake in an all-too-familiar way, "we enclose [the] bill to you."[25] Charlie's marriage had ended, but Frank's involvement in it had not. He continued to support Margie for the rest of his life and made provision for her benefit in his will.

A domineering husband, a distant father, but a dutiful son and a thoughtful family member, Blake proved complex and contradictory. His reactions to his brother's travail are easily understood and quite admirable. But his relationship with his father-in-law, Charles T. Hubbard, is immeasurably more difficult to comprehend. During Frank's courtship of Lizzie, Hubbard showed remarkable forbearance with an impatient and demanding young man. He respected Frank and, though cautious, always acted with dignity and with the best interests of his daughter and future son-in-law in mind. The Hubbards accepted Frank into their family—sometimes on a nightly basis—though he offered little to the marriage other than a promising, though not a lucrative, career. The Hubbard wealth awed Frank and left him with a painful sense of inferiority. The Hubbards wanted their daughter to live in a fine home, even an elaborate one. But Blake's presumptuous spending of his in-law's money possessed a quality of revenge that appeared calculated to compensate for the sense of shame he endured. Even after establishing himself professionally and financially, Blake could not make peace with Charles Hubbard's wealth and social status, and seemed intent on surpassing him in every way possible.

By any measure, Blake had achieved enviable success and enjoyed enormous respect from family, friends, and professional peers. Few Americans could match his intellectual gifts, accomplishments, or wealth. Yet Blake could not reconcile himself to his former dependence upon the Hubbards and Sewalls, and while on a day-to-day basis he could treat his father-in-law with civility, the relationship remained deeply troubled. Blake's strong characteristics, his intensity, intolerance, and need for control, became magnified when dealing with Hubbard. It took little to provoke him. The earlier shocking dispute with his father-in-law over a servant's trivial conduct foretold greater conflicts to come. Two issues, a dispute over the cost of maintaining a gas line and the management of the Benjamin Sewall Trust testified to Blake's inability to make peace with Hubbard or with himself.

In August 1880, Hubbard expressed to Blake some indecision he had regarding his plans to build a new house at Woodlands, adjacent to Keewaydin. If he kept his Louisburg Square home in Boston, then the new house would be an informal summer place. If he sold the Boston home, then he would build a much more formal house. Blake arranged to have his own home supplied with gas from the Newton & Watertown Gas

Company in Auburndale. Hubbard thought the gas from the Hanlon Company was better and cheaper. In any event, Hubbard advised Blake, "Do not depend on me for taking it with you from the Newton Co."[26]

Hubbard decided to build two houses at Woodlands, one for himself on the brow of the hill just west of Keewaydin, and one for his daughter Anne Davis east of the reservoir on the land bought from Benjamin Cutter. On behalf of his father, Charles W. Hubbard, Lizzie's half-brother, negotiated the business to connect the two houses with gas. Writing to Blake on November 28, 1882, Charles referred to Blake's "ultimatum" that Charles Hubbard's father pay two thirds of Blake's original cost to supply gas to Keewaydin—$1,666—and to connect the two houses. Charles then wrote to the Newton & Watertown Gas Company asking if they would buy out Blake's interest in the gas line, and then sell gas directly to the Hubbards. The company advised Charles that Blake had no interest in the line and that when they made their original deal with him, Blake had promised that Hubbard would eventually buy their gas for his home.[27] Whatever the true arrangement with the gas company, and despite whichever company Hubbard had wanted to buy gas from, he felt morally obliged to pay Blake the $300 it would cost for a gas connection. The confusing claims, the lack of documentation, and the relatively small amount of money, led Hubbard to consider the matter easily settled and quickly forgotten. So Blake's response, addressed to his brother-in-law, arrived with the shock of an earthquake:

> I cannot conceive the mode of reasoning which could lead you to take the course you have with reference to the gas question. And as I contrast the spirit with which I acted at the time I introduced the gas to your father's and our own estates with the spirit shown in your letter I am led to congratulate myself that I have not been brought up in the business atmosphere of life. Upon second thought, however, I cannot believe that business men as a class are inclined to discard all principles of equity in dealing with their fellow men. I shall not accept the sum you offer and the question of my having any legal claim against you is

Charles T. Hubbard. By Sarony's (New York, N.Y.), n.d. #39.267

too contemptible a one for me to consider a moment. Our ideas of ethics, as shown by this affair, are opposite; and I shall take good care to avoid any intercourse with you which may open the way to a like occurrence in the future.[28]

The matter lay dormant until July 23, 1884, when Blake advised the Newton & Watertown Gas Company that he planned to establish a private gas works for himself and for those neighbors who wished to join him. Thus, he asked the company to terminate his service at the same time that they supplied Hubbard. He also advised the company that he had put this matter before "some thirty gentlemen" and felt fully justified in believing that the gas company should not have been supplying Hubbard with gas on a line that Blake had paid for without just compensation from Hubbard. A week later, Hubbard decided to buy gas from the Newton & Watertown Company and sent Blake a check for $750, which he thought would cover whatever he owed Blake. Hubbard's letter appeared to calm Blake, leaving him with the impression that Hubbard had conceded to him and was installing an independent gas-making machine, rather than using the line that Blake had established.[29] Blake provided Hubbard with a diagram of the pipeline and details as to how he arrived at the figure of $1,258.96, which he considered to be Hubbard's fair share of the costs. Blake and Hubbard exchanged a series of letters about the matter, with Blake changing from time to time the amount of money he believed Hubbard owed. Because Blake simply refused to drop the matter, Hubbard decided that for the sake of family comity he would bring it to an end.

My dear Mr. Blake,

The Newton & W. Gas Co have put gas in my house. I have your note of the 15th making a distinct claim on me of $1,076 96/100 in the gas matter. After all the correspondence on the subject, you have failed to convince me that I owe you anything. And I have also failed to convince you that I do not. We are both honest in our convictions. Let each keep his own.

Money is no object with me, compared with the perfect good feeling that should exist between us, & I therefore send you a check for the amount. Let us never mention the subject again, & let the gas bring light and not darkness to both houses.

Yrs. Truly,

Charles T. Hubbard[30]

If a minor dispute over gas could rupture relations between Blake and his father-in-law, what could one expect from the always troubling issue of inheritance? Benjamin Sewall's death on October 12, 1879, left an estate of $1,460,000—perhaps the modern equivalent of $65 million—to be divided among his heirs.[31] The will included a provision that made an outright bequest of $30,000 to each of his granddaughters, "to her own use, free from the control and interference of her husband." It also established a trust with Charles T. Hubbard and Moses H. Day as trustees to invest and manage $300,000 "with a view to safety rather than profit," and to divide the income among Sewall's three granddaughters and Hubbard. Hubbard wrote to Lizzie on January 30, 1880, advising her that he hoped to divide some income among the heirs the following week, and thereafter she received a monthly distribution of at least $1,500. Blake may have resented the provision that prevented a husband from interfering in the bequest, although this had been a common feature of wills for many generations. He disputed Hubbard's interpretation of what the will said regarding deductions from the initial $30,000 bequest. The original will stated that money given to the heirs subsequent to May 1, 1868 for a home or for furniture would be deducted from that granddaughter's bequest, although other evidence suggested that the date had been revised to November 30, 1877.

The date change made an enormous difference to the Blakes, as the earlier date would have required them to deduct all the money that Grandfather Sewall had given them for their original house. The controversy dragged on for about two years, during which time Blake was convinced that his father-in-law either misunderstood the will or simply did not care to turn over the money to Lizzie because of his unhappiness with Frank. Hubbard, on the other hand, believed that a genuine ambiguity existed in the will and wanted a ruling from a judge. Each side engaged counsel. As was often inevitable in such cases, long delays ensued. Depositions had to be obtained, and because Louisa Jackson, Lizzie's sister, lived in Paris, a resolution remained even farther away. Hubbard, in Rome during the beginning of 1880, responded to a prodding cable from Blake that tried to elicit from him some indication of exactly what he would do about the bequest. Hubbard explained to Blake that his own wishes were irrelevant; everything depended upon what the court would decide. He had complete confidence, however, that the court would ascertain Sewall's intentions. But no decision came, and the matter dragged into another year just as the squabble over the gas lines heated up. In April 1881, Blake again prodded Hubbard for an answer about the will. This time replying from London, Hubbard expressed his dismay that Blake believed that he deliberately put obstacles in the way of a settlement and disregarded the best interests of his children. His dismay at the latter accusation harkened back to the incident with the servant and must have riled Hubbard considerably. In response to Blake's hectoring, Hubbard asked his lawyer to explain the situation more fully to Blake and, perhaps, prevent further friction.[32] Several days later, another exchange of cablegrams indicated additional misunderstandings. Not until November 5, 1881, did Blake's lawyer, Moorfield Storey, finally inform him that the judge had found in their favor and Elizabeth would receive $24,090.82. When the Blakes finally received payment on December 22, 1881, the total with interest came to $25,817.[33]

With the exception of the struggle over the gas line, three years of relative peace passed between Frank and his father-in-law. But the calm would not last. Blake learned that Hubbard had not been distributing the additional income the trust produced to his daughters, instead preferring to add it to the principal. He penned an astonishing letter to his father-in-law on January 4, 1884, accusing him of interfering in "the peculiar privilege of man and wife." Shocked and perplexed, Hubbard replied two days later that he had no desire to interfere in Frank's marriage and that he had no grounds for such an accusation. He explained that Sewall had intended to benefit his granddaughters and their heirs and allow his granddaughters' husbands to have access to this income. When Hubbard assumed control of the property as trustee, he had said that the heirs could count on an income of $1,500 per month, but he neglected to add that in order to achieve that amount, he would have to reinvest the extra funds the trust produced back into the principal.[34]

Accepting Hubbard's explanation, a slightly contrite Blake expressed his regret that he had written that first letter. He now understood Hubbard's concerns and intentions and could put that portion of their disagreement behind them. But he could not let the matter drop. Hubbard's position would matter considerably if the income from Sewall's bequest represented their only source of income. It did not, and Blake wished to establish with absolute clarity just how little he needed the Sewall money or, indeed, Hubbard:

> The fact is, however, that it has been, and may be, small in comparison with the income from our own property. Our income during the last five years has been $482,733.47 or 95,546.69 per annum of which, as you show, the Estate has yielded an average of only $30,954.93. While I do not anticipate so large an income yearly in the future, I am confident that the increase in the ordinary profits of our telephone investments will more than counter-balance any decrease in the annual yield of the trust estate.
>
> You must remember too, that the time cannot, in the nature of things, be far distant when I shall receive in fee my 1/12 interest in the valuable Trumbull estate at Worcester. Also that, having the ultimate interests of our children in view, we know that they are heirs to at least 1/24 more of the principal of the B. S. Estate than we now receive the income of.
>
> You are wrong in your assumption that we have spent our entire income. Much of it is invested in our homestead estate; and it thus affords us much more acceptable interest than dollars and cents can bring with them. But, aside from this, we have about $25,000 invested in good dividend-paying property; and the close of the last year finds us with about $10,000 cash in hand after all bills are paid.
>
> To sum up, I do then think our financial methods and results are

such as can afford [no] reasonable grounds of alarm to ourselves or our friends. And above all our characters are such that we can without compromising our happiness reduce our living expenses at least two thirds within a month if circumstances should demand it.[35]

Powerful emotional and psychological forces lay behind Blake's response and clearly colored his entire relationship with his father-in-law. Although this was the last major conflict between the two men, precious little time was left for Blake to enjoy a more normal relationship with him. Three years later, on January 18, 1887, Hubbard died.[36]

Endnotes

1. Cunard to Blake, Nov. 11, 1881, FBP.
2. Russell Sullivan to Blake, June 15, 1882, FBP.
3. The source of information for Blake's voyage and purchases are the bills preserved in vol. 4, FBP.
4. John H. Garland to Blake, Oct. 5, 1883, FBP.
5. Elizabeth Blake, Diary, Aug. 9, 1885, FBP; bills for the theatre's construction are in vol. 6, FBP.
6. An undated and unidentified newspaper clipping in vol. 45, FBP.
7. Bills and correspondence throughout the Blake papers indicate that such parties went on year after year, see vol. 6, FBP.
8. Most of Blake's wine records are in vol. 30 and "Wines, 1882–1901" series, FBP.
9. The bills for the labels, dated Nov. 6, 8, 1882, are in vol. 5, FBP.
10. John Power to Blake, Nov. 20, 30, 1883, FBP; Blake, Diary, Nov. 27, 1883, FBP. A barrique is a large cask containing 225 liters.
11. Blake to John Osborn, Oct. 9, 1885, FBP; Blake to A. Binninger, June 29, 1888, vol. 30, FBP. Vol. 30 is a scrapbook in which Blake placed correspondence with wine merchants, bills, and copies of labels for wines bottled at Keewaydin.
12. Elizabeth Blake, Diary, Dec. 25, 1885, FBP.
13. Charlotte Young, Diary, Oct. 3, 1883, FBP. A bill from the city of Newton for tuition for Benjamin Blake at the Williams School, from January through June 1889, is in vol. 10, FBP.

14. Elizabeth Blake, Diary, Dec. 20, 1885, May 16, 1886, FBP.
15. Elizabeth Blake, Diary, Jan. 31, 1885, FBP.
16. Elizabeth Blake, Diary, July 11, 1886, FBP.
17. Blake to Lisa and Charles Wells, June 15, 1882, FBP; bills for Wells's care are in the "Health, 1880–1911" series, FBP.
18. Louise C. Trumbull to Blake, Dec. 30, 1880, FBP.
19. Louise C. Trumbull to Blake, Apr. 15, 1883, FBP.
20. Blake to William Lincoln, Apr. 17, 1883, FBP.
21. Margie Blake (Mrs. Charles) to Blake, Dec. 26, 1880, Apr. 21, May 1, 1881, FBP; John T. Langford to Blake, April 20, 1881, FBP; Charles Blake to Blake, Apr. 13, 1881, FBP; Blake ledger, vol. 40, p. 24, FBP.
22. Charlie Blake to Blake, Sep. 5, 1881, FBP. Accounts and receipts for Charlie can be found in vol. 40, FBP.
23. A copy of the undated letter is in the "Private Letters, 1866–1912" series, FBP.
24. Blake kept a draft confidential memo, apparently sent by someone associated with the Mexican Central Railroad, inquiring about Charlie Blake. "Private Letters, 1866–1912" series, FBP.
25. Thurston, Ripley & Co. to Blake, Jan. 4, 1888 and other relevant correspondence regarding Charles Blake and his family are in "Private Letters, 1866–1912" series, FBP. The bill for Margie's divorce is in vol. 9, FBP.
26. Charles T. Hubbard to Blake, Aug. 1, 1880, FBP.
27. Charles W. Hubbard to Blake, Nov. 28, 1882, FBP.
28. Blake to Charles W. Hubbard, Nov. 29, 1882, FBP.
29. Blake to the Newton & Watertown Gas Company, July 23, 1884, FBP; Charles T. Hubbard to Blake, July, 29 1884, FBP; Blake to Charles T. Hubbard, July 31, 1884, FBP. For an unknown reason, the Blake letters on the gas question are copies. The papers also include a memorandum and a list of the friends Blake consulted on the dispute.
30. Charles T. Hubbard to Blake, Aug. 19, 1884, FBP.
31. A copy of the appraisal of Sewall's estate and Sewall's will is in the "Benjamin Sewall Trust, 1879–1902" series, FBP.
32. Charles T. Hubbard to Blake, Apr. 30, 1881, FBP.
33. Moorefield Storey to Blake, Nov. 5, 1881, FBP. This letter reported that the court had settled on Nov. 30, 1877 to be the date after which deductions would be made. Information about the telegrams is contained in the correspondence. The telegrams are not preserved in the Blake papers.

34. Blake to Charles T. Hubbard, Jan. 4, 1884, FBP; Charles T. Hubbard to Blake, Jan. 6, 1884, FBP.
35. Blake to Charles T. Hubbard, Jan. 8, 1884, FBP.
36. Blake to Charles W. Hubbard, Jan. 7, 1889, vol.10, FBP. To honor Hubbard, the Blakes contributed $2,000 to the Hubbard Memorial Library in Ludlow, Massachusetts.

CHAPTER 9

PHOTOGRAPHY

T HE KEEWAYDIN ESTATE, the telephone transmitter, and photographic innovations constituted Blake's greatest achievements. But
rapid strides in technology soon rendered Blake's transmitter obsolete,
and within two generations Keewaydin had fallen to the wrecking ball.
The photographic images Blake created, however, endure. During his
lifetime, Blake's photographs earned him awards and an international
reputation. More importantly, he became one of the few individuals in
the United States and Europe in the late nineteenth century to experiment with high-speed photography. Blake's scientific genius, keen sense
of composition, and fresh eye—unspoiled by professional training—permitted him to "see" in new ways and create images that remain fascinating
to this day. But Blake never possessed the slightest interest in becoming a
professional photographer and set out only to follow his curiosity.[1]

Blake first became familiar with photography during his service with
the Coast Survey, a time when only professionals cared to handle the necessary bulky and complicated photographic equipment. The great Boston
photographer Joseph A. Whipple had travelled with Blake on the Shelbyville mission in 1869, and two years later photographer John Moran had
accompanied the Darien expedition. But Blake left no record of any personal interest in the medium prior to 1884. Like others of means, he had
hired professionals to photograph his family. W. A. Webster of Waltham,
Massachusetts, photographed the Blake children on numerous occasions,
and in 1883 Blake hired him to document his creation of Keewaydin.[2] Per-

haps watching Webster do his work sparked Blake's interest. On April 9, 1884, he bought his first camera, a 5 x 8 from a Boston shop on the recommendation of William deYoung Field, a friend and amateur photographer. Characteristically, Blake bought one of the best cameras available. "This 'machine' is so much better than mine," Field wrote, "that I did not hesitate to pay at a little higher price for you."[3]

Field had given Blake his start in photography and even helped him set up his own darkroom. During the summer of 1884, they spent much time together at one or the other's homes, sharing equipment and learning the best techniques for developing photographic plates. For all the help Field had provided, Blake felt much gratitude. In July, as a gesture of thanks, Blake gave Field a "Blair 5x8 R. B. Double Swing Camera." "I can think of nothing better than a gift of the accompanying camera," Blake wrote, as "evidence of my appreciation of your many kindnesses in the manner of my introduction to the art of photography." Field, on the other hand, felt equally grateful for all he had learned from Blake, both technically and esthetically. "It has been a real pleasure to me to watch your nice work & note the many points I thought were so good. . . . [W]orking with some one of taste & skill was in itself enough to make me your debtor."[4]

Blake had learned enough photography from Field to plunge ahead independently. Friends and colleagues suggested books for him to read, and he borrowed books by the leading English authority on photography, Sir William de Wivelslie Abney, likely his *Instruction in Photography* (1874) or *Photography with Emulsions* (1882). Blake also purchased books and quickly expanded his knowledge.[5] He started working with Beebe gelatine dry plates and soon searched for other lenses and shutters. He had some difficulty finding the best equipment, and two camera shops, one in Boston and one in New York, chased after the Dallmeyer equipment he demanded. A 10 x 12 Dallmeyer lens did not reach Boston until September.[6]

Blake developed his talents by photographing Keewaydin, and in the summer of 1884 he recorded one of the family's late-summer annual visits to the Glen House resort in the White Mountains. He photographed the view up the drive, the interior of the resort, and scenes of the surrounding landscape and mountains.[7] He shot woodland trails, trees, mountain streams, even mushrooms. He also captured dramatic images of Thompson's Falls, Crystal Cascade, and Glen Ellis Falls, and photographed various local characters such as B. F. Osgood, who sold rustic canes and other tourist items at the entrance to the Crystal Cascade, and Franklin Leavitt, a New Hampshire mapmaker. A bartender became one of his favorite subjects and Blake took a number of careful, contemplative images of him.

Indeed, Blake's interest in the scenes of everyday life paralleled similar trends in the art of the era. This is especially true for the many photographs Blake took during the family sojourn in the spring of 1885 to

Sheep shearing at the Payson farm. By Francis Blake, 1887. #57.478

the Payson farm, home of Elizabeth's cousin Henry Silas Payson, in Mossville, Illinois. Blake made a full photographic record of rural life there, including the land, buildings, farm chores, and various colorful individuals, especially farm hands and family members, either capturing them as they worked or putting them in formal poses. Blake's attention to the details of farm life is striking, and the images he created are crisp, evocative, and free of the formalism that still dominated the world of high art at the time.

Family and friends immediately recognized Blake's talent with a camera. Silas Payson let Blake know that everyone at his home greatly admired the photographs he had taken of them. Cousin Russell Sullivan characterized the photographic portrait that Blake had made of him as truly "inspirational."[8] Blake's success fueled his burgeoning fascination with photography and he quickly expanded his technical expertise. In January 1886, he began purchasing enlarging equipment and wasted no time in putting it to use.[9]

One can easily imagine Blake enthusiastically setting to work with his newest equipment, practicing his new skills on his wide circle of friends. He photographed the literary lion William Dean Howells, who intended to use the image to publicize a new work, perhaps *The Rise of Silas Lapham*, which had come out late the previous summer. Blake enlarged the image for Howells, who proclaimed that the "photograph as enlarged is magnificent. . . ." He placed a copy of the picture in his own home and a duplicate in Boston's Tavern Club, the famed private watering hole for Brahmin men. But Howells believed that another image by Blake, a "¾ face—would 'give more satisfaction' to the public." Blake's response to Howells's preference revealed his attitude toward fame and typified his deeply personal approach to his professional work and all intellectual inquiry. "I send you with this an 'artist's proof' from the best negative I have of you. Pray accept it as a souvenir of our mutual struggle to obtain the (for me) unattainable—that which shall please the public. I venture to prophesy that your endeavors to 'give satisfaction' to this hydra will ultimately leave you in 'The public be damned!!' frame of mind."[10]

*William Dean Howells. By Francis Blake from a glass
plate negative, n.d. #6.3.805m*

Despite Blake's "public be damned" attitude, his work began to attract much attention in photographic circles. He had joined the Society of Amateur Photographers of New York in October 1885, and his pictures began appearing in public exhibitions.[11] Blake's most famous image, *New York Express, 48 Miles an Hour*, appeared at Allen & Rowell, a Boston photographic supply store and gallery, sparking requests for copies, and on October 7 the influential Boston Camera Club elected Blake a member. He addressed a club meeting later that month and explained his methods of measuring the speed of drop shutters, illustrating with the apparatus he used and negatives enlarged with a lantern projector.[12]

A version of "48 Miles an Hour." By Francis Blake. The photograph's inscription, in Blake's hand, reads "Building the terraces and greenhouses at Keewaydin, late 1880s." #57.797

Much of Blake's fascination with photography resulted from his love for well-crafted, precision instruments. He developed this appreciation while working for the Coast Survey and his photographic work served to increase this passion. In October 1885, he bought shutters for his Euroscope cameras and an "Instantaneous Shutter" from the New York importer and manufacturing optician William T. Gregg.[13] This reference to an "instantaneous shutter" is the first reference in Blake's records to high-speed photography, an area in which Blake would become a pioneer and make his greatest contributions. He soon began experimenting with fast shutters, using family members as subjects. The photos he took of family members laughing, Silas Payson and John G. Hubbard in particular, are extraordinary.

Until Blake began his work, photographs typically depicted seemingly somber or stern individuals. In part, nineteenth-century photographic conventions were dictated by the limitations of the equipment. Shutters required minutes, not milliseconds, for exposure. Any movement by the subject would blur an image, a costly mistake. But more importantly, a photograph, like a formal portrait, sought to capture the "true character" of an individual. Subjects inevitably wished to have dignified and responsible images, perhaps even proud, but never superficial. In taking photographs of subjects in natural expressions of laughter or even silliness, Blake completely broke with social convention and gave photography new purposes. The personalized, more natural portraits that Blake captured are modern in every sense of the word, even revolutionary.[14]

With a genius for mechanics, Blake concentrated his energies on improving the camera shutter. He quickly mastered its workings and familiarized himself with the quality of the various shutters then available. As in nearly every mechanical or electrical device he examined, Blake found deficiencies, and even the best shutters in existence could not meet his exacting standards. One particular shutter he examined operated with such a violent jar that it actually damaged the camera and deposited a fine white powder across the inside of the lens. Blake disdained such flaws, and

Henry Silas Payson laughing. By Francis Blake, n.d. #57.289

he set himself to improving shutter design and speed and tested the best shutters he could find.

The measurement of action in milliseconds lay far beyond the capacity of most people in the 1880s. Blake devised and built his own measuring apparatus, which he sometimes used with the assistance of his daughter Agnes. He exhibited his device at the October 21, 1886, meeting

of the Boston Camera Club. His description of its operation, published a few years later, is worth quoting at length.

> Before beginning original work, it was thought best to test the speeds of the best market shutters. This was done by means of an apparatus which I devised, and had the pleasure of exhibiting to the Boston Camera Club some years ago. The principal of the apparatus is simply photographing the image of the sun as reflected by a freely falling silvered ball, and deducing the time of exposure by applying a law of gravitation to the linear value of the distorted image.
>
> My apparatus consists of a vertical staff about 6 feet in height, rigidly attached to an iron bed-plate. The staff is painted dead black, and is graduated downward on its front face in white lines to feet and hundredths. At the top of the staff is a movable piece, readily adjusted to the height which brings the image of the sun as seen upon the surface of the ball exactly in line with the zero of the staff graduation. The silvered brass ball, 2⅜ inches in diameter and 2 pounds 2 ounces in weight, is suspended by a short piece of silk trout-line attached to a small vulcanite ring, which, in turn, is held by a spring-clip attached to the adjusting piece. On opening the spring-clip the ball is released, and falling parallel to the graduated staff is received into a padded box attached to the bed-plate.
>
> It is perhaps needless to say that the exposure is made while the ball is falling, and that the length of the exposure is computed from the scale of readings of the beginning and end of the black line, which marks on the negative the path of the reflected image of the sun.[15]

Blake's address before the Boston Camera Club immediately established him as an expert in high-speed photography to whom photographers and manufacturers of photographic equipment would turn for information and advice. Edward H. Lyon of the American Bell Telephone

Left: Agnes Blake dropping weight. By Francis Blake from a glass plate negative. #6.3.992m

Company laboratory was one of many who asked Blake to test equipment, in this case a Prosch shutter. Blake's test revealed that the shutter had rebounded, opening a second time, which spoiled the definition in the negative. When he returned the shutter with his analysis of its problems, Lyon praised the accuracy of Blake's work:

> I am greatly obliged to you for measurement of my Prosch shutter, and also for the pleasant outing afforded me by a visit to you.
>
> The rebound exposure, so beautifully shown in the negatives, is indeed a serious defect, and will account for the difficulty I have had in getting good definition in instantaneous exposures.
>
> The extreme precision of your test discloses the fact that the specific elasticity of the metal causing the rebound remains pretty much the same although the force of the impact varies. This suggests to my mind the possibility of making a shutter wherein the exposure could be effected by a rebound, constructing the parts of material whose specific elasticity would give great rapidity.[16]

For the next two years, Blake—assisted by his cousin John G. Hubbard—tested numerous makes and varieties of shutters. They found the average working speed of a commercial shutter to be about 0.03 seconds. While some shutters could be forced to operate more rapidly for test purposes, they usually lost enough light to be rendered useless. Blake found no commercial shutter that admitted more than 50 percent of the light that fell on the lens during operation. For high-speed photography, Blake concluded, that was disastrous.

> Three-hundredths of a second is too slow a speed for photographing the quickest motions of animate or inanimate nature; and the successful pictures obtained with shutters of that speed are due to the fortunate coincidence between a moment of exposure and a slower phase of motion. Thus, with such a shutter, the most rapid phases of motion produce blurred plates, which are thrown into the waste box;

and science receives but a few special—and therefore misleading—data, in place of the many which the art of photography should be made to yield.[17]

After two years of patient research of all forms of shutters, including those placed before, between, or behind the lens, Blake and Hubbard reached the conclusion that a satisfactory shutter required an entirely different approach. Blake discovered a long-neglected idea that caught his interest. In Thomas Sutton's *Dictionary of Photography* (1867), Blake found a description of an unusual shutter: "A guillotine sort of shutter, with a slot cut across it, which falls immediately in front of the sensitive plate. As the slot passes the plate the parts thus exposed to light receive the full effect of the whole power of the lens." Sutton considered it to be in some respects the best instantaneous shutter, although its operation created an undesirable vibration.[18] For the next three years, Blake worked to develop and perfect this idea of a focal plane shutter.

Blake kept abreast of all new developments in camera technology and technique and subscribed to photographic journals such as Edward Anthony's *Photographic Bulletin* and Scovill's *Weekly Photographic Times*. He also corresponded with leading photographic authorities, especially on high-speed photography. Eadweard Muybridge, the world's recognized authority on high-speed photography, proved Blake's most important contact. His *Animal Locomotion* (1887) set the international standard for high-speed photography, and Blake formed an important professional relationship with him.[19] Muybridge respected Blake's work and asked Blake to keep him informed about progress in the development of new camera shutters. The two men met in December 1888, and Muybridge glowingly advised Blake that "I saw a photograph of a gray horse while trotting, a few days ago, the negative of which I was told was made by you in the 1/1000th part of a second. Allow me to congratulate on the result. I have no doubt of the one tenth of a thousandth part being attained with a proper exposing apparatus."[20] In turn, Muybridge enjoyed the praise he received from Blake, but freely recognized Blake's great talent. "Your very gratifying letter came duly to hand," Muybridge wrote on December 5. "I am greatly pleased with your appreciation of my work, but shall be equally resigned to take a back seat when you get your new exposer in operation."[21]

By the close of 1889, Blake had achieved a new level of confidence in his research and agreed to address the Boston Camera Club in the spring. In anticipation of the talk, club president Henry N. Sweet arranged to have an extensive variety of shutters available for discussion. At Blake's request, he had a Blair 6½ x 8½ camera and a lantern slide projection in place for the April 14, 1890, meeting. Blake reported on the results of his tests of nineteen different shutters. He criticized shutters placed at the lens because they significantly reduced the amount of light that reached the photo plate and praised the focal-plane shutter design with its ability to pass on close to 100 percent of the light that passed through the lens during operation. Despite the focal-plane shutter's advantages, shutter manufacturers and photographers had neglected it for twenty-five years.

The focal-plane shutter which I now show you is the outcome of the experimental work carried on by Mr. Hubbard and myself during the last four years. It consists of a mahogany case attached to the backboard of a 6½ x 8½ camera. The case is 18½ inches long, 9½ inches high, and ⅞ inch thick, outside measurements. At its centre is an opening in which may be placed a focusing screen or a 4 x 5 plate holder.

Within the case are two screens, 5½ x 5¾ and 4½ x 5¾ inches in size. They are made of a very light framework of bamboo, covered with thin tissue-paper rendered thoroughly light-proof by the application of a mixture of lamp-black and shellac. These screens run freely on two brass wires strained lengthwise across the wooden case above and below the plate-holder opening.

Attached to the base of the larger screen is a piece of thin sheet steel pivoted to the corner of the base at one end and divided on its lower edge into ten notches one-tenth of an inch from centre to centre. Attached to the opposite corner of the smaller screen is a screw stud, over

Pigeons in flight. By Francis Blake from a glass plate negative. #6.3.418s

which the notched piece may be slipped. By this simple bit of mechanism the two screens may be at will attached to each other, with a slot between them varying for 1/10th of an inch to 1 inch in width by tenths. The exposure is made while this slot is passing over the sensitive plate, motion being imparted to the screens by means of a steel pin connecting them with a wooden piston, which in turn is driven through the brass tube by compressed air.

With a 1/10-inch slot in connection with a 2 B Dallmeyer lens three tests for the speed of this shutter have given the following results:

First test 0.0006
Second test 0.0006
Third test 0.0005
                                          _____
Mean 0.0006

This speed, which we may call half a thousandth of a second, is a severe tax upon the ability of the most rapid lenses and plates to produce pictures. It is obvious that the speed of the shutter may be increased to any desired extent by simply narrowing the width of the slot; but until the market affords us quicker lenses or plates there will be no practical advantage in making exposures of less than half a thousandth of a second.

The lantern slides of pigeons in flight, which will now be thrown upon the screen, were made from negatives taken with this shutter, using a slot two-tenths of an inch wide. The length of the exposure was therefore one-thousandth of a second; but you will note that the eyes and feathers of the birds are as sharp as if they had been standing still.[22]

Blake's remarks at the Camera Club confirmed his already considerable reputation as an authority on shutters. The following fall, the Society of Amateur Photographers of New York asked him to repeat his talk, and Sweet induced Blake to prepare his paper for publication. Sweet praised the address, considering it a "most interesting and valuable paper and when published will I am sure be of great benefit to photographers generally."[23] Others fascinated with advances in photography soon contacted Blake. A. L. Colton, private secretary to the chief of the United States Weather Bureau, expressed his interest in Blake's work and sought his advice on camera equipment. He raised the interesting matter of distortion caused by the failure to expose the entire plate at once. A moving train would be lengthened or shortened depending upon whether the shutter was moving in the same or opposite direction the train was moving. Colton's observations appealed to Blake, who responded with a gift of photographs and an offer to test a shutter for him. The Camera Club held additional meetings devoted to shutters, and for years afterward photographers sought Blake's advice on shutter design.[24]

From shutters, Blake moved on to lenses, and he tested many with equipment he had designed and fabricated. His series of pigeons in flight was taken with a 3 B Dallmeyer lens. "During the last four years I have tested a great many lenses by means of an apparatus devised for the purpose, but I have yet to find one which excels this in optical qualities."[25] When he mated a high-quality lens with a shutter of his own design, the results proved unmatched. Blake sent to J.H. Dallmeyer, his favorite lens maker, a set of the five high-speed photographs he had entered in the exhibition of the Photographic Society of Great Britain. "These pictures were all taken with your 3 B Portrait lens and a 'focal-plane' shutter and camera of my own make; and they have excited the wonder and admiration of all the experts on this side of the water who have seen them."[26]

Blake's reputation as a pioneer and expert in high-speed photography soon equaled or exceeded his reputation as a telephone inventor. He became known as "not only one of the highest authorities living on photographic lenses, but is also an unusually skillful photographer and chemist. . . ." It brought many admirers to his door, most seeking his advice. Wilfred French said he would be "highly honored if you could spare the time to try these fine lenses, giving us, if not asking too much, a detailed report of their merits and capacity." And F. A. Laws of the

Thomas Pettit playing tennis. By Francis Blake, 1891. #6.3.285s

Massachusetts Institute of Technology asked Blake to recommend a lens for "all around amateur work."[27]

Keewaydin provided Blake with a dazzling photographic backdrop. Blake could look out across his property and capture a train as it sped by his house and gardens. Family members in natural poses, his son leaping or riding a bicycle, one of his wife's relations practicing a golf swing, bursting with humor, or simply riding a horse, all proved excellent subjects for his stunning high-speed photographs. With the exception of his train images, most of Blake's photos did not reach an audience beyond a coterie of professionals and serious amateurs. But Blake's work would gain its greatest recognition with a series he did in the 1890s on lawn tennis.

On May 31, 1891, Blake shot photos of Silas Payson in tennis costume playing on the grass courts at Keewaydin. Blake liked to share copies of his favorite images with friends, and somehow word of these photographs reached James Dwight, five-time U.S. doubles champion. Dwight, then writing *Practical Lawn Tennis* (1893), thought that Blake's images would prove essential to his book. That summer, Blake photographed some of the country's leading lawn tennis athletes, including Edward L. Hall, winner of several tennis tournaments, Richard D. Sears, champion of the United States during most of the 1880s, Thomas Pettitt, professional lawn tennis champion of America, and Dwight.[28]

The results proved quite amazing. Until that time, no one had ever systematically photographed athletes in action, breaking down their motion in such clear and sharp detail. Blake not only had significantly advanced the art of photography, but he now offered athletes a new and exciting tool to analyze their play. After seeing his images, Pettitt told Blake that he had never seen anything quite like these photographs. Dwight found Blake's photographs to be stunning and ultimately included about thirty of them in his book. The images proved so unusual, so strange to the public, that Dwight had to assure his readers that the photographs actually depicted players in action, with real strokes. Despite all appearances, he insisted, the tennis balls were captured in flight and not fastened to the rackets.[29]

The photographs seemed so unfamiliar, indeed almost bizarre, to late nineteenth-century readers that Dwight felt compelled to include in his preface a letter from Blake verifying the reality of the images along with an explanation about how he made them.

My dear Dr. Dwight,—I have just received your letter, asking me to say a few words as to the methods and apparatus used in making the photographs which are to serve as illustrations to your forthcoming book on "Lawn-Tennis," and it is with pleasure that I comply with your request. The finished prints are direct enlargements of about three diameters from the original un-touched 4 by 5 negatives, taken on my tennis courts with a Dallmeyer "3 B. Patent Portrait Lens," worked at full opening, in connection with a "focal-plane shutter" and camera of my own device and make. The lengths of exposure were, for Mr. Hall half a thousandth of a second, and for the other players one thousandth of a second. The photographs of Mr. Sears were taken on a cloudy day. The success attending these short expo-sures is due to the light advantage of the focal-plane shutter over mar-ket shutters, which are all placed either before, between, or immediately behind, the lens. The distinguishing feature of the focal-plane shutter is a slotted screen placed immediately in front of the sensitive plate; so that, as the slot passes the plate, each part thereof receives the full effect of the whole power of the lens. In view of the fact that each point in nature is reproduced upon the photographic plate by the apex of a cone of light rays, the base of which is formed by the lens, it is evident that the "light value" of a slot of given width increases with its approach to the plate. Opposed to this tremendous advantage there is only the theoretical objection to the principle of the focal-plane shutter, and that is, that all parts of the sensitive plate are not exposed at the same time. But practically this objection does not hold good, since the velocity of the slot motion may be made so great that there is no sensible distinction of the phase of motion of the moving object. Moreover, the possibility of any distinction may be eliminated by setting up the camera at such a distance from the moving object that the angular value of its image on the sensitive plate shall be equal to or slightly less than the width of the shutter slot. The tennis exposures were made with a slot two tenths of an inch wide, working in a plane about one quarter of an inch in front of the plate, and under these conditions there can be no sensible distinction in the resulting prints. In conclusion, I will say that the focal-plane shutter is the outcome of series of experiments to which I devoted much of my leisure during nearly four years. . . .

The first public showing of Blake's high-speed photographs took place in Boston on May 2–7, 1892, at the Fifth Joint Annual Exhibition of Photography, sponsored by the Photographic Society of Philadelphia, the Society of Amateur Photographers of New York, and the Boston Camera Club. Blake contributed forty-five images in six groups. They included thirty-six tennis players, four images of a pony at sharp canter, two images of pigeons in flight, a bicyclist, an express train, and a portrait. Not only did he come away from the event with a medal—one in a group that included Alfred Stieglitz—but also with great popular acclaim. The *Boston Transcript* declared that Blake had proven himself as the world's foremost scientific photographer. Under the headline "Blake's Great Feat" the *Boston Record* described his photographs as "the most wonderful specimens of this art." Using the highest praise, the *Record* declared that Blake had surpassed both Muybridge and Ottomar Anchütz of Prussia—two of the world's leading high-speed photographers. Blake, according to the paper,

> took up amateur photography as a diversion and a recreation, and it shortly developed into a passion. His inventive genius could not be held in check. He became greatly interested in the wonderful results of the experiments made by Muybridge, whose instantaneous photographs of animals in motion, a feat never before accomplished and hitherto regarded as impossible, created so much talk a few years ago.

But it is commonly conceded that today Francis Blake has eclipsed not only Muybridge, but Anchütz, in this peculiar department of human effort, which is at once an art and a science.[30]

Over the next year, Blake continued to exhibit his images, winning praise and awards in addition to much attention. In July, the Massachusetts Charitable Mechanic Association invited him to participate in their Eighteenth Triennial Exhibition. "Our attention has been called to the excellence of your work of which we would like to have a number of selected specimens, or if possible a portion of your exhibit contributed to the recent exhibition held at the Boston Art Club." Blake submitted the images he had previously exhibited and won a silver medal.[31] In April 1893, he won another silver medal at the Sixth Annual Exhibit of the Photographic Society of Philadelphia. The next month *Anthony's Photographic Bulletin* invited Blake to show some of his work in their 4th International Annual Exhibition. In July, Walter Sprange requested some of his prints to illustrate his forthcoming *Blue Book of Amateur Photographers*. Alfred Stieglitz and F. C. Beach, editors of the *American Amateur Photographer*, asked Blake for a personal photograph to include in a series of portraits of the "most prominent amateur photographers of the world." Even the Camera Club of Hartford, Connecticut, asked Blake for a series of his photos to include in a exhibition. This great burst of attention might have been gratifying to most people, but, as Blake tried to convince William Dean Howells, the "hydra" of publicity still left him in a "public be damned!!" frame of mind.[32]

Blake had been interested in adaptations of his photographic work for scientific research. In 1888, he contacted John Trowbridge of Harvard's Jefferson Physical Laboratory, who wanted to photograph electric sparks. In 1890, Blake corresponded with Frank H. Bigelow of the Nautical Almanac Office of the Navy Department to explore application of photography to the transit instrument. High-speed photography seemed to offer great promise to help improve the accuracy of the Coast Survey's longitudinal measurements. Adaptation of his focal-plane shutter to astronomy should have captured his interest, but Blake never pursued any of these ventures. He never tried to patent his focal plane shutter or explore the possibility of commercial production. Soon, improvements in conventional shutters rendered Blake's more cumbersome focal plane shutter obsolete. For several years, Blake had captured the photographic world's imagination. But then he let it go.[33]

Blake's 1893 exhibition in Philadelphia effectively marked the end of his interest in public showing of his photographic work. He occasionally shot special projects, and in 1898 he created a high-speed series of golfers. But the work only repeated his previous photographic efforts, and Blake's interest trailed off. Despite numerous requests, he never even bothered to sell a single photograph or promote his work; he was content with his accomplishments and enjoyed simply giving copies of favored images to friends and a few admirers. Nor did he have any interest in publicity, viewing it as shameless self-promotion that would have garnered only unwanted attention. Blake's photographic work simply represented an extension of the man: precise, scientific, ordered, and unique.

Blake's work marked the cutting edge of late-nineteenth-century photography. Its realism strikes us today as bold, innovative, adventurous, and very modern. Blake perceived the world in a new way, and through his photography helped create a new aesthetic concept and a new artistic temperament. This socially conventional man, ironically used the camera in most unconventional ways. He did not set out to change the way we see the world, but in the process of solving technical and scientific challenges that interested him, he did so.[34]

Endnotes

1. For the most thorough appreciation of Blake's photographic work, see Keith F. Davis, "The High-Speed Photographs of Francis Blake," *The Massachusetts Historical Review* 2 (200):1–26.

2. Webster billed Blake for twenty-two negatives and thirty-dozen prints, many to be sent as gifts to Blake's friends. Webster's bills dating from Feb. 1, 1884, for work done in January, June, October, and December 1883, are in vol. 6, FBP.

3. William deYoung Field to Blake, Apr. 9, 1884, FBP; bills for the purchase of Blake's first camera equipment are in vol. 6, FBP.

4. William deYoung Field to Blake, June 2, July 1, 1884, FBP; Blake to William deYoung Field, July 1, 1884, FBP. A bill for the purchase is in vol. 6, FBP.

5. Dr. Crehore to Blake, June 1884, FBP. A bill from Cuppler, Upham, & Co. dated July 9, 1884, lists the following books: "one by Abney, *Photographs* by Edward L. Wilson, *Photographics* by Edward L. Wilson, *Photographer* by Wallace, and *How to Make Photographics*, by T. C. Roche" is in vol. 6, FBP. William de Wivelslie Abney, *Photography with Emulsions: A Treatise on the Theory and Practical Working of Gelatine and Collodion Emulsion* (New York, 1882), FBP; *Wilson's Photographs: A Series of Lessons Accompanied by Notes on all the Processes which are Needful in the Art of Photography* (Philadelphia, 1883); T. C. Roche, *How to Make Photos: A Manual for Amateurs* (New York, 1883), are all in FBP.

6. Channing Selee to Blake, July 21, 1884, FBP; E.& H. T. Anthony & Co. of New York to Blake, July 22, 1884, FBP.

7. Although Blake did not date his images, these photographs and negatives can be accurately dated because the Glen House resort burned to the ground just after the end of the 1884 season.

8. "The finished photographs Papa had taken at the farm came & much pleasure they give." Elizabeth Blake, Diary, June 28, 1885, FBP; Russell Sullivan to Blake, July 6, 1885, FBP.

9. Benjamin French to Blake, Jan. 1, 1886, FBP.

10. William Dean Howells to Blake, Feb. 6, 1886, FBP; Blake to William Dean Howells, Feb. 10, 1886, FBP.

11. Bill for corresponding membership, The Society of Amateur Photographers of New York, Oct. 7, 1885, vol. 7, p. 165, FBP.

12. Albert F. Hall to Blake, Sep. 23, 1886, FBP; minutes of meetings of the Boston Camera Club, Oct. 7, 21, 1885, Boston Athenæum.

13. A bill from William T. Gregg for three shutters, Oct. 4, 1885, is in vol. 7, p. 65, FBP.

14. Elizabeth Blake, Diary, Jan. 27, 1886, FBP; Davis, "The High-Speed Photographs of Francis Blake," 8–9.

15. This passage from Blake's second talk to the Boston Camera Club of Apr. 14, 1890, repeated his description of his method of timing shutters. It was published under the title "Photographic Shutters," in several periodicals in-

cluding *The American Amateur Photographer* 3 (Feb. 2, 1891):67–73 and *Anthony's Photographic Bulletin* 22 (March and April, 1891):144–146, 174–177, 234–236.

16. Edward H. Lyon to Blake, Oct. 25, 1886, FBP.

17. Blake, "Photographic Shutters,"*American Amateur Photographer*, 71.

18. Thomas Sutton, ed., *Dictionary of Photography* (London, Eng., 1867), 156.

19. *Dictionary of American Biography* (New York, 1964); Eadweard Muybridge, *Animal Locomotion: an Electro-photographic Investigation of Consecutive Phases of Animal Movements* (Philadelphia, 1887); Eadweard Muybridge to Blake, May 12, 1888, FBP.

20. Eadweard Muybridge to Blake, Dec. 1, 1888, FBP.

21. Eadweard Muybridge to Blake, Dec. 5, 1888, FBP.

22. Blake, "Photographic Shutters," *American Amateur Photographer*, 72–73.

23. Harry N. Sweet to Blake, Nov. 27, 1890, FBP. The published address included the gravitational formula for testing the speeds of shutters and a table showing the time in ten-thousandths of a second for each hundredth of a foot for a falling body. See note 15.

24. A. L. Colton to Blake, Dec. 15, 1891, FBP; Benjamin French & Co. to Blake, Feb. 23, 1894, FBP; N. L. Stebbins to Blake, July 12, 1898, FBP; Minutes of the Boston Camera Club, Feb. 5, 1894, Boston Athenæum.

25. Blake to Anthony & Co., Mar. 27, 1891, FBP.

26. Blake to J. H. Dallmeyer, Ltd., Oct. 17, 1892, FBP.

27. Benjamin French & Co. to A. L. Colton, Feb. 27, 1892, a copy of French's letter to Colton in Blake's handwriting, FBP; Wilfred French to Blake, Nov. 22, 1894, FBP; F. A. Laws to Blake, Sept. 24, 1898, FBP.

28. Elizabeth Blake, Diary, May 31, 1891, FBP; James Dwight, *Practical Lawn Tennis* (New York, 1893).

29. Thomas Pettitt to Blake, July 7, 1891, FBP; James Dwight to Blake, July 15, 1891, FBP.

30. *Boston Record*, May 7, 1892; also see Davis, "The High-Speed Photographs of Francis Blake," 18–19.

31. W. Jay Little to Blake, July 1892, FBP; *Report of the Eighteenth Triennial Exhibition of the Massachusetts Charitable Mechanic Association* (Boston, 1893), 135, 136, 182.

32. Robert S. Redfield to Blake, Aug. 24, 1893, FBP; Arthur H. Elliott and Frank P. Smith of *Anthony's Photographic Bulletin* to Blake, May 15, 1893, FBP; Walter Sprange to Blake, July 24, 1893, FBP.
33. John Trowbridge to Blake, Jan. 28, 1888, FBP; Frank H. Bigelow to Blake, Nov. 26, 1890, FBP.
34. Davis's "The High-Speed Photographs of Francis Blake," stresses the modernity of Blake's achievement in photography.

CHAPTER 10

BLAKE AT HOME

A s his interest in photography waned, Blake returned to his greatest passion, Keewaydin. For the next decade, scarcely a week passed without a tradesman on the grounds. In the spring of 1893, Blake decided to have his entire house encased in a shell of Perth Amboy brick, and install new sills and lintels of Nova Scotia sandstone. He also decided to expand the house further. At the beginning of the summer, 32,700 pounds of brick arrived. In June, after returning to Keewaydin from a trip to Chicago, Elizabeth found the estate in "confusion & the house surrounded with workmen." Nevertheless, she liked the house's new look and tolerated the slow pace that had been set: "Weeks more will be needed to finish the work."[1]

Construction continued through July and into August. Blake, who closely managed all construction at Keewaydin, recorded in his diary the names of the workmen, what they did each day, and changes in agreements with contractors. By the time the bricklayers had reached the roof and towers, the Blakes had departed for the Adirondacks, their new late-summer resort. Work finally tapered off toward the end of September. George Metcalf, a friend from nearby Framingham who had viewed the estate while passing on the train, wrote Blake to say how delightful the house appeared. Train riders now enjoyed an enhanced view of the estate as a result of the installation of the new Boston & Albany tracks, which rested on higher ground than the original ones, making the house more visible above the balustrade at the top of the terraced gardens.[2]

The same summer, Blake also built a cow barn into a hillside northeast of the Cottage complex. It rested on a stone foundation about twenty-two by sixty feet in size and contained two calf pens, two horse stalls, and six cow stalls with mangers. It also had gutters leading to a trap door that opened to a manure pit in the center of the ground floor. Grain and hay chutes led from the loft above, and a dormer with doors and tackle for

Keewaydin in brick from the sunken garden. By Francis Blake, 1893. #57.528

hoisting hay sat over the main entrance. When construction ended in August 1893, Blake possessed a beautiful structure, complete with custommade iron gutters, matching spruce floorboards in the loft, blind hinges and T irons, a hay chute, a hayfork run, hay doors, ramps to cow and horse stalls, oat and sand bins, feed troughs, mangers, stone drinking troughs, dressed stone thresholds, iron window bars, a concrete manure pit, and a pigeon house with a laid floor. Few other Americans would do so much for ten animals, but Blake would settle for nothing less than the very best.[3]

While Blake spent lavishly on Keewaydin, he did not spend foolishly. His meticulous oversight continued to frustrate contractors. A plumber's bill for $1,698.39 for a new bath left Blake fuming. He demanded that the plumber submit daily reports of the work done on his property for the previous three years. After examining and annotating the account, comparing its materials' prices with a Walworth catalog, and reviewing all the records from March 1892 to February 1895, Blake contacted the plumber, Henry Hussey of Henry Hussey & Co. He informed Hussey that his bills included "grossly inaccurate charges for labor and exorbitant charges for stock. I therefore decline to pay it. To avoid the annoyance of a lawsuit, . . ." Blake offered $1,300 to settle the account. If Hussey did not like the settlement, he could contact "my counsel, Messrs. Storey & Thorndike of Boston who will answer for me any proceedings you may take toward the collection of your bill." The plumber elected to settle.[4]

Although Blake had once again become preoccupied with developing Keewaydin, he did not lose his interest in the process of invention. He continued to dabble in a variety of areas, with a special interest in the health field. Back in 1887, he had discovered that six of his herd of ten cows had become infected with tuberculosis, and his subsequent correspondence with veterinarians and doctors led him to discuss his experience at the Thursday Evening Club in February 1890. Blake related how, for all he knew, he had owned one of the healthiest herds in the commonwealth, so a veterinarian's diagnosis of tuberculosis in six of his animals had come as a shock. Autopsies of the diseased animals later confirmed the diagnosis.

But when a microscopic analysis of one of his cow's milk could not confirm presence of the disease, Blake said that he became concerned. He met with the official inspector of milk in Boston and learned that, while the city stood ready to punish a particular dairyman for watering down his milk, it ignored the transmission of deadly diseases. Blake urged club members to test their herds and obtain regular health certificates for those herds that supplied milk to their homes. He further urged them to use their influence to "secure prompt and decisive legislative action in the interest of humanity."[5]

Perhaps his herd's illness led Blake to greater interest in the field of medicine. In the late 1890s, he applied his mechanical genius to the microtome, an instrument used to slice single micron specimens for the preparation of microscope slides. In May 1897, Charles S. Minot, an anatomical physician from Harvard University, informed Blake that he had been using the new microtome in his laboratory and found that it worked far better than any available. Blake apparently had yet another microtome in preparation that "greatly bettered the wheel microtome." The two men, along with Blake's laboratory assistant, Tom Cloonan, cooperated to improve the device.[6]

On June 3, Blake demonstrated his new microtome to Dr. J. H. Wright of the Pathological Laboratory at the Massachusetts General Hospital. Following its successful operation, Blake asked Minot if he approved of the new name he had given to the instrument, the Minot-Blake Microtome. Minot preferred "to have your microtome known as the Blake-Minot Wheel Microtome."[7] Blake and Cloonan continued to refine the device, and in February 1898 Wright and another physician visited Keewaydin to test the refined instrument. "Both of them seemed to be much astonished and delighted at the results attained with two and single micron feeds." The following day Wright used it at Massachusetts General Hospital, where he found that it "proved to be most satisfactory under the microscope." After some additional refinements, the device was ready for general use. In January 1899, Blake presented a paper to the Boston Society of Medical Science, describing his new microtome, which the society published in its journal that month. Blake sought no compensation for his work, seemingly content with the knowledge that he had helped science.[8]

In 1887 Blake had purchased sixty acres of land between the Charles River and the Boston & Albany Railroad from William S. Seaverns. He learned after the purchase that the town of Weston had plans to build a road through the property. In a July 1887 letter to Alonzo Fiske, chairman the road commissioners of Weston, Blake complained that he had not received an invitation to a meeting the Weston road commissioners and county commissioners held regarding the town's plans. In his letter, Blake revealed that he intended to establish "Riverside Village," a subdivision of moderately priced houses, on the former Seaverns farmland. Blake's astonishing "village" proposal might simply have been a bold attempt to halt the town's plans. In July, Blake met with the commissioners, and eventually the town dropped the idea of a road across Blake's property. But Blake did hire his landscape architect Ernest Bowditch to draw up plans for the village.[9]

Clearly, Blake did not intend to build anything in the near future. No plans for "Riverside Village" survive among his papers (although they may remain in private hands), but receipts in the Blake papers indicate that Bowditch surveyed the land and produced plans for the project. Creating a moderately priced housing project in a bucolic setting along the Charles River most likely appealed to Blake. Some of Blake's happiest childhood years took place in a similar setting when the Blake family lived in David Sears's Brookline community. Furthermore, the passing of the elder Hubbards and Sewalls positioned Blake as the new family patriarch. As time passed, his role as clan leader strengthened, pleasing him enormously. His contemplated village would have greatly expanded the world of Keewaydin and its essential idea, that of a relatively self-contained compound created and governed by Blake.

Prior to any development of his plans for the village, the Boston Athletic Association (BAA), in April 1890, approached Blake about acquiring some of the Seaverns land along the Charles River. Blake hesitated, but indicated that he might agree to lease the property. The association examined Bowditch's topographical survey and requested ten to twelve acres, including river front. Bowditch suggested that, as part of the plan, the two parties share the cost of building a span across the Charles River to link the Riverside railroad station to Blake's land across the river.[10]

For about two years, the proposal languished. Then in May 1892, Arthur Hunnewell of the BAA again approached Blake about the property. By that time, however, the Boston & Albany Railroad had plans to realign their tracks and add two additional ones, thus requiring more land and possibly threatening the views that Blake and his neighbors so dearly prized. Charles W. Hubbard, who owned the land beyond the railroad, granted an easement to Blake and two other neighbors and agreed to allow no building on the land other than that suitable for a public park. He then conveyed the property to the town of Weston to be used as a park.[11] Blake, who also became committed to the park idea and to preserving the character of the Charles River Valley, initiated a series of land swaps and sales with Hubbard and the railroad company to increase his holdings, protect the area from industrial development, and provide the railroad some of the land it needed.[12]

While continuing with his property reorganization, Blake resumed negotiations with the BAA, and in May 1893 he sold the association over twenty acres. To maintain the beauty of the area, the deed included restrictions designed to retain the rural character of the land. There was to be no factory, mill, machine shop, slaughterhouse, hospital, or asylum placed there, and all fences were to be "neat and usual," without advertisements. Moreover, there were to be no buildings on the property other than a boathouse or park building.[13]

With their agreement in hand, Blake and the BAA cooperated on erecting a bridge across the Charles River. In May 1894, Blake acquired a strip of land adjacent to the Newton Boat Club, fronting on the river and Charles Street, which provided the access they needed to erect the bridge. Ernest Bowditch designed a new access road and William G. S. Chamberlain, a civil engineer of the Boston & Albany Railroad, designed the bridge.[14] "With the deepest regret," the Newton Boat Club opposed Blake's plans. A railroad bridge already stood near their property, and an additional bridge on their facility would, the club asserted, seriously interfere with the pleasure the public derived from the river. They argued that no compelling need for an additional structure existed, because access for Blake and the BAA could be established by suspending a footbridge from the railroad bridge. Blake rejected the club's views, stating that both he and the BAA considered their plans absolutely essential to the development of their properties. He would, however, make every effort to produce a bridge that would be "as unobjectionable as possible, from an aesthetic as well as a practical point of view." Blake assured the club that both he and the BAA considered preservation of the river's natural beauty their priority.[15]

But the Newton Boat Club did not accept Blake's assurances and attempted to preempt his scheme. The club petitioned the Newton Park Commissioners to designate a public park on the property between the boat club and the South Avenue Bridge, which included the property Blake had purchased for his bridge. Blake immediately urged Henry Parkman, the BAA's president, to buy property on the Newton side of the river to establish standing as a claimant for damages should their right of way across the river be taken. Fearing what the club might do, Blake warned the BAA to act swiftly. "If things were in my hands alone, I would have the bridge in place within the next ten days, and talk about it afterward." On June 13, the BAA bought a half interest in Blake's Newton property.[16]

Chamberlain had designed a bridge for Blake and the BAA, but the controversy smoldered for a year without resolution. Then on May 3, 1895, the club's new president, Charles W. Hubbard, informed Blake that the Newton Boat Club had withdrawn its objections to the bridge. Once again, family contacts proved crucial to Blake. Before the end of the month, nine men and four horses were pulling trees, and the King Bridge Company received a commission to erect a steel bridge for Blake and the Boston Athletic Association. By October, workers had installed piers and abutments. On February 5, 1896, Blake met with the foreman of the Riverside Bridge erecting gang to finalize acceptance of their work, a bridge 189 feet long and 20 feet wide. Blake and the BAA had spent $4,360.46 for convenient access to their properties.[17]

With construction of the bridge and an elaborate new entrance to Keewaydin, Blake dropped any further development plans for the Seaverns property. Although the remaining farmland provided valuable support to his stable and barn, Blake recognized the need to preserve the beauty of the Charles River. Having become a Weston town selectman in 1886, Blake investigated relevant laws and described his plans for the land along the Charles River at a December 31, 1892, town meeting. He overcame any existing opposition and gained the town's approval for the park, thereby preventing the railroad from taking it. Boston's Metropolitan Park Commission's plans for the Charles River Reservation dovetailed perfectly with Blake's desires, and he hoped that the commission would ultimately take over the town's park. As part of his campaign to preserve the region, in January 1893 he wrote to the *Boston Traveller*, pledging that when the MPC agreed to create its reservation and take over the park, he would donate the half-mile of riverbank that he owned between the Riverside and Weston bridges.[18]

In answer to an MPC inquiry, Blake wrote in June 1894 that he wished to preserve all his land bordering the Charles River in Weston as a public park.[19] Blake attended many meetings and hearings on the Charles River, and in March 1896, addressed representative Charles F. Sprague, chairman of the committee on Metropolitan Affairs, asking him to help move along plans for the reservation. "Having lived for nearly a quarter of a century in full view of one of the most beautiful reaches of the Charles River," Blake wrote, "I am impressed with the fact that it has, from year to year, made steady progress toward becoming to the inhabitants of Boston and her suburbs what the upper Thames is to the inhabitants of London." The stretch of the Charles River beyond Newton and Weston, Blake reminded Sprague, "has preserved its natural beauty to a remarkable degree; and I believe that the broadest and most persuasive reasons exist in favor of such beneficent action by the Commonwealth as shall result in our handing down to posterity this example of Nature's choicest handiwork."[20]

Blake's lobbying was influential, and the same year the commission filed a plan to take land along the Charles River, including Blake's and Hubbard's property, for the reservation. Blake had made a considerable personal investment in this early effort at conservation. He even opened Keewaydin to public viewing of its gardens and landscaped property. Beginning some time prior to June 19, 1897, Blake invited the public to his estate one day a week. The commission received the final land contribution in August 1898, leaving Blake a half-acre wedge that allowed him access to the river.[21]

Blake added electricity to his estate in the winter of 1896[22] and a squash court in 1901. For a time, Blake's interest in physical activity had declined. But he recovered his old enthusiasm and returned to regularly rowing on the Charles and at Lake Saranac in the Adirondacks during the family's summer retreat. His desire for a squash court certainly testified to Blake's renewed vigor. The seventy incandescent lightbulbs that illuminated the court allowed Blake to play well into the evening.[23]

By the turn of the century, Blake had erected all the major facilities he desired for Keewaydin, but the estate's grounds and gardens offered endless opportunities for development. Each year, Blake's correspondence and account books revealed the extraordinary lengths he took to make Keewaydin a paradise. The terraced gardens overlooking the railroad lines provided an excellent location for espaliered fruit trees, and in July 1890, James Bowditch advised Blake that he would tour nurseries in New York and Pennsylvania in search of appropriate stock. A year later, Blake recorded the results of Bowditch's tour: pears, apricots, nectarines, plums, peaches, cherries, and dwarf apple trees.[24]

In addition to the Bowditch brothers, Blake also sought the landscaping advice of Benjamin Watson of Harvard's Bussey Institute. In her diary for June 1892, Elizabeth Blake noted that:

Professor Watson comes here every Tuesday to look over the place & decide about the thinning out of the trees. We have many fine specimens but too many to do well. [H]ad they been moved when small we should not have had to do the terrible work now necessary—over a hundred trees have been cut down. On the lawn near the west of the house is a Boncolor. [F]urther off another & better one to which everything else must be sacrificed. The inner boughs of the two lines of spruces on the border of the lawn have been cut out, they were not thriving, in fact, nearly dead, & the space left by the trimming make an arbor or a grove.[25]

Francis and Elizabeth Blake on the lawn of Keewaydin.
Unknown photographer, June 24, 1898. #57.788

Before the end of the month, Blake had cut down 410 trees, but they would hardly be missed. Blake planted thousands in their place. In 1895, he planted hundreds of white pines in the former Boston & Albany Railroad gravel pit and added 1,000 more a year later. When nearly all died, he replaced them the following summer. White pine planting reached a frenzied state in May 1905 when Elizabeth noted in her diary that the last of 12,000 pine trees arrived from Maine and had been planted on the remaining portion of the old William Seaverns farm property. Dry weather killed many of the trees, but another 1,600 replacements soon arrived.[26]

Blake painstakingly labeled many of his trees, but after a short time, few labels remained in place—so Blake invented a better one. His patent for the device (granted in April 1897) claimed that, "The herein—described label for trees, consisting of a plate adapted to bear against the tree, a nail passing through the plate and adapted to be driven part way into the tree, and means for yieldingly holding the plate upon the nail to permit the plate to move along the nail as the tree grows." During June and July 1895, Blake affixed his new label to hundreds of trees on his estate.[27] The labels attracted the attention of Olmstead, Olmstead, & Eliot, the famous Brookline landscape architects. Blake's reply to a correspondence between them stated that he had been using the new labels successfully for two years. Not only did they stay on the trees, but they accurately measured growth. "Before contriving this arrangement I had fastened each label to its tree by a zinc nail driven to the head. But at the end of two years fully 80% of the labels so attached were on the ground, having been forced over their nail heads by the growth of the trees." Blake sent Olmstead, Olmstead, & Eliot a sample label, but apparently nothing further developed. Although Blake had secured a patent for his invention in 1901, when Henry Voorce Brandenburg & Co, New York patent brokers, offered their services to sell or put the invention into manufacture, he showed no interest.[28]

To maintain the estate's grounds, Blake hired a permanent staff of five full-time gardeners and groundskeepers, employing additional part-time help during the summer. According to family tradition, Blake had no difficulty hiring workers because Keewaydin enjoyed a reputation for feeding its employees exceptionally well. Each year's collection of bills and receipts shows the purchase of vast amounts of flowers and shrubs for the estate. When he wanted geraniums in 1890, for instance, he ordered 1,328 from Charles Evans in Watertown. In 1892, he ordered 3,600 tulips and 2,100 narcissus. And his greenhouses contained multitudes of tomatoes and roses, which he often gave away to family and friends. Blake planted so many flowers of so many varieties that he had to ask Ernest Bowditch to draw up detailed plans of the gardens. Then in 1912, he hired the Olmstead brothers to redesign them.[29]

The Blake children, Agnes and Benjamin, enjoyed every advantage life could bring. Following her home schooling, Agnes went on to Dana Hall School in 1890 and then to The School at 6 Marlboro Street in Boston. Benjamin attended the Williams School in Newton in 1890 and then studied with a series of private tutors, including Ernest Jackson, who prepared students for Harvard. Agnes received dancing lessons from August Papanti and from a Miss Post at Pierce Hall in Boston. On January 14, 1895, she was able to display her dancing at her debutante ball. The event exceeded even Blake's standards of quality and set the pattern for debutante balls in Boston. Elizabeth Blake's diary recorded some of the splendor.

Tomorrow at this time we expect to be in town, where we shall pass the night, nearly all of it at our party at Peirce Hall, the rest of it at the Hotel Vendome. We shall go in after dinner at 7-19 P. M. dress at the Vendome & go to the hall at ten oc. We have invited about two hundred & sixty exclusive of the aunts & uncles. They have not all answered but 72 girls & 118 men have accepted. The hall is to be decorated by Galvin the florist who employs someone to attend to the furnishing aside from flowers. It is to be in gold & white. Red has been used also pink at parties there this winter & I like white & gold & am glad to know that it has not been used. Smilax which grows at the South is to nearly cover the walls, & gold tinsel will be used. The curtains, sofas, & mirrors will have white & gold. The flowers will be white lilies, roses & white carnations.[30]

"The party at Pierce Hall last Monday was beautiful," Elizabeth wrote. "The hall was then ready the decorator arranging vases of flowers in the small rooms. Agnes received a beautiful bouquet of Mermet roses with white hyacinths on one side & smilax from Mr. L. C. Deming, Sy's friend, also pink roses from Mr. F. W. Welch & from Mrs. Charles H. Pitts. Agnes' dress white tulle over white satin with white lilacs & white satin ribbon trimming is a very pretty, dainty dress & she was lovely. . . . It was said to be the prettiest ball ever given there. It was even prettier than I had expected & that was much for I felt sure it would be a beautiful sight."[31]

Outside Pierce Hall, Blake had set up an awning with two policemen and carriage checks to expedite the arrival and departure of guests. For the guests' coachmen, who had to stand by throughout the night, Blake engaged a night lunch-wagon to provide coffee, cocoa, frankfurters, milk, and sandwiches. He also arranged for two special streetcars to run from Copley Square to Harvard Square at 4:30 A.M. The Boston newspapers enthusiastically reported the ball, praising especially the floral decoration, the beauty of the gowns, and the provisions for the coachmen, which represented yet another Blake innovation. The event was not only a defining moment in Agnes's life, but symbolized Blake's ascent to the crest of Boston society.[32]

Expectations for Benjamin proved more rigorous, and the results less satisfactory. Despite Ernest Jackson's tutoring, Ben did poorly in school, and his first attempt to enter Harvard in the fall of 1896 failed. After another year of tutoring and preparation he made a second effort to enter the class of 1901, but won acceptance only through special pleading on his father's part. "Would it be possible to reexamine his paper to see if there is more proof of knowledge than a routine examination would disclose?" Blake asked Professor John W. White, who administered the Greek entrance examination.[33] Benjamin struggled through Harvard, and the next year only the intervention of his father allowed him to register as a sophomore without probation. Harvard agreed to permit Benjamin to reach the junior class only if the combined records of his first two years justified the promotion. Blake assured Dean Le Baron Briggs that his son fully "appreciates the obligation he is under to exert himself to the end that his record for the current year may justify the consideration he has been given."[34] Benjamin justified his father's efforts, and with additional tutoring graduated with his class.

Agnes presented an entirely different type of problem to her father. A pretty, eligible young lady, Agnes was bound to attract promising young men. Alfred Rodman, who had been one of the ushers at her debutante party, soon began calling at Keewaydin. His increasing attentiveness toward Agnes aroused Blake's notice and before long "he had practically offered himself to Agnes and that she has neither refused nor accepted him." Blake, despite his own overheated romance with Elizabeth, felt compelled to deflect Rodman's advances. In May 1896, he wrote the young man, declaring that we "cannot ignore the fact that in many grave particulars— for which you alone have been responsible—your life has not been one which entitles you to the life of our daughter."[35]

What Blake had in mind at this point is unclear. But Rodman left for Europe, which temporarily resolved the problem. When he returned that fall, Rodman again appeared at Keewaydin for dinner. Blake became alarmed when his wife informed him that "Agnes has about decided to accept him."[36] On November 21, Rodman informed Blake that he and Agnes wanted permission to announce their engagement. Blake's suspicions about Rodman's intentions were confirmed by his daughter, who had opposed Rodman's desire to seek her parents' permission to marry. After a family discussion, Elizabeth wrote to Rodman that he was not to visit Agnes again.[37]

Despite the decision, the persistent Rodman returned to Keewaydin, and on February 19, 1897, the two announced their engagement at a tea party for about sixty guests. Blake did not attend and instead lunched at the Somerset Club and played whist until early evening. When he returned home—the family stayed at 246 Beacon Street in Boston for the winter—very few relatives remained. Clearly, something was amiss.

A suspicious silence about wedding plans broke on June 7 when Agnes told her father that Alfred Rodman had accumulated over $1,000 in debt and that unless he immediately came up with $500, creditors would bring him to court. Agnes then told her father that she did not wish to marry Rodman, but she cared enough for him to sell her two shares of American Bell Telephone Company stock and to give him the $500. Instead, Blake gave Agnes a check for the amount, and that night she induced Rodman to accept it and break their engagement.

Rodman continued to haunt Agnes's life. Irate, Blake hired a private detective to investigate him, and the news could hardly have been worse. Rodman, under the assumed name of Gibson, lived with a woman in Boston. The end had come. "At the request of my daughter," Blake wrote Rodman, "I write to inform you that her knowledge of your intercourse with 'Mrs. Alfred Gibson' at No. 116 Dartmouth Street, Boston, prevents her from taking any further interest in your life."[38] In 1906, Agnes married Stephen Salisbury Fitzgerald. The couple lived at Keewaydin until 1911, when Blake gave them a house and lot on his property. Benjamin married Ruth Field in 1908, and after a period of living at home, they moved into Pine Cottage, a nearby building Blake had acquired in one of his earlier transactions.

Blake considered the care of his family to be his absolute duty, a responsibility he extended to his and Lizzie's siblings, including his wife's, nieces, nephews, aunts, uncles, and cousins. His assistance came in the form of advice, trusteeships, direct financial aid, and abundant hospitality.[39] He managed the Trumbull estate in Worcester and the estate of his sister-in-law, Louisa S. Jackson, who had been living abroad for many years after leaving her husband. Blake handled her assets and sent her quarterly payments right up until a few days before his death. In 1901, Blake became a trustee of the Benjamin Sewall Trust, the principal source of income for members of the Hubbard family since Benjamin Sewall's death. Upon the death of his brother-in-law, Charles B. Wells, on March 3, 1902, Blake became executor and sole trustee of his estate as well.[40]

Blake continued to support his poor sister-in-law Margie Blake with a monthly allowance. When her son William entered Brown University, Blake increased the allowance and financed young Charles's education at Worcester Polytechnic Institute. When college did not work out for him, Blake supported his nephew's search for an appropriate career. He also came to the aid of his cousin and best friend, Russell Sullivan. They remained close throughout Blake's life and in December 1893, when Russell succumbed to disease-induced blindness, Blake offered financial support until his full recovery. To the degree that Blake had been self-absorbed as a younger man, he was now caring and responsible.[41]

Endnotes

1. Blake, Diary, Apr. 24, 1893, FBP. According to a memorandum at the end of his 1897 diary, Blake spent $4,167.60 for the bricks and other improvements. Elizabeth Blake, Diary, July 9, 1893, FBP. This entry describes the condition of the house as the Blakes found it on June 19, FBP.

2. J. A. DeLacey to Blake, Sept. 22, 1893, FBP; George Metcalf to Blake, Sept. 17, 1893, FBP.

3. Andrews, Jacques & Rantoul to Blake, Nov. 23, 1892, FBP; Blake, Diary, May 20, 1893, FBP. In the fall of 1892, Blake engaged the Boston firm of Andrews, Jacques & Rantoul to develop plans for the cow barn.

4. Blake to Henry Hussey, May 11, 1895 (copy), June 1895 (undated copy), FBP; Henry Hussey to Blake, May 20, 1895, FBP; "Beware of all Claims," Henry Hussey to Blake, June 20, 1895, vol. 14, 122–128, FBP.

5. While the complete text of Blake's talk has not been found, there is an article about it including some quotations clipped from a newspaper in his scrapbook in vol. 43, FBP.

6. Dr. Charles S. Minot to Blake, May 10, 1897, FBP; Blake, Diary, May 22, 1897, FBP.

7. Dr. Charles S. Minot to Blake, June 9, 1897, FBP.

8. Blake, Diary, Feb. 17, 1898, FBP.

9. Blake to Alonzo Fiske, July 9, 12, 1887, FBP; Ernest Bowditch to Blake, Aug. 5, 1887, FBP; Middlesex County Registry of Deeds, vol. 1789, p. 481.

10. Meredith & Nelson to Blake, Apr. 24, 1890, FBP; Ernest Bowditch to Blake, Aug. 1, 1890, FBP.

11. Arthur Hunnewell to Blake, May 26, 1892, FBP; Middlesex County Registry of Deeds, vol. 2166, p. 589; vol. 2166, p. 590.

12. Middlesex County Registry of Deeds, vol. 2216, pp. 229 and 231 and Plan Book 82, plans 46 and 47, vol. 2259, p. 312; vol. 2387, p. 184; vol. 2389, p. 201.

13. Blake to Arthur Hunnewell, Mar. 24, 1893, FBP; Middlesex County Registry of Deeds, vol. 2192, p. 326, 329; Plan Book 81, p. 48.

14. Blake to William G. S. Chamberlain May 26, 1894, FBP; Middlesex County Registry of Deeds, vol. 2278, p. 245.

15. Newton Boat Club to Blake, May 25, 1894, FBP; Blake to Severance Burrage, Secretary, Newton Boat Club, Aug. 26, 1894, FBP.

16. Blake to Henry Parkman, May 31, 1894, FBP; Middlesex County Registry of Deeds, vol. 2386–2386. Although dated June 13, 1894, the deed was not recorded until July 24, 1895, suggesting the two parties wanted to get the transfer in writing and retain some flexibility.

17. Charles W. Hubbard to Blake, May 3, 1895, FBP; Blake, Diary, May 30, 1895, Feb. 5, 1896 FBP.

18. Blake to F. T. Fuller, Jan. 5, 1893, FBP.

19. Blake to S. Parkman Blake, June 4, 1894, FBP.

20. Blake to Charles F. Sprague, Mar. 14, 1896 (copy), FBP.

21. Middlesex County Registry of Deeds, vol. 2681, p. 201; vol. 2885, p. 579; Blake, Diary, June 19, 1897, FBP.

22. Blake's diary provides a daily room-by-room account of the progress of the wiring.

23. Keewaydin plan book, pp. 44, 45, FBP; Blake to Dr. William S. Bigelow, July 12, 1901, FBP.

24. James Bowditch to Blake, July 31, 1890, FBP. A bill from James Bowditch to Blake for fruit trees, May 18, 1891, is in vol. 11, p. 120, FBP; Blake, Diary, Mar. 25, 1891, FBP.

25. Elizabeth Blake, Diary, June 5, 1892, FBP.

26. Elizabeth Blake, Diary, June 19, 1892, Aug. 9, 1895, May 28, Oct. 1, 3, 1905, FBP.

27. Blake, Diary, June and July 1895, *passim*, FBP.

28. Olmstead, Olmstead, & Eliot to Blake, May 22, 1896, FBP; Henry Voorce Brandenburg & Co. to Blake, July 3, 1901, FBP.

29. Mrs. Arthur Blake to Blake, Feb. 15, 1893, FBP; Ernest Bowditch to Blake, Apr. 13, 1898, FBP; bill from Charles Evans to Blake, July 30, 1890, bill from Benjamin Watson, Oct. 1892, bill from Olmsted brothers to Blake, Aug. 1, 1912, FBP; Elizabeth Blake, Diary, Oct. 23, 1892, FBP; Keewaydin plan book, p. 21, FBP.

30. Elizabeth Blake, Diary, Jan. 13, 1895, FBP.

31. Elizabeth Blake, Diary, Jan. 14, 1895, FBP.

32. Bills for the ball are in vol. 14, FBP; unidentified newspaper clipping in "Elizabeth Hubbard Blake, 1842–1908" series, FBP.

33. Blake to Professor John W. White, July 3, 1897, FBP.

34. Dean L. B. R. Briggs to Blake, Oct. 25, 1898, FBP; Blake to Dean Le Baron Briggs, Oct. 27, 1898 (copy), FBP.

35. Blake, Diary, May 16, 1896, FBP; Blake to Alfred Rodman, May 29, 1896, (copy), FBP.

36. Blake, Diary, Nov. 5, 1897, FBP.

37. Blake, Diary Nov. 2, 22, 1897, FBP.

38. Box 69 contains reports from detective James R. Wood about Rodman's activities. Vol. 17 contains the bill covering Nov. 25 to Dec. 9, for Wood's services. Blake to Alfred Rodman, Dec. 10, 1898, FBP.

39. Middlesex County Registry of Deeds, vol. 3570, p. 60; vol. 3623, p. 442. Blake acquired the Herbert Seaverns farm on Dec. 16, 1910 and conveyed it to Agnes on July 29, 1911.

40. "Trumbull Estate, 1881–1910" series, FBP. The final account was rendered Oct. 31, 1910. "Louisa S. Jackson Trust, 1889–1913" series and "Charles B. Welles Estate 1902–1912" series, FBP.

41. Charles B. Blake to Blake, Mar. 13, 1901, FBP; Blake to Charles B. Blake, Nov. 14, 1901 (copy), FBP; Blake to Margie Blake, Nov. 15, 1901 (copy), FBP. Correspondence between Blake, Sullivan, and Mary L. Cochrane in Dec. 1893, describes Sullivan's illness and Blake's assistance.

CHAPTER 11

LAST YEARS

I N THE REMAINING YEARS of his life, Blake devoted himself to his family and to public service. Relatives and friends in need could count on Blake for assistance. He had completed his major Keewaydin projects, and now increasingly turned his attention to the community beyond his estate. His support for the Charles River Reservation and his many years as a town selectman typified Blake's strong sense of civic responsibility, but by no means fully encompassed his commitment to public welfare. Blake also served as chairman of a visiting committee at Harvard University, a member of the corporation of the Massachusetts Institute of Technology, trustee of the Massachusetts General Hospital and the Museum of Fine Arts, Boston, and treasurer of the American Academy of Arts and Sciences.[1]

Blake became a central figure in Weston town government. He helped secure new fire fighting equipment, calculated the cost of a new bridge across the Charles, and helped build the town's new library. As was the custom, Blake returned his token pay as selectman to the town for the purchase of library materials. When Weston outgrew its new library within a few years, in part due to Blake's many contributions, he oversaw construction of its replacement. He even helped design the town's first official seal.[2] As Clerk of the Board of Selectmen, Blake was involved in nearly all of the town's routine business, including management of the schools and water supply, road maintenance, fire protection, and regulation of utilities, in addition to his role as an overseer of the poor. He also drafted warrants for town meetings and prepared annual reports. Seeing firsthand the precarious condition of the town's early records, Blake oversaw their transcription and eventual publication. In all, Blake devotedly served Weston as a selectman for nineteen years.[3]

Politically, Blake fell into the stalwart Republican camp. He detested Massachusetts governor Benjamin F. Butler, a controversial Democrat. A request from his cousin Stanton Blake to assist the Republican state executive committee "in conducting the fight against Butler," elicited a $250 contribution from Blake.[4] But like so many other state Republicans, he was not stalwart enough to support the party's 1884 presidential nominee, James G. Blaine. He not only gave to the opposition, but became president of Weston's Independent Club. The club's July 26 broadside proclaimed that the Republican candidate's "official record denies him the title of an honest man." While on the other hand, Grover Cleveland's "official record is above reproach" and his "political actions have alienated him from all that is bad in his own party." Blake's name stood at the top of a list of twenty subscribers who supported the Democrat party's candidate for president.[5]

On August 20, 1884, the once-radical-abolitionist and Civil War hero Col. Thomas Wentworth Higginson spoke at an Independent Club meeting. As president of the meeting, Blake introduced Higginson and welcomed those present, "Not as Republicans—not as Democrats—but as honest men." For Blake, the issues at stake in the election could not have been simpler or more fundamental. He defended his abandonment of the Republican party as a necessity.

This independent movement may fairly be said to be a protest against the corruption which has sprung up within the Republican party during the long years that it has had control of our national affairs. A grand old party it has been in the past! and a grand old party it may yet be in the future; but just at the moment when it calls upon us to give our votes to him who represents the very worst elements of its corruption—who has used his public office as an instrument of private gain we proudly throw off our party allegiance and pledge our votes to him who although called a democrat has been in his official life all that a true republican should be.[6]

Blake's independent reform spirit proved short-lived. After Cleveland's victory, he returned to the Republican party, remained a major contributor at the local, state, and national levels, and always voted the straight party ticket. In 1895, Elizabeth Blake became the first woman to vote in a Weston local election, but she and her husband voted against municipal suffrage for women. The Democratic party, particularly under the sway of the great commoner William Jennings Bryan, horrified Blake. Although he didn't regret his previous support for Cleveland, Bryan "has convinced me that it is my duty to become heart and soul a member of the Republican Party. There are, of course, faults to be corrected therein; but to my mind they become infinitesimal when compared to the monstrous faults of the Democratic Party."[7]

Blake's interest in reform did not go much beyond civic betterment and promotion of good government. Beginning in 1888, he had served as a director of the Massachusetts Society for Promoting Good Citizenship. From time to time, he also had maintained membership in the Citizens' Association of Boston, the National Club of Massachusetts, the Election Laws League of Massachusetts, and the Massachusetts Civil Service Reform Association, but never became especially active in any of them.[8] Beginning in the fall of 1899, Blake joined the New England Watch and Ward Society, formerly known as the New England Society for the Suppression of Vice. Blake apparently joined the society without much awareness of its activities or history. Dr. W. S. Bigelow, a friend from the Thursday Club, explained to Blake that the Watch and Ward Society "used to be run by a set of prurient fanatics (who had dragged in a number of innocent and respectable people) for the Promotion of Virtue by the Abolition of the Social Evil—a task which they went at by raiding & closing all the most quiet and respectable assignation houses as well as the dives, & did a lot of mischief by stirring up the sediment which was perfectly quiet at the bottom of the bottle & scattering the whores all through the community—to say nothing of the effect on the men." He urged Blake to read some of the society's annual reports to see if they had given up their annoying war on vice.[9]

Blake, on the other hand, did not need to read "their ancient reports" to conclude that the organization's "crusade against the 'Social Evil'—so called was unwise and unworthy . . . of anyone who does not wish to over-throw a system which, while it may be open to narrow minded moral ob-jections, on the whole—taking society as it is—ensures the greatest good to the greatest number." He believed that the society could perform a valuable function in mitigating the worst aspects of prostitution, but he found its busybody moral absolutism repugnant. It needed, to his mind, more "liberal" voices to "act as a balance wheel against such erratic or fa-natic impulses as may naturally proceed from a machine which is driven by the super-heated fervor of religion and morals rather than by the low pressure of common sense." Although Blake remained a member for sev-eral years, the change of heart he sought for the organization failed to ma-terialize. The society's moral campaign against local booksellers in 1904 finally drove Blake out. "After mature consideration," Blake wrote, "of the action of the Society in prosecuting reputable Boston book-sellers for hav-ing on sale books which (in my opinion) should be found in every library of classical literature, I ask that my name be stricken from the list of its life members."[10]

Blake preferred to invest his energies in those institutions that helped to increase knowledge, not restrict it. The Jefferson Physical Laboratory at Harvard became one of his chief interests. Although he never attended Harvard University, or any other college, Blake had developed a close re-lationship with Harvard's observatory and science departments during his days with the U.S. Coast Survey. Beginning in 1881, he had served as a member of the "Committee on Mathematics, Physics and Chemistry"—renamed the "Committee to Visit the Physical Laboratory and Depart-ment of Physics" in 1889. Such committees, with long histories at Harvard, brought together specialists from a variety of fields to monitor the quality of teaching, staffing, and facilities for the university's many departments. In December 1890, Blake became chairman of the "Committee to Visit the Jefferson Physical Laboratory and Department of Physics." He arranged the annual inspection tour and submitted a written report to the board of overseers. In addition to commenting on improvements in the laboratory over the previous year, Blake suggested further ways the university might advance the laboratory's work.[11]

Blake's close relationship with laboratory director John Trowbridge proved an important asset to the Jefferson Physical Laboratory. Trowbridge encouraged his students to carry on original research and worked hard to furnish his facility with the best equipment, which won Blake's enthusiastic support. He understood that technological advancement depended upon companies such as the American Bell Telephone Company having access to well-trained and able young men. The laboratory could fill that vital role, and Blake wished to do whatever he could to help it. After one of Trowbridge's visits to Keewaydin, Blake donated a Brown & Sharpe universal milling machine to the laboratory. In 1890, Blake assumed leadership of the effort to create a $50,000 endowment in honor of Joseph Lovering, the laboratory's first director. A weakened economy frustrated Blake's plans, but he raised enough funds to hire a full-time mechanic to maintain the laboratory's equipment, which had been one of the campaign's objectives.[12] Despite this all-too-common failure, Blake proved an important contributor and retained Harvard's gratitude.

In October 1896, Blake informed Dr. Alexander McKenzie, secretary of the board of overseers, that he wished to retire from the visiting committee. The news alarmed Trowbridge. "It is the opinion of the Physical Department," he advised his colleague Charles Francis Adams, "that the retirement of Mr. Francis Blake from the Committee, appointed to visit the Laboratory, would be a great loss to the department. We have profited in every way by his knowledge of the proper mechanical equipment of the laboratory, and the department would regard his resignation as a calamity."[13] Blake read Trowbridge's letters and agreed to continue his service. Six years later, Blake suggested that Professor Elihu Thompson of the Massachusetts Institute of Technology should succeed him as chairman of the visiting committee. Blake's appointment by Harvard's board of overseers to head the visiting committee for twelve successive years had been, he asserted, a "most agreeable surprise." But he advised the board that if the university expected the Jefferson Physical Laboratory to attain international stature, the chairman of its visiting committee must possess a worldwide scientific reputation. Whatever the merits of Blake's argument, Harvard had no intention of giving up someone of Blake's experience and wealth. In 1902, Harvard recognized his service by awarding him an honorary Master of Arts degree.[14] Blake had provided expert guidance for the committee, and his influence on the university board of overseers made the laboratory a better place to perform basic research. He continued as chairman until April 27, 1905, when weakening health finally compelled him to resign. Representing the board of overseers, Charles Francis Adams expressed the university's appreciation for all he had contributed and its "regret at your inability to serve further, and the sense of loss to the University thereby incurred. . . ."[15]

Blake also proved an important advocate for the Massachusetts Institute of Technology, and in May 1889, he was elected to MIT's corporation. But after three years, when he tendered his resignation in March 1892, President Francis A. Walker refused to accept it. Blake's resignation, Walker explained, "Would be a loss to the school, which distinctly needs such influence as you can exert upon its instruction & management." He informed Blake that he would ask the executive committee of the corporation at its next meeting to appoint a new visiting committee on electrical engineering with Blake as chairman. Blake agreed to stay on, serving as chairman of that committee and also as a member of the committees on physics, mechanical engineering, chemistry and chemical engineering, and, later, biology.[16]

Blake also took great interest in several of MIT's staff members. In July 1897, one of them, Professor Silas Holman, informed Blake that he had written a book-length manuscript on matter, energy, force, and work. Holman described it as a "plain, logical exposition of certain fundamental ideas and definitions in Physics . . . somewhat novel in matter as well as in treatment." Although colleagues found the book valuable, Holman's publisher, Macmillan, believed that, whatever the book's merits, it would not be commercially successful. Holman sought Blake's advice. About to sail for France, Blake could not give the manuscript the reading it deserved. Nevertheless, "I have so much confidence as to the scientific and commercial value of your work," Blake wrote, "that I do not hesitate to offer to guarantee Messrs. Macmillan & Co. against any loss they may incur in publishing it." Blake's $500 subvention guaranteed the successful publication of Holman's book.[17]

In 1900, MIT chose Henry S. Pritchett as its new president. Pritchett, according to Herbert Putnam, the Librarian of Congress and a Blake correspondent, "Combines strikingly the scientific spirit with administrative ability and social aptitude."[18] Much to Blake's delight, Pritchett also had been superintendent of the United States Coast Survey. Blake lost no time in meeting the new president and making him feel welcomed, even proposing him for membership in the St. Botolph Club, one of several Brahmin eating establishments in Boston. When Pritchett visited Keewaydin in the summer of 1900, just before beginning his duties at MIT, Elizabeth Blake found him "very agreeable and it is delightful to see & hear someone so much interested in our dear, old Coast Survey. He must be sorry to leave it, but his new position is a great one & will I believe be made even greater by him. We like him very much."[19]

Pritchett's first year at MIT proved trying, and Blake's support encouraged the new president to remain at his post. He found in Blake an ideal advisor with whom he could discuss proposals before bringing them to the MIT board, as he apparently did in May 1901. In a letter written soon after, Blake assured Pritchett that the "more I think of it the stronger is my belief that the success of the Institute depends upon your ability to carry into effect the radical changes you have in mind." He encouraged Pritchett to stand his ground, believing that he would also get "a free hand and much better pecuniary compensation for the great work which lies before you."

But Pritchett had additional motives for confiding in Blake; he wanted the inventor to fund a "new building for the Department of Electrical Engineering." As much as he admired the former head of the Coast Survey and supported MIT, Blake had no interest in the project. "The popular estimate of my wealth must be much exaggerated," he told Pritchett. He lived on a fixed income and, as large as that might be, he already gave more than a sixth of it away to a variety of charities. "This fact and a prudent provision for the time when my estate must be divided between my two children," prevented him from providing the support MIT sought. "I wish, indeed, that I might be a second Carnegie to the Institute, the Massachusetts General Hospital, the Museum of Fine Arts, the Arnold Arboretum, the Jefferson Physical Laboratory, and the Harvard Medical School, the special needs of which have been brought to my notice during the last few years." Pritchett thanked Blake for his candor and assured him that "you can perform, and are so doing, in our Corporation a far higher service than giving money, namely to call attention in effective way to needed progress."[20] Blake continued his service for MIT until Pritchett left in 1909.

In Boston, someone of Blake's wealth and influence would be expected to fulfill an important philanthropic role. Indeed, the many charities and cultural institutions in the city depended upon Brahmin leadership and increasingly newer money like Blake's. Thus, in 1881 the American Academy of Arts and Sciences elected Blake a fellow. He served on the academy's library committee and was its treasurer from 1899 to 1906. He also became a member of the American Association for the Advancement of Science, the American Institute of Electrical Engineers, the Boston Society of Civil Engineers, and the International Electrical Congress of the 1893 Columbian Exposition. From 1897 to 1909, he served on the board of trustees of the Massachusetts General Hospital, and from 1898 through 1907 he was a trustee of the Museum of Fine Arts, Boston.

While men and women of Blake's class became involved in various philanthropies, many simultaneously turned a blind eye to their own employees. Blake's sense of civic responsibility ran deep. The Ludlow

Corporation, the principal business of Blake's father-in-law, Charles T. Hubbard, manufactured jute bagging, sacking, and twine. Hubbard had reorganized the business in 1868 from the remains of the defunct Springfield Manufacturing Company and its successor, the Ludlow Mills Company, and served as its treasurer. The firm grew dramatically over the years and employed scores of men and women. A true factory town, much like those of the early nineteenth century, Ludlow provided housing, a school, a bank, a library, water and electrical service, and parks and recreational facilities to the community. By 1901, thirty-three years after receiving its original charter, the company found itself operating well outside limitations placed on Massachusetts corporations. In an attempt to comply with state law, a board of nine trustees assumed control of the company on January 1, 1902, operating under a declaration of trust and renamed it the Ludlow Manufacturing Associates.[21]

In 1891, construction of a new plant in Allston, Massachusetts, placed Sewall & Day Cordage Company, another Hubbard family business, into debt. In a long letter to his brother-in-law, Bancroft Davis, husband of Anne Hubbard, Blake urged the Ludlow company to buy the new plant from Sewall & Day. To finance the purchase, Ludlow would issue additional stock and the Hubbard family would purchase a majority share to maintain its control. The purchase gave Ludlow the additional manufacturing capacity it needed, relieved Sewall & Day of its threatening debt, and, thanks to Blake, preserved the Hubbard family's assets.[22]

When Blake made the proposal, he acted as only a stockholder, albeit an important one, of the Ludlow company. By December 1897, Blake had become a central figure in the company's management and an auditor of its books.[23] With the establishment of the Ludlow Manufacturing Associates trust in 1902, he became its most influential trustee, one of a group that included Richard Weld, a Boston commission merchant, Charles W. Hubbard, who had succeeded his father as treasurer, Cranmore N. Wallace, president, John E. Stevens, manufacturing agent, Ernest W. Bowditch, Blake's landscape engineer, Henry Oliver Underwood, president of the William Underwood Company, packers of canned goods, and Emor H. Harding, a Boston realty trust lawyer. With few exceptions—Stevens, for instance, lived in Ludlow—the trustees were wealthy, accomplished, and respected Bostonians. While some became deeply involved in management, others, such as Blake, served in an advisory capacity with responsibility for policy and financial decisions. Blake assumed his role as trustee with intensity—others noted that Ludlow had become Blake's "particular pet."[24]

One need not go far to understand the reasons for Blake's interest in Ludlow. The company's stock could command at least $200 a share and earned 25 percent on its par value. Its earnings over dividends had been reinvested into the main plant, which by all accounts was magnificent. Blake believed that the company would enjoy a bright future and be extremely profitable. Four years later, a Boston stockbroker declared that Ludlow Associates did an annual business of $7,000,000, employed 3,000 people, and paid 10 percent regular and 2.5 percent extra dividends on its stock.[25]

By the summer of 1911, Blake's health began to decline. On July 19 he submitted his resignation to Wallace, Ludlow's president. The very idea of Blake's departure struck Wallace with a "deep sense of personal loss" and he urged Blake to delay any decision until the next annual meeting in December. Philip Dexter, lawyer for the Sewall estate, encouraged Blake to remain a Ludlow trustee, given the substantial amount of Sewall wealth invested in the company and Blake's unequaled talent. Blake relented and agreed to remain, a decision that proved critical to the company and to the town of Ludlow.[26]

Back in April 1911, Charles W. Hubbard had prepared a detailed report of the company's expenditures unrelated to manufacturing: housing, utilities, and especially the company's hospital. Because the Ludlow Associates represented the only significant source of town tax revenue—about 80 percent—and employment, the company found it reasonable to conduct business in the same manner that a municipality might. Because the company eventually paid for any town services through taxes, trustees concluded that they could provide those services directly at less expense, rather than funneling the money through town officials. In fact, the company waterworks and electric system proved profitable and supplied the necessary utilities to the factory during the day and to the town in the evening. The trustees also supported, as had been the case since the beginning of the industrial revolution in New England, the company's provision of cottages and tenements for its employees, together with schools and stores, to create the desired moral, social, and economic order. By the close of the nineteenth century, most industries had long abandoned what had been known as the Waltham system and adopted the more recognizable wage-labor system of today. But Ludlow could profitably supply the housing, hospital, church, utilities, athletic facilities, and other municipal services, at considerable cost, and still turn a profit.[27]

When Hubbard reported his findings at the January 1912 trustee meeting, he defended these community costs as business necessities and social duties that had formed the basis of the company since its founding by Charles T. Hubbard in 1868. Without such investments, Hubbard argued, the company would not have the community of loyal, healthy, able, well-trained employees of good character who currently ran its plant. Prosperity depended upon maintaining his father's original vision. But the $1,268,102 worth of property that the company owned in the village and the $23,025 it spent annually on nonmanufacturing activity caused grave concern among the other trustees.

Several restless trustees pointed directly at the $3,682 that the company spent every year on Ludlow's hospital, officially under the management of the Ludlow Hospital Society, which served both Ludlow employees and other citizens of the community. Additionally, in March 1912, C. E. Gowen, financial secretary of the Ludlow Hospital Society, contacted each Ludlow trustee and requested a personal contribution to the hospital. Perhaps the time had come, many of the trustees thought, to end all such drags on profitability, particularly at a time of keen competition from low-wage factories in the south.[28]

In March, Blake wrote a letter to fellow trustee Ernest Bowditch expressing his support for the hospital. He pointed out that the "Massachusetts General Hospital found its 'social service department' of great aid in its work. The Ludlow community is one in which the Trustees should, at least for business principles, support methods to make good health in the family." Clearly, Blake saw a paternal role for the company, not unlike his own governance of Keewaydin, that responsible trustees ought to have felt morally obliged to continue.[29] With his health failing and beginning to experience difficulty in speaking, Blake asked Bowditch to read his letter at the next meeting of the trustees. Bowditch happily agreed and suggested that he might also ask for a vote on the issue. Bowditch, however, did not share Blake's sentiments about the hospital. As a trustee, he accepted his share of responsibility for the amount of money the company currently expended on social services. Nevertheless, to his mind it came at the expense of Ludlow's primary manufacturing role. Most worrisome, Bowditch believed that other than Hubbard, Blake was the only trustee who favored continuing the company's commitment to the hospital.[30]

The previous summer, Benjamin Loring Young, Blake's nephew and trustee of the Benjamin Sewall estate, had investigated Ludlow's hospital. About a week after Blake wrote to Bowditch, Young reported his discoveries. A hospital or other form of regular medical assistance for Ludlow's employees and their families, he advised Blake, did not represent charity or even welfare work. Sound business sense and common decency demanded that the company continue to fulfill this obligation to the town. To drive home his point, Young cited the example of one female employee at Ludlow whose hand had been badly lacerated by a machine. Without readily available medical service, she might have become crippled or even died. Instead, she received prompt treatment and soon returned to work.[31]

Blake used Young's letter at the trustees' next meeting to stunning effect. On April 10, 1912, the Ludlow trustees, on Blake's motion, resolved that "in the opinion of the Trustees, the Ludlow Social Work is based on strong business principles displayed by its founders, the Managing

Trustees; and that all its departments should be efficiently maintained." We cannot know the depth of the original opposition to the hospital among the trustees, but if Bowditch correctly understood his colleagues' opinions, for a time Blake had stood virtually alone. By the close of the meeting, however, most opinions supported Blake.[32]

If any of his colleagues had questioned Blake's resolve, the next trustee meeting erased all doubt. On June 26, he advised his colleagues that "if the Trustees at this meeting do not take steps toward the re-organization of the staff for conducting the business of the Associates, I shall inform my co-trustees of the Benjamin Sewall Estate that is it my opinion that we forthwith should sell our holdings of the Ludlow Manufacturing Associates." The April vote had represented a tremendous achievement, now fortified with irresistible power.[33]

"This has been a great day for Ludlow," Blake exclaimed to Philip Dexter. Strong-willed, resourceful, and powerful, Blake was accustomed to achieving what he wanted. In the case of Ludlow, he not only protected the interests of the employees, but simultaneously preserved the power of stockholders and the influence of his family over the company. "At the morning's meeting of the Trustees," Blake proudly wrote, "I had read the enclosed statement of my position; and, thereafter, such votes were passed unanimously that the executive powers will be, hereafter, so conducted that the business will ensure the best interests of the share-holders to be preserved."[34]

The June trustees' meeting was Blake's last significant involvement with Ludlow or any other of his numerous responsibilities and interests. Since 1904, Blake had suffered intermittently with nagging health problems, particularly insomnia and a loss of speech. In November 1904, Elizabeth noted a slight improvement in his condition: "He more frequently makes a remark, It must be called that, for he does not talk, that is converse."[35] A few years later, Blake suffered an attack of aphasia. Although physically vigorous and still rowing on the Charles River, Blake's continued inability to speak clearly signaled a more serious aliment, perhaps foreshadowing an aneurysm or stroke. The family returned to their late summer retreat to the White Mountains; in the fall, Blake attended at least two board and trustee meetings and kept a number of workers busy making additional improvements to his beloved estate. On Sunday, January 19, 1913, Blake paid his trusted handyman Tom Cloonan for some work done to Keewaydin's conservatory and sent a small donation to Harvard's physics department. That night, just three weeks past his sixty-second birthday and without warning, Francis Blake died.[36]

Endnotes

1. Blake to John W. Denny, Mar. 28, 1902 (copy), FBP. Blake belonged to many associations and clubs. In this letter to Denny, Blake emphasized several of those institutions that meant the most to him. See "Clubs and Societies, 1879–1908" series, FBP.

2. Blake to D. S. Lamson, Nov. 19, 1890 (copy), FBP; Blake to Dr. Benjamin A. Gould, Feb. 27, 1891, FBP.

3. Mary Frances Pierce, ed., *Town of Weston Records of the First Precinct, 1746–1754, and of the Town, 1754–1803* (Boston, 1893); Mary Frances Pierce, ed., *Town of Weston Records of the Town Clerk, 1804–1826* (Boston, 1894); Mary Frances Pierce, ed., *Town of Weston, The Tax Lists, 1757–1821* (Boston, 1897); Blake materials concerning Weston town government are in "Weston Town Letters, 1887–1908" series, FBP.

4. Stanton Blake to Blake, Oct. 29, 1883, FBP.

5. A copy of the July 26, 1884 broadside, dated in Blake's hand, is in the "Republican Club of Weston, 1884–1912" series, FBP.

6. Autographed text of Blake's introduction of Thomas Wentworth Higginson, "Republican Club of Weston, 1884–1912" series, file 893, FBP.

7. Blake, Diary, Nov. 5, 1895, FBP; Blake to Andrew Fiske, Nov. 5 1896 (copy), FBP.

8. Records pertaining to Blake's membership in various clubs and organizations, 1879–1908, can be found in vol. 28, FBP.

9. Dr. W. S. Bigelow to Blake, Nov. 24, 1899, FBP.

10. Blake to Dr. W. S. Bigelow, Nov. 25, 1899, FBP; Blake to Secretary of the Watch and Ward Society, Jan. 4, 1904 (copy), FBP.

11. A copy of Blake's report of Jan. 11, 1895, FBP. Committee memberships can be traced in the annual catalogs of Harvard University.

12. Blake contributed $1,000 to the endowment and obtained subscriptions for about $6,500 more.

13. John Trowbridge to Blake, Dec. 14, 1892, FBP; Blake to Dr. Alexander McKenzie, Oct. 13, 1896, FBP; John Trowbridge to Charles Francis Adams, Oct. 29, 1896, FBP.

14. Blake to Charles Francis Adams, May 7, 1902 (copy), FBP.

15. Charles Francis Adams to Blake, May 11, 1905, FBP.

16. Blake to Francis A. Walker, March 8, 1892 (copy), FBP; Francis A. Walker to Blake, Mar. 30, 1892, FBP.

17. Silas W. Holman to Blake, July 2, 1897, Nov. 13, 1898, July 31, 1899, FBP. See Silas Whitcomb Holman, *Matter, Energy, Force, and Work; a Plain Presentation of Fundamental Physical Concepts and of the Vortex-Atom and other Theories* (New York, 1898).

18. Herbert Putnam to Blake, Mar. 3, 1900, FBP.

19. Elizabeth Blake, Diary, June 3, 1900, FBP.

20. Blake to Henry S. Pritchett, May 25, 1901 (copy), FBP; Henry S. Pritchett to Blake, May 27, 1901, FBP.

21. Herbert L. McChesney, *A History of Ludlow Massachusetts* (Ludlow, Mass., 1978), 217–230.

22. Blake to Bancroft Davis, Mar. 8, 1891, FBP.

23. Cranmore N. Wallace to Blake, Dec. 11, 1897, FBP.

24. Philip Dexter to Blake, Apr. 10, 1908, FBP.

25. Blake to Philip Dexter, Apr. 10, 1908 (copy), FBP; Curtis & Sanger, stockbrokers, Boston, circular, Dec. 17, 1912, FBP.

26. Blake to Cranmore N. Wallace, July 19, 1911, FBP; Blake to Philip Dexter, Aug. 3, 1911, FBP.

27. Charles W. Hubbard, Report to the Trustees of the Ludlow Manufacturing Associates on Social Work Carried Out by the Associates, Apr. 10, 1911, "Ludlow Manufacturing, 1902–1912" series, file 1061, FBP.

28. Ludlow Manufacturing Associates, Treasurer's Report on Social Work, Jan. 11, 1912, FBP; C. E. Gowen, Financial Secretary of the Ludlow Hospital Society to Ludlow Trustees, Mar. 11, 1912, FBP.

29. Blake to Ernest Bowditch, Mar. 21, 1912 (copy), FBP.

30. Blake to Ernest Bowditch, Mar. 21, 1912 (copy), FBP; Ernest Bowditch to Blake, Mar. 22, 1912, FBP.

31. Benjamin Loring Young to Blake, Mar. 26, 1912, FBP.

32. Typed memorandum of Blake's motion and note, Apr. 10, 1912, FBP.
33. Typescript of statements enclosed with Blake to Philip Dexter, Jan. 28, 1912, FBP.
34. Blake to Philip Dexter, June 28, 1912, FBP.
35. Elizabeth Blake, Diary, Sept. 25, Nov. 6, 1904, FBP.
36. Blake to W. E. Sedgewick, May 15, 1912, FBP; Francis Blake, Diary, 1912 *passim*, especially Dec. 17, also Jan. 8–19, 1913, FBP.

AFTERWORD

How wealthy was Francis Blake? He asked himself that question nearly every year and annually evaluated his worth. With his usual precision, Blake calculated the value of his stocks, land, buildings, and all his other real and personal estate. By January 1911, Blake believed his assets totaled $763,943, very roughly equivalent to $34 million in today's currency. With control of so much land in exclusive Weston, Blake's true wealth (in contemporary figures) was undoubtedly much higher. But this would be the wrong calculus of Blake's worth.[1]

Dollars aside, Blake was an important American inventor and scientist. A.T.&T. proudly deemed his famed transmitter "the best transmitting and most effective telephone in existence and was produced most opportunely for the company. . . . Mr. Blake's invention not only came opportunely, but was so superior to all other transmitters then in existence, that is soon became a very large factor in the upbuilding of the Bell System as it is today."[2] Our modern phone system developed because of Blake's inventiveness. As a philanthropist, Blake performed very useful services to a number of local institutions, especially Harvard, MIT, and the Massachusetts General Hospital.

It is in the world of photography, however, that his legacy is most enduring. Blake deserves recognition as one of the most important photographers of the late nineteenth century. As no one else before him, Blake combined scientific analysis with a clear and unassuming aesthetic. In extraordinary ways, Blake's photographs awaken us to the "wonder of the real." In his pigeons, bicycles, trains, laughing faces, and working hands, the everyday objects and events of our lives, Blake found what his good friend William Dean Howells discovered in the great Concord sage, Ralph Waldo Emerson: "Man is surprised to find that things near are not less beautiful and wondrous than things remote. . . . The foolish man wonders at the unusual, but the wise man at the usual." Francis Blake was a very wise man.[3]

Endnotes

1. "Francis Blake trial balance, 1881–1912" series, vol. 41, FBP.
2. Theodore N. Vail, concluding statement, in American Telephone & Telegraph Company, *Annual Report* (1912), 39.
3. Davis, "The High-Speed Photography of Francis Blake," 20, 22.

APPENDIX

FRANCIS BLAKE PAPERS AT THE MASSACHUSETTS HISTORICAL SOCIETY

Francis Blake Papers 1804–1917

The papers of Francis Blake and the Blake family are held in two substantial collections at the MHS. The first collection, "Francis Blake Papers 1804–1917," contained in eighty-three document boxes and forty-six volumes, came to the Society in May 1964 through a family donation. It is arranged by series, each section largely devoted to a single subject or period of Francis Blake's life.

The most important series are those containing private and business letters, diaries, photographs, and the enormous number of receipts and bills that Blake retained for virtually every purchase he ever made, whether for family members, business, or the construction and reconstruction of Keewaydin. The series "Private Letters, 1866–1912" holds thousands of Blake letters in forty-two boxes and is chronologically arranged. It includes Blake's incoming correspondence and copies of occasional outgoing letters chiefly regarding personal, family, and some business matters in Boston and Weston, Massachusetts. Much of the correspondence deals with Blake's attempts to sell his transmitter patents to national and international telephone companies. Also included is correspondence with Brown & Sharpe Manufacturing Company of Rhode Island, Charles Follen McKim, Alexander Graham Bell, Blake's brother, Charles H. M. Blake, and Boston area photographers. Some interesting references are to the performances of Edwin Thomas Booth (1833–1893) and the imprison-ment of Jefferson Davis at Fortress Monroe, Virginia.

For Blake's early years, the "U.S. Coast Survey, 1843–1889" series is critical. This chronological record group has incoming correspondence, especially from Charles O. Boutelle and Thomas Oliver Selfridge about the Darien Exploring Expedition to survey the Isthmus of Darien (Panama). It holds pay accounts, charts, and notebooks of weather, birds, and general observations at Observatory Island. This series also has in-structions from Julius Erasmus Hilgard, material related to Blake's trans-atlantic longitudinal measurement surveys, letters and newspaper clips regarding a federal investigation for alleged misappropriation of funds by Boutelle and Hilgard, and a scientific ledgerbook charting survey points at Keewaydin.

The series "Telephone, 1877–1917" is devoted to Blake's most lucrative inventions. This especially important series has letters and diagrams de-tailing the development of the Blake transmitter for the telephone, patent offers to Bell Telephone and New England Telephone, and his attempts to patent the transmitter worldwide. There are also materials related to Blake's other electrical inventions, the work of other inventors, tables and graphs recording the number of telephone calls made from selected Boston metropolitan phone lines, and one volume of monthly earnings reports of American Telephone and Telegraph Company. Correspondents include Alexander Graham Bell, John Elbridge Hudson, Theodore N. Vail, and Thomas A. Watson.

Two other series hold the voluminous diaries of Blake and his wife Elizabeth Hubbard Blake. Both proved indispensable to this biography. Between 1866 and 1913, Francis Blake recorded his thoughts and activities for each year in fifty bound volumes; in six additional ones (1885–1906), Elizabeth recorded Blake family domestic life.

"Photographs, c.1860–1900" contains the majority of Blake's finest work. Hundreds of photos and negatives of Blake's are preserved, amount-ing to one of the nation's most important late-nineteenth-century photo-graphic collections. It is complemented by five albums of cartes de visite, cabinet cards, and cyanotypes of the Blake, Hubbard, and Sewall families. There are also many images of Keewaydin, various Blake vacation spots, and the Blake ancestral home in England.

Complete Series Title List, Francis Blake Papers

Account books, 1842–1912

Agnes Blake, 1895–1904

American Academy of Arts & Sciences, 1877–1903

Benjamin Sewall Trust, 1879–1902

Bills, Domestic, 1875–1912

Bills, Housebuilding, 1874–1875

Blake Genealogy, c. 1849, 1891–1913

Charles B. Wells Estate, 1902–1912

Charles H. M. Blake, 1877–1901

Clubs and Societies, 1879–1908

Davenport Stone and Mt. Feake, 1895, 1902

Diaries, Elizabeth Hubbard Blake, 1885–1906

Diaries, Francis Blake, 1866–1913

"Editors" Word Contest, 1897

Edward L. Wilson, 1901–1903

Elizabeth Hubbard Blake, 1842–1908

Elizabeth M. Crosby, 1870–1892

Greenhouses, 1891

Harvard University, 1902

Health, 1880–1911

Investments, 1893–1912

Keewaydin Water, 1883–1902

Lane Family, 1804–1883

Louisa S. Jackson Trust, 1889–1913

Ludlow Manufacturing Associates, 1902–1912

Massachusetts General Hospital, 1899–1902

Massachusetts Institute of Technology, 1896–1910

Miscellaneous Scrapbooks, 1862–1909.

Oversize

    Photographs, c.1860–1900

    Private Letters, 1866–1912

    Republican Club of Weston, 1884–1912

    Robert Craighead, 1903–1904, 1911

    St Mary's Episcopal Church, 1903–1912

    Telephone, 1877–1917

    Thursday Evening Club, 1882–1913

    Trumbull Estate, 1881–1910

    U.S. Coast Survey, 1843–1889

    Weston Town Letters, 1887–1908

    Wines, 1882–1901

*

Blake Family Papers, 1867–1964

The second important collection of Blake papers at the MHS is the "Blake Family Papers, 1867–1964." These documents came to the Society in a series of gifts, particularly in 2001, and with the assistance of the Oliver family. They are in seventeen record cartons, two oversize volumes, and one additional oversize photographic box. Primarily, this collection holds the papers of family members other than Francis Blake, principally his wife Elizabeth Livermore (Hubbard) Blake and children Agnes (Blake) Fitzgerald and Benjamin Sewall Blake. The papers are organized into ten separate series, with the bulk of the material consisting of family correspondence, 1867–1964 (primarily, 1880–1918). The family correspondence consists mostly of letters written to Elizabeth (Hubbard) Blake from family and friends, her sisters Charlotte and Louise, and her son Benjamin S. There are many daily runs of letters from Agnes to her mother, written whenever the two were separated. A number of letters written between Benjamin's wife Ruth (Field) Blake and her mother Amelia D. (Mrs. Joseph W.) Field are also contained in the collection.

The various series in the Blake Family Papers hold materials related to Benjamin S. Blake's education, particularly at Harvard; family bills and receipts; medical papers, consisting mostly of prescriptions and later (1950s) medical charts; First Corps Cadets papers; charitable solicitations; Commodore George S. Blake miscellaneous papers; and landscaping at Keewaydin. Bound volumes hold financial material, memoranda, Benjamin S. Blake's engagement diary, material related to Agnes Blake Fitzgerald's marriage, scrapbooks, and Elizabeth Hubbard Blake's records of her children's infancies.

The Blake photographs in this collection cover the period from about 1860 to 1920 and consist mostly of portraits of family and friends, travel views, a series of photographs of drawings of early telephone apparatuses, and two of Francis Blake's experimental images.

Complete Series Title List, Blake Family Papers
   Bound Volumes, 1873–1943
   Charitable Solicitations, 1887–1941
   Correspondence, 1867–1964
   Financial Papers, 1881–1938
   First Corps Cadets Papers of Benjamin S. Blake, 1896–1909
   Harvard and other School Papers of Benjamin S. Blake, 1893–1902
   Medical Papers, 1870–1956
   Miscellaneous Papers
   Miscellaneous Printed Matter
   Photographs, 1860–1920

Detailed finding aids for both Blake collections are available at the Massachusetts Historical Society.

INDEX

Weston, Mass., 185–186
  See also, Keewaydin
Whipple, John Adams, 61, 142
Whipple, Joseph A., 25
White, John W., 179
White, Stanford, 98
Whiting, Blake & Hindro, 3
Whitwell, May, 30–31

Williams, Charles, 75, 80
Williams, Charles, Jr., 77
Wilson, Edmund, 77
Winlock, Joseph, 16, 24, 26
Worcester Spy, 4
Wright, J. H., 170

Young, Benjamin Loring, 55, 196

ELTON W. HALL received his M.A. from the University of Delaware in the Winterthur Program in Early American Culture. Following service in the U.S. Navy, he became curator of the New Bedford Whaling Museum. He is presently executive director of the Early American Industries Association. His other publications include *Sperm Whaling from New Bedford: Clifford W. Ashley's Photographs of Bark Sunbeam in 1904* and *Frederick Garrison Hall: Etchings, Bookplates, Designs.*